A Matter of Hours

Women, Part-time Work and the Labour Market

Veronica Beechey and Tessa Perkins

University of Minnesota Press, Minneapolis

Published by the University of Minnesota Press 2037 University Avenue Southeast, Minneapolis MN 55414.
Published simultaneously in Canada by Fitzhenry & Whiteside Limited, Markham.
Printed in Great Britain.

Library Cataloging-in-Publication Data

Beechey, Veronica.
   A matter of hours.

   (Feminist perspectives)
   Bibliography: p.
   1. Women—Employment—England—Coventry (West
Midlands)   2. Part-time employment—England—Coventry
(West Midlands)   3. Coventry (West Midlands, England)—
Economic conditions.   I. Perkins, Tessa.   II. Title.
III. Series.
HD6136.Z6C683   1987   331.4'12'0942498   87-12459
ISBN 0-8166-1641-8
ISBN 0-8166-1642-6 (pbk.)

The University of Minnesota
is an equal-opportunity
educator and employer.

Contents

Acknowledgements

Many people have helped us in the preparation of this book, which would probably never have been written had Colleen Chesterman not done an MA dissertation on the same topic. Our debt to Colleen's research is evident throughout the book. Nor would our research have been carried out had we not been funded by the EOC/SSRC Joint Panel. The research was housed in the department of sociology at Warwick University, which provided a stimulating and supportive environment for us during the project. Carole Brigden, Beth Hensman and Pam Smitham all worked as half-time secretaries on the project (though we could easily have used time and a half), and all helped us with the research as well as wading through numerous tapes and manuscripts. A great number of people gave willingly of their time to talk to us about part-time work: part-time women workers, shop stewards, trade union officials, managers, and employees of Coventry City Council and the Area Health Authority. Many of our colleagues and friends shared their own work with us and advised us about different aspects of our research: Mick Carpenter, members of Coventry Workshop, Pat Dutton, Tony Elger, Peter Elias, Bob Fryer (who also wrote a case study of the school meals service for us), Ken Grainger, Margaretta Holmstead, Marjorie Mayo, Ceridwen Roberts, Sheila Roche and Ann Sedley. Paul Allin, Fred Bayliss, Irene Bruegel, Beatrix Campbell, Simon Clarke, Angela Coyle, Simon Frith, Jennifer Hurstfield, J. A. Lakin, Jill Liddington, Jan Pahl, Mandy Snell, Jackie West, Sheila Wild and David Winchester read and commented, in whole or in part, on our research report and/or draft chapters of the book, and Judy Dougall typed the manuscript of the book for us. We are extremely grateful to them all for their help. Finally, we owe a special debt of thanks to Simon Frith and Bob Fryer who acted as consultants to the research project and gave us endless support and advice, and to Michelle Stanworth whose perceptive criticisms, support and tact helped us greatly as we struggled to transform our research report into a book.

Abbreviations

APEX	Association of Professional, Executive, Clerical and Computer Staff
BIFU	Banking, Insurance and Finance Union
CBI	Confederation of British Industry
COHSE	Confederation of Health Service Employees
CPSA	The Civil and Public Services Association
DHSS	Department of Health and Social Security
EAT	Employment Appeals Tribunal
EC	European Community
EIRR	European Industrial Review and Report
EOC	Equal Opportunities Commission
GLC	Greater London Council
GMBATU	General, Municipal, Boilermakers and Allied Trades Union
IDS	Incomes Data Services
ILEA	Inner London Education Authority
IR-RR	Industrial Relations Review and Report
MLH	Minimum List Headings
NALGO	National Association of Local Government Officers
NATFHE	National Association of Teachers in Further and Higher Education
NCCL	National Council of Civil Liberties
NHS	National Health Service
NUPE	National Association of Public Employees
OECD	Organization for Economic Cooperation and Development
PSI	Policy Studies Institute
SIC	Standard Industrial Classification
SRN	State Registered Nurse
SSRC	Social Science Research Council (now ESRC, Economic and Social Research Committee)
TGWU	Transport and General Workers Union
TUC	Trades Union Congress

Introduction

One of the most striking changes in the structure of the labour force in Britain in recent years has been the increase in part-time working. Part-time work is not itself a new phenomenon. Historical studies show that a lot of work (especially women's and children's work) in agriculture, in trades like sewing and in service occupations (cleaning and taking in washing, for example) has often been done on a part-time basis. What is new, however, is the extent of part-time employment and the fact that whole occupations and sectors of the economy – among them cleaning, food preparation and serving, and caring work in the health and social services – are now being organized on a part-time basis.

Part-time work has grown steadily since the Second World War, but since the early 1970s its increase has been especially dramatic. Over one million part-time jobs were created in the 1970s alone, in a period when the British economy was experiencing its most severe recession in 40 years. The number of full-time jobs, in contrast, has declined. Thus, the composition of the workforce has recently been undergoing a fundamental transformation. One in five of Britain's employees worked part-time in 1980; by 1990 the figure is likely to be nearer to one in four. What is so significant about part-time work is not merely its vast numerical increase. It is that over the past 30 years or so in Britain we have witnessed the development of a new form of work which is highly exploitative and heavily gender-specific.

The decline in full-time work and the expansion of part-time work are part of a more general process whereby the working population is changing. Men's working lives are becoming shorter as young men find it increasingly hard to get jobs, and are therefore on the dole or on youth training schemes, and men in their fifties and early sixties are increasingly being offered inducements to take early retirement. Women, on the other hand, are working more, and today the vast majority of women are in paid employment for most of their working lives. Whereas in the early post-war years the majority of women ceased employment on marriage, most now work until they have children, and they return to the labour market quite quickly afterwards. Today, the major difference between women and men is not that men work and married women do not. It is that most men do full-time paid work and very little else, while most women combine paid work with unpaid housework and caring work. Women's actual hours of work are often more than full-time, but only a certain proportion of these is recognized as 'work' and remunerated accordingly.

Part-time work is overwhelmingly women's work. Over 90 per cent of part-time workers in Britain are women. Moreover, women's jobs are increasingly being constructed as part-time jobs. Nearly half of all women's jobs are part-time, and it is becoming more and more difficult for women who want to work full-time to find jobs. Despite the fact that opportunities for a handful of women have expanded in recent years as a result of the growth of equal opportunities policies, for most women opportunities in the labour market are extremely limited. And for the increasingly large number of women who return to work part-time after having children, the opportunities are particularly limited. A good number of these women experience downward mobility. Thus, while from some vantage points the mass entry of women into the labour market represents an advance, an examination of the form of work done by many women and their conditions of employment suggests the need for caution in proclaiming this as *ipso facto* emancipatory. Moreover, since women's work is increasingly being organized on a part-time basis, the formal and informal discrimination against part-timers and the overwhelmingly underprivileged status of their work are matters of serious concern. They must be tackled by everyone interested in eradicating inequalities between the sexes.

Part-time jobs are highly segregated from full-time jobs, especially from full-time men's jobs. It is extremely rare to find a woman working part-time doing the same job as a man. In the main, part-time jobs are manual jobs in service industries and occupations, and they are usually located at the bottom of the occupational ladder. Even those women who work part-time in higher-level jobs – in administration, for example, or the nursing, teaching and social work professions – are almost always in the lowest grades. They often work in 'Cinderella' jobs like nursing on night duty or in jobs which are construed as marginal.[1]

While many men's jobs have some kind of promotion prospects, most non-professional women's do not, and part-time jobs in particular are dead-end jobs. Men's jobs are more likely to be classified as skilled than women's, and it is most unusual to find a woman doing a part-time job which has been defined as skilled. This is true even where the jobs clearly involve complex competencies and responsibilities, as many women's jobs in the welfare services (like home helping) do.

Part-time jobs are not simply segregated from full-time ones on a 'different but equal' basis. People working in them lack many of the advantages that accrue to people in full-time employment. Full-time workers (especially men) are considerably better paid than part-timers, because they are usually in higher-graded jobs and they more often benefit from overtime pay, shift premiums and bonus payments. Part-time workers are also frequently excluded from benefits such as sick pay and maternity pay, paid holidays and occupational pensions schemes. Moreover, part-timers are often hired for the absolute minimum number of hours deemed necessary to do a specific job so it is much less likely that there will be any slack in their work time. Employers, trade unionists and full- and part-time workers often commented to us on the 'intensity' of much part-time work. It is somewhat ironic therefore that these part-time workers are so frequently talked about as if they were not proper workers. They are undoubtedly an underprivileged section of the working population.

A Matter of Hours approaches the question of part-time work from a variety of perspectives. It contains a detailed analysis of part-time employment in a number of different industries, based on fieldwork which we carried out in Coventry (a city in Britain's West Midlands) between 1979 and 1981. It develops a theoretical framework which we hope will contribute to the analysis both of part-time work and of women's employment and labour markets more generally. It also discusses questions of policy, focusing not only on specific policies towards part-time work but also on more general policies concerning equal opportunities, the restructuring of production and the future of work.

The Coventry Study

Our analysis is developed on the basis of a research project which looked at part-time work in Coventry between 1979 and 1981.[2] Coventry was the fastest growing city in Britain in the first half of this century at least, with a population in 1951 which was more than three times its population in 1901. It is known as a car town, a boom town of the fifties which paid high wages, especially to its skilled male engineering workers. It is also known as a city whose centre was almost completely destroyed by bombing during the war. Something like 75 per cent of the shops in the city centre disappeared, and with them of course went jobs. By the mid-1960s, however, the city centre had been redeveloped as a massive shopping precinct, and a new large hospital was built on the edge of the town. A polytechnic and a college of education, and later a university, were also opened.

Even when compared with other towns in the 'manufacturing Midlands', Coventry's industrial structure has been more dominated by manufacturing industry than is typical. Moreover, manufacturing in Coventry has been less diversified than in other Midland towns. Since the nineteenth century, a high proportion of Coventry's employment has been concentrated in metal-based manufacturing, and in the twentieth century it has specialized in car production. This industrial concentration has been a source both of Coventry's strength and its vulnerability. It benefited enormously from the car industry in the long post-war boom, but as the industry virtually collapsed in the recession the effects have reverberated throughout the city. It moved rapidly from being a boom town to a 'ghost town' (as it was called by The Specials, a Coventry band).

We studied part-time work in a number of different areas of Coventry's manufacturing industry – telecommunications, baking, vehicles and mechanical engineering – and in three areas of the welfare state: the health service, social services and the education system. We investigated the ways in which employers used various kinds of labour (part-time and full-time, men and women) in different forms of labour process, and we analysed the relationship between part-time and full-time work throughout the occupational hierarchies in the workplaces we studied, attempting thereby to break with a tradition which has largely ignored work in service occupations and industries. We also tried to identify similarities and differences in the ways in which part-time workers had been used in the early post-war period, and in the more recent recession.

We began our research using a fairly conventional Marxist framework of analysis. In the late 1970s two main arguments were used to analyse the trends in part-time employment. In *The Part-time Trap*, Jennifer Hurstfield (1978) argued that part-time workers had been substituted for full-time workers, especially in service industries like catering and retailing which paid low wages and experienced difficulties in recruiting full-time workers. Irene Bruegel (1979), on the other hand, argued that part-time workers were used as an industrial reserve army of labour, particularly in manufacturing industries, and were being disposed of in the recession. She also suggested that low wages made it unlikely that men would take over women's jobs in the service sectors of the economy.

We approached our fieldwork with these two theories in mind, and with a specific set of questions to address. We wanted to examine the actual conditions in which part-time workers were recruited or disposed of in a variety of labour processes. Did part-time workers constitute an industrial reserve army of labour, and, if so, in what conditions? Alternatively, were women part-timers being substituted for full-time men or for full-time women workers? Were the patterns of part-time employment similar in the manufacturing and service sectors of the economy, and was there a relationship between the expansion of part-time employment in the service sectors and the decline in manufacturing?

Our analysis suggests that the incidence and pattern of part-time work is quite variable: there is not just one kind of part-time work nor single pattern of use.[3] In some sectors (mainly the engineering industries), part-time workers had mostly been disposed of, while in others (baking, for instance, and in all areas of the welfare state) they have continued to be important and are often central to the labour process. We found that the reasons for the employment of part-time workers had changed over time. In the years following the war, the general labour shortage led employers to devise a number of strategies to attract workers, among them the construction of part-time jobs, and the expansion of the welfare state and of the private service sectors of the economy also played a key role in creating a demand for part-time workers. Employers anxious to extend the length of the working day or week also employed part-time workers – on evening shifts in factories and during the evenings and at weekends in many jobs in the welfare state. Part-time workers were also employed in domestic and caring jobs. The fact that there was a labour shortage during this period meant that women frequently had some say in the hours that they worked, and employers were often forced to take account of women's own commitments and responsibilities in organizing their workforce.

In recent years there has been no shortage of labour although there has been a scarcity of trained personnel in particular areas like computer programming and some jobs associated with new technology. Despite the large increase in the number of people of both sexes who are unemployed, many employers have opted to create part-time jobs. Since the 1970s the dramatic increase in part-time work has been mainly associated with the expansion of the service sectors of the economy, although there is some evidence of part-time employment continuing in manufacturing industry. During the recession, employers have used part-time workers for reasons of flexibility, to cover peaks and troughs of work and to extend the length of the working day and week, and women have also been employed part-time in a wide range of domestic and caring jobs. Much of the opportunity which women had in the early post-war years to have some say in their hours of work seems now to have disappeared. With a few exceptions, in recent years employers have reorganized part-timers' hours with little or no consideration of women's needs.

Theoretical Questions

A principal aim of *A Matter of Hours* is to develop a framework for analysing part-time work, for as yet there have been very few theoretical analyses of this new form of work. Moreover, the prevailing assumptions that 'real' work is full-time and that part-time workers are marginal to the world of work have often been unquestioningly reflected in discourses on work. Conventional sociological approaches to work reveal two rather different and mutually exclusive perspectives.[4] On the one hand, there are the studies which fall within the province either of a general sociology of industrial societies or the more specific areas of industrial sociology and industrial relations. These invariably adopt a masculine conception of industry and work, or what has sometimes been called a 'job model', and their focus is generally narrow.[5] They concentrate almost exclusively on manufacturing industries and on men's manual jobs within these. Moreover, the conception of workers which they adopt is also narrow. It is assumed that people either work full-time and have no family obligations or are unemployed.[6] On the other hand, there are the studies which grew out of the sociology of the family, the 'women's two roles' perspective. These, in contrast, adopt a 'gender model' of work, analysing women's attitudes to work and their work experiences almost entirely in terms of their role within the family. They assume that a woman's primary role is that of wife and mother, and discuss how a second role, that of wage-earner, can be combined with this. Part-time work often features in these studies as one of the means by which women can combine their two roles. These studies have the advantage of highlighting the ways in which many women are forced to balance the competing demands on them, but they are theoretically unsatisfactory. They do not analyse the sexual division of labour within the family and they also ignore the ways in which women's relationship to the labour market is affected by the organization of production.

Analyses of work have developed considerably in recent years as people have become aware of the inadequacies of the old frameworks and as work itself has been restructured. Sociological approaches to work in particular have been affected by feminist theory and research. Both our theoretical and our empirical knowledge about work have been broadened appreciably by studies of housework and of women's work histories and their experiences of paid work, and by analyses of the relationship between paid and unpaid work and of the international division of labour. Workplace ethnographies have focused attention on questions which were missing from earlier studies of work: the persistence of job segregation, the role of gender in the construction of jobs, the importance of ideology and the role of culture (not just workplace cultures but also family and community cultures) in the formation of people's consciousness and their experiences of work,[7] and studies of new technology have called into question the view that technology is neutral (see, for example, Cockburn, 1983, 1985).

Studies of the labour market and the labour process have also developed considerably in recent years. As the recession has led to a restructuring of work and of labour markets, new theories have emerged. These have been particularly popular among economists and 'economically minded' sociologists, and have emphasized divisions within the working population. Marxist theories have tended to focus on the process of 'deskilling', while dual and segmented labour market theories have focused on the differentiation of the labour market into primary and secondary sectors. Like the older sociological studies, many of the newer labour markets and labour process analyses have been dominated by a masculine model of work and they have not always paid sufficient attention to part-time work. However, a few writers have recently begun to recognize the significance of part-time work, a recognition which stems from the rapid expansion of part-time jobs in recent years and the growing realization that these are likely to be the only major areas of employment growth in the near future. In so far as they tackle the question of part-time working, these theories generally see the growth of part-time work as a product of other more general features of the labour market or labour process: the process of deskilling, the segmentation of the labour market into primary and secondary sectors or the growing differentiation of core and peripheral workers. These wider processes are conceptualized in predominantly economic terms.

Our own analysis has some common features both with recent feminist studies of work and with the new approaches to the analysis of labour markets. We share with the new labour market theorists a belief that 'demand' factors are important in explaining the growth of part-time work and the location of part-time workers within the labour market. We also share their assumption that part-time work should be placed within a more general analysis of the process in which work is being restructured. Where we depart from labour market and labour process theories, however, is in our specific analysis of restructuring, for it is a major finding of our research that employers have gender-specific ways of organizing their labour forces. Where the labour force is female, our research suggests, employers use part-time workers as a means of attaining flexibility. On the other hand, where men are employed, other methods of attaining flexibility are used. Thus, in our view, many of the characteristics of part-time work do not stem from some general economically defined process like deskilling or the segmentation of the labour force into primary and secondary or core and peripheral workers, but from employment strategies which are related to

gender. It is a central argument of *A Matter of Hours* that gender
enters into the construction of part-time jobs and that the division
between full-time and part-time work is one crucial contemporary
manifestation of gender within the sphere of production.

We take issue, therefore, with theories which analyse production in purely economic terms, and try instead to develop a way of
thinking about economic life which analyses the relationships
among economic conditions, social relations and gender ideology.[8]
We also take issue with theories which see part-time work as some
kind of 'natural' outgrowth of relations within the family, as the
older sociological studies tended to do. Crossnational comparisons
show that part-time working is not always as closely correlated
with married women's employment as it is in Britain. In France,
for instance, married women with dependent children tend to
work full-time. Such comparisons suggest that the articulation of
the family with the labour market varies from one country to
another, and that both state policies and gender ideology play a
crucial role in determining the form of this articulation and
whether or not women are constructed as marginal workers.

Policy Implications

The final chapter of *A Matter of Hours* is concerned with questions
of policy. We discuss policies designed to improve the situation of
part-time workers which have recently been taken up by some
trade unions and a few employers – policies to grant part-time
workers *pro rata* pay and benefits with full-time workers, for
example. We also discuss a range of other policies which are rather
more indirect in their effects on part-time workers but which are
none the less important – for instance, equal opportunities policies
and policies to deal with low pay. In conclusion, we also raise
rather briefly a number of issues which are part of current debates
about the future of work: 'the flexibility debate', which has
recently developed in Britain (with employers showing an interest
in more flexible ways of organizing work) and the question of
shortening working time, which is barely on the policy-making
agenda in Britain but has been important elsewhere in Europe.

The current climate in Britain is not a hospitable one for those
who are interested in egalitarian labour market policies. The
present Conservative government has consistently pursued a whole

range of policies which are in sharp conflict with egalitarian goals – deregulating the economy, cutting back on public expenditure and privatizing services like cleaning – and most employers have gone along with these initiatives. Moreover, the government has pursued social policies which are predicated on the notion of the male bread-winner/dependent wife, and has also cut back on social service provisions, a move which places additional stress on women in the family. In almost any area one cares to consider – provision for paid holidays, minimum wage legislation, maternity leave or parental leave – the statutory policies in Britain are among the worst in Western Europe, and the British government has also vetoed a range of measures designed to introduce social considerations into the oper-ation of labour markets for the European Community as a whole.

Nevertheless, it is our contention that the position of women in the labour force is only likely to be significantly improved if the organization and structure of work more generally is transformed, because not only does women's work need to change, but also that of men. And it is arguable that, despite the policies of the Conservative government, the current situation (in which produc-tion processes are being restructured and new technology is being introduced) has considerable scope for change. Not only is the organization of work changing in a technical sense, but it is becoming more and more apparent that 'traditional' ways of organizing work and 'traditional' notions like 'the family wage' and 'the 8 hour day' are not particularly relevant to the world today. This opens up space for new possibilities.

As yet in Britain the question of women's employment has been somewhat marginal to debates about the future of work, and in any event such debate has been less widespread here than in many other countries in Western Europe and the United States of America. In Western Europe, in particular, there has been interesting discussion within left-wing political parties, trade unions and the European Parliament about the organization of work, and several radical ideas have emerged. It is important, in our view, that questions about the future of work should find a more central place in political discussions and on policy-making agendas in Britain than they have in the past, and that the concerns of women should become central to discussions about how work might be organized in years to come. The arguments in this book will, we hope, contribute to this end.

1
Part-time Work in a Changing Labour Market

Changes in the Structure of the Workforce

Part-time work on the scale we know it today is a relatively recent phenomenon and is part of a much broader series of changes in the structure of the workforce which have been taking place in Britain this century, and particularly since the Second World War. Overall, the proportion of the adult population which is economically active has increased, and this has had a gender-related dimension to it. Women have been participating in the labour force at higher levels than at any period (other than war-time) since the Industrial Revolution, while men's particip-ation in the labour force has declined steadily. In recent years there has also been a rapid rise in the number of self-employed and an enormous increase in the proportion of the economically active population which is unemployed.[1]

Although men's activity rates in Britain have remained consis-tently higher than women's throughout this century, they have fallen in recent years. The activity rate for men was 65 per cent in 1901, 69 per cent in 1931 and 67 per cent in 1951, but since then it has fallen steadily and in 1981 it was just under 60 per cent (Beacham, 1984, p. 6). Having remained relatively stable at 15.5 million between 1977 and 1981, the male labour force fell sharply between 1981 and 1983 with the loss of a further 500,000 men from the workforce (*Employment Gazette*, July 1985).

The decline in the male activity rate is mainly the result of changes in the participation in the labour force of two groups of men: those aged 16–17 and those over 55. The decline in paid employment among younger men is in part an expression of a long-term trend towards later entry to the labour market due to the raising of the school-leaving age and the expansion of further and higher education, a trend common to all developed societies. However, the recent decline in participation in the labour market by young men aged 16–17 in Britain also results from the development of government training schemes (first YOP and subsequently YTS) which have been developed as a means of reducing youth unemployment. In 1983 less than half (40 per cent) of young men aged 16 and 17 were economically active, while the remainder were still in education or were on youth training schemes run by the Manpower Services Commission (Office of Population Censuses and Surveys, 1983). The present government (and, it seems, future governments of other political complexions) clearly intends to cope with the increasing levels of unemployment by promoting training schemes for young people.

At the other end of the spectrum, the decline in older men's participation in the labour market is due mainly to the spread of early retirement. The sharp decline in the proportion of men over 65 (the 'official' state retirement age) in paid employment, from 31 per cent in 1951 to 9 per cent in 1983, indicates that more men retire when they reach the state retirement age than previously (Office of Population Censuses and Surveys, 1983; Walker, 1984–5). Over the past decade, the proportion of men aged between 60 and 64 in the labour force has also declined dramatically. In 1971, 83 per cent of this age group participated in the labour force but by 1984 the figure had decreased to 57 per cent (Central Statistical Office, 1986). Furthermore, if the men in this age group who are registered as unemployed are included in the figure, only half of the men aged between 60 and 64 were in work in 1984. The activity rate among men in the 55–59 age group has also declined sharply since the mid-1970s from 94 per cent in 1975 to 83 per cent in 1984, and 10 per cent of this group of men were unemployed in 1984 compared to only 4 per cent in 1975. This recent and dramatic decline in the level of older men's employment is largely a result of mechanisms used to shed labour. There is a broad consensus that early retirement is a good way of reducing unemployment, as a recent Marplan opinion poll has shown, but a study by the Policy Studies Institute found that the Job Release Scheme, which is said to have been designed to alleviate unemployment among younger workers, has more often been used as a direct means of reducing overall manpower than as a mechanism of job creation (White, 1981; Walker, 1984–5).

Although there are very few men working part-time in Britain – only 9 per cent of part-time workers were male in 1981, according to the census – the vast majority of these are over 60 years of age. Thus, while it is most unusual to find younger men doing part-time work, it is by no means uncommon among men around or over retirement age. Hallaire pointed out in 1968 that firms had created jobs for 'a substantial minority' of older workers who qualified for retirement pensions, which suggests that this is not a recent phenomenon. However, whereas the creation of part-time jobs for older men in the early post-war period was mainly a response to the acute labour shortage experienced in the long, post-war boom, more recently it has resulted from measures designed to alleviate unemployment. Men taking early retirement are often allowed to go on working part-time, and their earnings are supplemented by their pensions.

It is clear that while it is still the norm for men to be economically active throughout their working lives, these working lives have been steadily decreasing in length over this century, and they have recently been shortened at both ends by state policies designed to alter the composition of the labour force and those who are to count as members of it. Furthermore, increasing numbers of men, while remaining formally 'in the labour market' in the sense that they are represented in activity rates, have been unemployed in recent years. The rate of unemployment has been considerably higher among certain groups of men – older men, younger men and black men in particular. And the duration of unemployment has also changed significantly so that many more men now experience long-term unemployment.

In sharp contrast to the decline in men's employment in Britain this century, women's participation in the labour market has steadily increased. Beacham (1984) estimates that the proportion of economically active women has increased from 25 per cent in 1901 to 36 per cent in 1981.[2] As with men, the employment patterns of different groups of women have varied markedly. Younger women's participation in the labour market has declined, and so has older women's (Dex and Philipson, 1986), but there has been a vast increase in the proportion of married women in paid employment as well as a growth in participation in the labour force by the mothers of dependent children. The married women's activity rate more than doubled between 1901 and 1981, increasing from 25 per cent to 55 per cent (Beacham, 1984). Since these increases have been significantly larger than the decline in the activity rates of younger and older women, women's overall activity rates have increased considerably. The major changes in the pattern of women's participation in the labour market during this century are illustrated in figure 1.1.

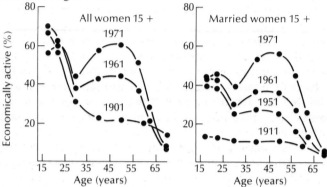

Figure 1.1   Emergence of the bimodal pattern in women's employment.
Source: Hakim (1979), p. 5, figure 1.

Figure 1.1 shows that at the turn of the century the predominant pattern was for women to participate in the labour market at a high level (averaging 61 per cent) between the ages of 15 and 27, and for their participation to fall in the 25–34 age group, and to continue falling until they reached retirement age. The typical pattern since 1961, however, has been for women to have a two-phase working life. The current trend is for women to participate in the labour market at a fairly high level before they have children, whether or not they are married, then to leave the labour market, returning again after a period of family formation. Thus, most women now return to the labour market. According to the *Women and Employment* survey (Martin and Roberts, 1984), 78 per cent of the women interviewed, and 95 per cent of those whose first baby had been born between 1960 and 1964, had returned to the labour market at some point since, mostly return-ing to part-time work. However, the survey also suggested that this two-phase pattern is becoming less common, and that younger women are now more likely to return to work *between* births or, in a small proportion of cases, to continue working throughout their child-bearing years. Between 1971 and 1981, then, the activity rates of younger women increased much more rapidly than they had in the previous decade. By contrast, the sharp increase noted in the activity rates of older women, especially the over-55s, appears to have slowed down.

There are three possible explanations for this slackening off of the rise in older women's activity rates. First, as with men, older women may be retiring earlier, voluntarily or not. Secondly, they may in the current economic situation be less inclined than younger women to try entering the labour market for the first time (the 'discouraged worker' effect may be stronger). And, thirdly, it may be that the activity rates of this group of older women has reached, or nearly reached, a ceiling. It is relevant to note here that while older women may be free of childcare responsibilities, many of them acquire responsibilities for elderly and dependent relations at this stage in their lives. The *Women and Employment* survey (Martin and Roberts, 1984) found that 21 per cent of women over the age of 40 provided care for sick or elderly dependents (compared to 12 per cent of the 30–39 age group). A total of 79 per cent of the non-working women who were interviewed said that they were prevented from going out to work because they were caring for someone, and 51 per cent of the working women who provided care said that their hours of work and the times at which they could work were affected. It seems likely, too, that a substantial proportion of women who make up the more or less unacknowledged and certainly uncounted voluntary workforce of this country comes from this age group.

There is some evidence that the sharp increase in women's activity rates between 1961 and 1971 has slackened off, and that the married women's activity rate may even have declined slightly since the late 1970s. This raises the question of whether the recession has been adversely affecting women's participation in the labour market, or whether women's participation has reached some kind of ceiling. Certainly the census figures suggest that the rate of increase in women's activity was less steep between 1971 and 1981 than it had been between 1961 and 1971, and the General Household Survey states that the married women's activity rate decreased slightly between 1980 and 1982, from 52 to 50 per cent (Office of Population Censuses and Surveys, 1983). However, on

close examination it appears that the falling off in the rate of
increase may be less significant than has often been supposed, or
indeed, that it may not have occurred at all.[3] What is quite clear
from the statistics is that women now comprise a higher proportion
of the total labour force than at any peacetime period this century,
and the increasing attachment of women to the labour market has
become a relatively permanent fact of life (cf. Paukert, 1984).

The number of women working part-time has increased dramatically since the Second World War, and it is largely the
increase in part-time work which accounts for women's higher
participation rate. The census shows a steady increase in the
proportion of women working part-time between 1951 and 1981
(table 1.1).

Table 1.1   Women employees working part-time 1951–81 (all ages)

Year	Unadjusted census (%)	Adjusted census (%)	Labour force survey consistent (%)
1951	11.5	12	13
1961	24.9	22	23
1971	37.8	34	36
1981	39.1	39	42

Source: Joshi and Owen (1984), table 4A.

According to the 1981 census, part-time women workers
comprised 39 per cent of the female labour force, but it has been
estimated that if allowance is made for women doing part-time
work who would have been undercounted by the 1981 census, the
percentage of women working part-time would have been higher –
closer to 42 per cent (Joshi and Owen, 1984). In the 1980s, the
number of part-time workers has continued to increase, as has the
proportion of married women who work part-time rather than
full-time (Central Statistical Office, 1986). Part-time work is
becoming a more and more important form of women's work.

Part-time workers in Britain are overwhelmingly female. The

UK has the highest proportion of women part-time workers of any OECD country (Paukert, 1984). According to the 1981 census, over 90 per cent of part-time workers were female and 87 per cent of these were marrried. The most common pattern is for women re-entering the labour market after a break for child-rearing to return to part-time work. A total of 52 per cent of the women interviewed in the *Women and Employment* survey (Martin and Roberts, 1984) returning to the labour force after a break went back to part-time employment (compared with about one-fifth who returned to full-time work). Women taking a longer break from work following the birth of a child were more likely to return to part-time employment, and almost half of those returning to part-time employment after having children returned to a job which was in a lower occupational category than previously. As a study of women's working lives based on evidence from the National Training Survey has clearly demonstrated, part-time work is frequently associated with downward mobility and skill downgrading (Elias and Main, 1982). The survey found that one in five women working part-time in 'other personal service' occupations had had a full-time job in some higher status occupational group 10 years earlier, and 4 per cent of the part-timers in this group had a teaching qualification, 8 per cent a nursing qualification, and 16 per cent had clerical and commercial qualifications (Elias and Main, 1982).

The *Women and Employment* survey (Martin and Roberts, 1984) showed very clearly that the presence of dependent children, and in particular the age of the youngest child, were the most critical variables affecting women's participation in the labour market. As table 1.2 shows, 69 per cent of the women surveyed whose youngest child was 0–4 years were economically inactive. Of the ones who worked, only 7 per cent worked full-time. By contrast, 31 per cent of the women with children aged 11–15 years worked full-time and only 19 per cent were inactive. Furthermore, the age of the youngest child is strongly associated with whether or not a woman is employed at all and if so whether or not she works full-time. Table 1.2 also indicates that older women without dependent children are more likely to work part-time than younger women.

The survey also found that women with younger children who worked part-time were more likely to work less than 16 hours. As

Table 1.2 Current economic activity by life-cycle stage: all women except full-time students

Economic activity	Childless women aged (%)		Women with youngest child aged (%)			Women with all children aged 16+ (%)		All women except full time students (%)
	Under 30	30+	0-4	5-10	11-15	Under 50	50+	(%)
Working full-time	82	67	7	16	31	40	27	35
Working part-time	3	12	20	48	45	37	32	28
Total working	85	79	27	64	76	77	59	63
'Unemployed'	11	6	4	4	5	5	5	6
Total economically active	96	85	31	68	81	82	64	69
Economically inactive	4	15	69	32	19	18	36	31
Total	100	100	100	100	100	100	100	100
Base	887	414	1,038	868	710	468	910	5,295

Source: Martin and Roberts (1984), table 2.11.

the age of the youngest child increased so too did the likelihood that a woman in part-time employment would work more than 16 hours or would work full-time. There were related findings in the attitude survey which found that more than half the women in the survey (60 per cent) felt that a woman with pre-school children 'ought to stay at home', and a further 25 per cent felt that she 'should only go out to work if she really needs the money'. Interestingly, the survey also found that 25 per cent of the women with children under 5 years who themselves worked actually thought that women in their situation (i.e. with children under 5) ought to stay at home. This was by far the highest discrepancy between what women thought and what they did, and Martin and Roberts (1984) imply that these women were particularly likely to be working under financial duress.

The women under most financial stress were the lone mothers: 43 per cent of all lone mothers had high financial stress scores compared to only 11 per cent of married mothers, and only 18 per cent had low scores compared to 55 per cent of married mothers. Although lone mothers were no more likely to work than married mothers (once factors such as the age of the youngest child were taken into account), if they did work they were more likely to be in full-time jobs. Half the lone mothers who worked were full-time, compared to only one-third of the married mothers.

The most likely explanation for this seems to be that for lone mothers who are receiving supplementary benefits the financial advantages of part-time work may be minimal – most of what is gained by working will be lost in benefit.[4] It has been suggested that the system of benefits for lone parents is so complex that it is unlikely that single mothers could make 'rational' economic choices about whether to work full-time, part-time or to rely in whole or in part on state benefits (Popay et al., 1983; Martin and Roberts, 1984). Although the system of benefits is extremely complex, it seems unlikely that this is the major barrier. It seems more likely that the financial advantage of working is so small that other factors achieve greater importance. Although it is important not to underestimate the significance of a few extra pounds a week to someone living on supplementary benefit, decisions about whether or not to work part-time for financial reasons are likely to be specific to individual circumstances, and to be affected by the availability of convenient work and adequate childcare. Lone mothers who are in receipt of some maintenance from their children's fathers may decide to do part-time work rather than have their income topped up by supplementary benefit in order to free themselves from what they may feel to be an unwarranted or intolerable intrusion into their lives by state agencies when they are in receipt of benefit. And since there are other advantages to part-time work – for example, as a possible stepping-stone to full-time work or for the social contact it provides – some lone parents on supplementary benefit may choose it despite its relative lack of financial reward.

The *Women and Employment* survey (Martin and Roberts, 1984) did not distinguish among women of different ethnic origins, but the limited available evidence suggests that varying patterns of employment exist among different ethnic groups, although it is not clear why these variations exist. Overall, the activity rate for West Indian women is much higher than that for white women, especially in the over 25 age group. Asian women, on the other hand, are less likely to be in the labour market than white women, but there are significant differences between Muslim and other Asian women. The survey by the Policy Studies Institute (PSI), *Black and White Britain* (Brown, 1984), found that only 18 per cent of Muslim women were working or unemployed, compared with 57 per cent of other Asian women, although Muslim women's employment may well be under-represented by official surveys. Non-white working women were more likely to be employed full-time than white women of the same marital status, according to the 1981 Labour Force Survey, and the ratio of full-time to part-time workers varied considerably among the different ethnic groups (*Employment Gazette*, October 1983). The PSI study (Brown, 1984) found that 44 per cent of the white women employees worked part-time, compared with 29 per cent and 16 per cent for West Indian and Asian women respectively. Asian and West Indian women working part-time were also found to work longer hours than white women. As the PSI study points out, the different levels of full-time and part-time working mean that 'the difference between the positions of white and West Indian women in the labour market is even greater than that shown by the comparison of overall activity rates; it also means that non-Muslim Asian women are, in terms of full-time work, more active than white women' (Brown, 1984, p. 151). We do not know why there are such pronounced differences in the levels of part-time working among the different ethnic groups, this is a question which needs further research. It is clear, however, that the presence of such distinct differences in the patterns of women's employment among various groups of women must have theoretical implications. It is therefore possible that the arguments advanced here about part-time work may be more appropriate to white women than to black women, who are far more likely to work full-time.

The Growth of Part-time Work

The Second World War

Undoubtedly a lot of work, especially casual and seasonal work, homework and work in service occupations, has always been done on a less than full-time basis, but it was not until the Second World War, with the massive mobilization of women workers,[5] that part-time work began to be used in a more systematic way – and even then it appears not to have been used very extensively or enthusiastically. Much of the discussion about women's work during the war centres on the experiences of women working in munitions factories, but the Wartime Social Survey conducted in 1943 found that part-time workers were employed principally in service industries, especially in distribution and transport, and in laundry, hotel and entertainment services (Thomas, 1944).

Part-time work was introduced into factories somewhat belatedly during the war, very much in response to the difficulties experienced by women in combining extraordinarily long hours of work with domestic responsibilities. Munitions factories often worked between a 65 and 80-hour week, and 10 or 12-hour working days were not uncommon, with just an hour's break for lunch (Riley, 1984). Since many women took longer lunch hours or time off in order to do their shopping, some employers began to introduce part-time shifts and shift-working in order to cope with the problems of absenteeism and avoid the consequent decline in productivity. Many employers introduced part-time work rather reluctantly, despite recommendations to do so by investigators, factory welfare officers, medical officers of health and industrial psychologists (Riley, 1984; Summerfield, 1984). Part-time work was seen less as a solution to women's domestic crisis (given that few of the burdens of domestic labour were lifted) than as a solution to the crisis in the supply and control of labour. The Ministry of Labour's attitude to part-time work was summed up by the North Midlands Regional Controller in 1941:

> Many married women would prefer part-time employment. This is not undesirable if it means attracting women who would not otherwise be in industry, but the danger, particularly in localities where there are large demands for female labour on essential war work is that it creates a tendency for women who can undertake full-time work to take part-time employment merely because it is less irksome. (Quoted in Summerfield, 1984, p. 142).

Factory employers gradually became more favourable to part-time working as the war progressed, and women began to be employed on a part-time basis either to cover for full-time women while they did their shopping or to extend the length of the working day. By the end of the war, employers' attitudes had shifted and part-time women were thought to be positively advantageous on a number of grounds: (a) they were more productive; (b) they stimulated a new and faster pace in the workshops; (c) they showed only half the rate of absenteeism and were better time-keepers; and (d) they were particularly good at doing the most unpopular kinds of work (Summerfield, 1984). This association of part-time working with the least desirable kinds of work was reinforced by the Ministry of Labour who recommended that 'all jobs where the onset of fatigue or boredom is relatively early' and 'work [that] is carried out in unpleasant surroundings caused by noise, dirt, smell or heat' should be organized on a part-time basis (Summerfield, 1984, p. 145). Furthermore, since part-time women workers received none of the supplements paid to full-timers – for instance, bonus and overtime rates, unemployment and accident insurance contributions – employers also made considerable direct economic savings from employing them (Summerfield, 1984, p. 145).

The Wartime Social Survey found that 7 per cent of the women interviewed worked part-time, that the vast majority of these were over 25 years of age and were married, and that just over half had children under 14 years of age (Thomas, 1944). A majority of the women interviewed said that they wanted to go on working after the war, and just under a third of the women working part-time said that they wished to go on doing so.

After the war, engineering and munitions work declined as the war industries were wound down, but while labour controls were lifted for the majority of women urgent appeals were made to women already in the labour force to remain in employment and to other women to take on paid employment. These appeals were amplified in the production drive of 1947 which aimed at increasing British exports. The *Ministry of Labour Gazette* in June 1947 specified where women were most wanted – in the cotton, wool and worsted, and clothing industries, in hospital domestic services and laundries, in the Land Army, iron and steel, boots and shoes and transport. In an address to women workers Aneurin Bevan emphasized that women were not being asked to do men's jobs. He said too that the labour shortage was temporary and that part-time work would be made available (Riley, 1984).

The Post-war Years of Boom

The labour shortage which Bevan had described as a short-term problem in fact continued throughout the 1950s and 1960s and many policy-makers pointed to married women as an untapped labour reserve which could be enticed onto the labour market and posed fewer problems than the employment of overseas workers (other than Commonwealth immigrants). The trend for the numbers of part-time women workers to increase, which has characterized the entire post-war period, began to emerge (table 1.3).

Geoffrey Thomas's second survey, *Women and Industry*, conducted in 1947 at the height of the post-war production drive, attempted to find out how far women were likely to remain in the labour market after the war, and concluded that a total of 900,000 more women might be persuaded to take up work if part-time as well as full-time jobs were available and if a sufficient number of nurseries could be provided. Part-time work, nurseries, improved industrial conditions and better shopping facilities were the main factors mentioned by women who were not in paid employment to improve women's situation at work; part-time work topped the list. Three-quarters of the prospective women workers interviewed

Table 1.3   Part-time women workers in Great Britain 1951–81

1951	779,000
1961	1,851,000
1966	2,562,000
1971	2,757,000
1981	3,781,000

The figures refer to employees in employment and are workforce-based. They therefore differ from the census of population, the Labour Force Survey and General Household Surveys, which count workers and not jobs, and are based on household surveys.

Source Derived from House of Lords' Session 1981–2, 19th Report, table 1, p. ix, and *Employment Gazette*, December 1983, Census of Employment 1981

Table 1.4   Working women in 1957 by type of occupation

| Type of work | Married women | | | Single women |
	Full-time (%)	Part-time (%)	Total (%)	Total (%)
Domestic workers, cleaners, canteen/ school meal helpers	15	45	31	10
Factory workers	22	10	16	14
Shop assistants	15	12	13	15
Clerical, office workers	10	15	13	19
Business: supervisory grades (shop managers, etc.)	14	3	8	7
Teachers, librarians, professional workers	7	5	6	10
Personal services (e.g. receptionist, hairdresser, dressmaker etc.)	6	4	5	7
Secretaries, typists, etc.	8	1	4	14
Other types of work	2	4	3	2
Not stated	1	1	1	2
Total (%)	100	100	100	100
Total (thousands)	122	137	259	137

Source: Klein (1965), p. 33

said they wanted part-time work (Thomas, 1948). The survey found that the largest number of women in the labour force (45 per cent) worked in unskilled occupations, while 27 per cent worked in personal services; 18 per cent were employed in distribution and 13 per cent were in routine clerical occupations. Unfortunately, it did not distinguish between full-time and part-time employment.

Ten years later, in 1957, Viola Klein conducted a study for Mass Observation which showed that nearly half (45 per cent) of part-time married women workers were employed in domestic occupations (Klein, 1965). She found that married women were also employed part-time in office work (15 per cent), as shop assistants (12 per cent) and as factory workers (10 per cent) table 1.4).

Klein pointed out that domestic occupations were predominantly part-time jobs (part-timers outnumbering full-timers by three to one), whereas among typists and secretaries the proportion of full-time to part-time workers was eight to one. Most of the part-time jobs were classified as unskilled and were described by Klein as 'types of work which have little or no appeal to middle-class women' (Klein, 1965, p. 32), and only a tiny proportion of women (3 per cent) were employed part-time in managerial and supervisory occupations. It appears that the association of the least desirable forms of work with part-time working, which was promoted by the Ministry of Labour during the war, continued throughout the post-war years. Klein also pointed out, as many have since, that a shift in occupation often takes place among women after marriage, and that while office work was by far the commonest form of employment among single women, domestic work ranked first among married women, with factory work in second place. Geoffrey Thomas's second survey, *Women and Industry* (1948), had also found that married and widowed women were found much more often in unskilled operative occupations but were much less likely than single women to be engaged in clerical work.

In the 1950s, as now, the majority of women were employed in service industries. It is ironic therefore (but not surprising, given the biases inherent in official statistics) that one of the few sets of official statistics on part-time work which were regularly collected before 1971 was on part-time working in manufacturing industry (table 1.5).[6] This shows that during the 1950s and 1960s part-time workers became a significantly larger proportion of the female labour force in manufacturing industry. In Coventry, the proportion of women working part-time in manufacturing industry was higher than it was nationally: in 1961 it was 26 per cent compared to 20 per cent nationally, according to the census.

The increase in the number of part-time workers in manufacturing industry was much slower than the increase in the number of married women workers *in toto*. Between 1950 and 1961 there was an overall increase of 82,000 part-time women workers in manufacturing industries compared to an increase of 306,000 married women workers in these industries (*Ministry of Labour Gazette* December 1962). This suggests that large numbers of married women were also being drawn into the labour force as full-time workers during this period. In Coventry, the number of women employed in the manufacturing sector increased by 3,453 between 1951 and 1961, although this pattern was to change during the 1960s when large numbers of women's full-time jobs in Coventry's manufacturing industry were lost.

The increase in part-time employment which had been gradual in the 1950s, became much more marked in the 1960s. Between 1960 and 1968 the numbers of female part-time workers increased in all manufacturing industries, regardless of whether the total female workforce was increasing or decreasing, or whether it was a 'male' industry such as vehicles or a 'female' industry such as clothing. Furthermore, the proportion of the female labour force working part-time increased in all manufacturing industries between 1960 and 1968 (table 1.5). Table 1.5 shows that the proportion of women employees working part-time in 1968 varied a great deal between manufacturing industries, from the very high proportion (30.6 per cent) in the food, drink and tobacco industry to the low proportion (10.3 per cent) in the clothing industry, both industries which have traditionally been heavily dependent on female labour. Such variation suggests that there is no simple correlation between areas of 'traditionally' female employment and part-time working, and that the form which women's employment takes in the different industries needs to be explained.

A study of personnel officers in manufacturing industry undertaken by Klein in 1960 analysed the reasons for the employment of part-time workers (Klein, 1965). Despite the fact that many of the managers interviewed expressed considerable reservations

Table 1.5 Part-time women workers as a percentage of total women's employment in manufacturing industries in Great Britain 1950–68

Industry order (1958 Standard Industrial Classification)	June each year (%)									
	1959	1960	1961	1962	1963	1964	1965	1966	1967	1968
Food, drink and tobacco	21.6	24.1	24.9	24.6	24.2	25.0	26.6	28.6	29.1	30.6
Chemicals and allied industries	12.3	13.0	14.1	14.6	14.1	15.1	15.4	17.9	16.4	17.5
Metal manufacture	11.0	11.7	12.1	12.6	13.8	13.9	14.3	14.7	14.5	15.3
Engineering and electrical goods	10.9	13.1	12.6	13.2	13.5	15.4	15.8	17.7	15.9	16.8
Shipbuilding and marine engineering	0.8	5.5	5.9	5.7	6.2	10.4	10.6	12.5	15.4	15.3
Vehicles	8.1	9.2	8.6	9.2	9.5	9.9	10.6	11.5	11.0	11.4
Metal goods not elsewhere specified	14.7	16.7	17.3	17.2	17.3	19.4	20.8	23.5	22.0	21.5
Textiles	9.9	11.5	12.6	12.3	12.3	13.4	14.5	15.9	15.1	15.9
Leather, leather goods and fur	9.8	10.9	12.8	11.5	11.8	14.2	15.0	16.2	17.3	15.7
Clothing and footwear	8.0	7.9	8.6	8.3	7.9	8.8	9.7	10.5	10.1	10.3
Bricks, pottery, glass, cement etc.	7.4	7.6	8.3	9.1	8.7	9.7	9.2	11.5	11.0	11.9
Timber, furniture etc.	10.8	11.4	12.1	12.8	12.3	13.1	14.8	14.9	15.8	14.4
Paper, printing and publishing	8.7	10.3	11.4	11.3	11.2	12.2	13.3	15.7	15.8	15.7
Other manufacturing industries	14.6	15.7	16.7	17.4	17.5	19.0	18.9	22.0	20.8	22.0
Total, manufacturing Industries	11.7	13.2	13.7	13.8	13.8	15.0	15.9	17.7	17.0	17.7

The data are derived from information supplied by employers. Part-time employment is defined as ordinarily involving not more than 30 hours per week. The percentage represents the proportion of the total number of women employed in the industry who worked part-time only. No detailed analysis is available for years before 1959.

Source: British Labour Statistics, Historical Abstract 1886–1968, table 142.

about employing part-time workers, Klein pointed out that only 14 firms out of the 120 who replied to the survey failed to employ any. The main reasons given by managers for employing women part-timers were that part-timers provided a source of labour in times of scarcity, that they constituted a labour force which was flexible enough to enable management to meet fluctuations in demand, and that they could easily be disposed of (cf. Hallaire, 1968). Part-time employment on the evening shift was a very common form of part-time work in manufacturing industry during the 1960s, as we discovered in our interviews in Coventry.

During the 1960s the government, faced by a severe shortage of labour, promoted the creation of part-time jobs in various branches of the public service, and some of these were in professional occupations. A census taken in the Civil Service in 1966 showed that the number of part-time workers had increased to 34,000, only 4 per cent of the total workforce but a considerably higher figure than a few years before. Whereas there had previously been no part-time workers in the Civil Service other than cleaners, there was a growing trend for part-time typists, telephone operators and book-keepers to be employed. The number of part-time nurses and teachers also rose during this period. According to Hallaire, strenuous efforts were made to recruit trained nurses back into the profession on a part-time basis. The Trades Union Congress (TUC) estimated that the ratio of part-time to full-time nurses was 1:3 in the mid-1960s. The number of part-time teachers in the United Kingdom grew from 13,830 in 1960 to 36,200 in 1966 as a result of propaganda campaigns aimed mainly at married women, and the government had a target of over 70,000 part-time teachers (Hallaire, 1968).

The development of part-time work in these occupations is noteworthy for three reasons. First, it signalled the end of the 'moral' ban on middle-class married women working, a ban which had forced women to resign their jobs on marriage in some professions (e.g. banking, teaching, the Civil Service). Secondly, it broke away from the model of part-time jobs as necessarily unskilled, uninteresting and unresponsible. These women were wanted precisely because they were qualified and experienced, although the part-timers working in the professions were, and still are, regarded as second-class citizens. Thirdly, the government's call to women to work part-time as teachers and nurses is significant in that it reflects a decision to offer reduced hours of work to married women rather than providing childcare facilities. The principal way, it was commonly assumed, of getting married women back into the labour market was to create jobs on a part-time basis. The creation of part-time jobs was not, however, the only way of enticing married women with children into paid employment. In the Lancashire textiles industry, for instance, there were far more workplace nurseries and fewer part-time jobs than in other parts of the country, and this was also true in countries like France. Although one must be cautious about conjecture in this area, it seems likely that more comprehensive provision of childcare facilities would have encouraged more women to work full-time, and that in the absence of such provision women who wanted paid employment had little option but to work part-time.[7]

The initiatives to create more part-time professional jobs in the 1960s led to some changes, but only in a very limited number of occupations. There is little evidence of any increase in part-time working in professions other than teaching and nursing (cf. Fogarty et al., 1971), and Audrey Hunt's survey of women's employment conducted in 1965 found that three-quarters of part-time women workers were employed in just four industries: miscellaneous services, distribution, professional and scientific services, and engineering, and that by far the highest concentration was in miscellaneous services (Hunt, 1968). Hunt also found that part-time working was substantially more occupationally segregated than women's full-time work.[8]

Furthermore, part-time women workers were found to be far more likely to be employed in 'less skilled' jobs than women working full-time. Three-fifths of the personal service workers interviewed were part-timers, as were nearly four-fifths of the unskilled manual workers. Managerial jobs, in contrast, were almost entirely done by women working full-time (Hunt,1968, vol. 1). One must beware of concluding from evidence such as Hunt's, however, that part-time women workers invariably lacked skills. Both theoretical discussions of the concept of skill and more recent empirical research suggest that many women's jobs are often not classified as skilled even when they involve complex competencies and responsibilties. That most of the part-time women workers' jobs were *defined* as unskilled, however, is undoubtedly true.

The 1970s

Unlike the first 25 years after the war, which were mainly characterized by a labour shortage, the 1970s and early 1980s have seen a deepening recession in the economy and moves on the part of many employers to restructure their labour processes. Labour shortage has given way to very high levels of unemployment among both men and women, and this has become a major political issue. There was much speculation in the early 1970s about what would happen to women's employment in the recession and whether or not women would be the first to lose jobs, but a clear trend has manifested itself over the past 15 years. Women's participation in the labour market increased steadily until 1977, then levelled off and has now begun to increase again. And women's part-time employment has increased dramatically and is now the only significant area of employment growth in the economy. The number of part-time jobs increased between 1971 and 1981 by over one million, an increase of 34 per cent. And the proportion of both men and women working part-time increased during this period. Despite a small increase in the number of male part-timers, however, part-time work remains a predominantly female form of work (table 1.6).

Between 1971 and 1981 part-time employment continued to increase in both the manufacturing and the service sectors of the economy, although the increase in part-time employment in manufacturing finally came to an end in 1978.[9] The major expansion, however, took place in the service sector of the economy with approximately one million new part-time jobs being created for women. Women's part-time employment became increasingly concentrated in this sector of the economy (table 1.7).

The largest concentrations of part-time women workers were in professional and scientific services, distributive trades and miscellaneous services, all of which had increased their employment of part-timers substantially since the early 1970s. In Coventry, women's part-time employment was also heavily concentrated in the service sector of the economy, and these same three industries accounted for more than three-quarters of Coventry's part-time

Table 1.6 Full-time and part-time employees in employment: by broad industry group

	1971^a	1978^a	1981^b
All industries and services			
Men			
Full-time	12,840	12,396	11,426
Part-time	584	704	709
Women			
Full-time	5,467	5,486	5,254
Part-time	2,757	3,688	3,759
Total industries and services	21,648	22,274	21,148
Manufacturing industries			
Men			
Full-time	5,475	4,949	4,174
Part-time	71	83	64
Women			
Full-time	1,869	1,604	1,318
Part-time	471	480	369
Total Manufacturing	7,886	7,117	5,924
Service industries			
Men			
Full-time	5,261	5,492	5,461
Part-time	473	578	597
Women			
Full-time	3,418	3,691	3,740
Part-time	2,206	3,117	3,294
Total services	11,358	12,878	13,091

[a] As at June.
[b] Interim estimates as at September.

The figures refer to employees in employment and are workplace-based. They therefore differ from the census of population, the Labour Force Survey and the General Household Surveys, which count workers and not jobs, and are based on household surveys.

Source Central Statistical Office, (1984), p. 63

Table 1.7   Growth in service sector employment and proportion of part-time work, 1971–8

Standard Industrial Classification	Total growth in employment	Growth in part-time employment	Growth in part time as % of total growth
Miscellaneous services	454,000	346,000	76
Professional and scientific	661,000	339,000	51
Distributive trades	169,000	208,000	123
Insurance, banking etc.	219,000	79,000	36
Other services	–3,000	34,000	n.a.
All services	1,500,000	1,006,000	67

Source: Clark (1982), p. 15.

female workforce in 1976. In both the manufacturing and service sectors, women tended to work part-time in jobs which were only done by other women, and they were much more heavily concentrated in manual work, often in jobs classified as unskilled. The *Women and Employment* survey (Martin and Roberts, 1984) found that 70 per cent of manual service workers were part-time, compared to 35 per cent of non-manual service workers. Some 60 per cent of sales assistants worked part-time, as did 80 per cent of semi-skilled and unskilled domestic workers. By contrast, only 19 per cent of intermediate non-manual workers and 22 per cent of teachers worked part-time (Ballard, 1984).

Part-time jobs are even more highly segregated than full-time ones. The *Women and Employment* survey found that two-thirds of part-time women workers were employed in just four broad occupational groups: catering, cleaning, hairdressing and clerical work (Martin and Roberts, 1984). More detailed information about the jobs that part-timers are doing is provided by the National Training Survey which shows that nearly two out of every five part-time jobs are concentrated in 'other personal service occupations', a group which includes waitresses, bar staff, other unskilled catering staff, school meals assistants, porters, caretakers, and all others in catering, cleaning and hairdressing who were not assigned a specific occupation. A further 12 per cent were found in 'other sales occupations', 12 per cent were in clerical occupations, and 11 per cent were classified as 'other operatives' (Elias and Main, 1982). The *Women and Employment* survey found that unlike full-time women workers, part-timers were as likely to experience job segregation in service industries as in manufacturing, and that in both sectors nearly three-quarters of the part-time women workers interviewed worked only with women (Martin and Roberts, 1984).

It is often assumed that the expansion of part-time employment in the 1970s can be explained in terms of the growth of the service sector of the economy. As table 1.8 shows, there certainly has been a growth in the number of people employed in service industries and occupations, but it is important to point out that the argument that this reflects a growth in the service sector is a tautological one. Measuring the growth or decline of a sector in terms of the number of people employed in it can be problematic when increasingly these are working part-time. If the people being counted are all full-time employees working a standard week, then (assuming that no significant changes in the organization of work have led to changes in productivity) comparisons can indeed tell us

Table 1.8   Percentage distribution of women in part-time jobs by sector

	1971	1976	1978
Manufacturing	17.0	13.5	13.1
Services	80.1	83.8	84.5
Base 100% (thousands)	2,757	3,646	3,679

The figures refer to female employees in employment only, and excludes employees in private domestic service, family workers, and HM Forces. Part-time workers are defined as those working for not more than 30 hours per week.

Source: Davidson and Cooper (1984), p. 22

something about the decline or growth of a sector. In recent years, however, the workforce in many service industries has been composed of constantly changing proportions of full and part-time workers, and the number of people employed has often increased while the number of employee hours has actually decreased. In these circumstances one can hardly accurately describe the industry as 'expanding'. The problem is further compounded by the fact that part-timers' hours may be reduced or increased from one year to the next, so that while the number of employees might remain stable or increase, the actual hours worked may change. Although full-timers' hours can also be variable (in that people may do overtime or be put on short-time) much better records of these variations are kept and the length of the basic working week is, relatively speaking, more constant.

These considerations are particularly relevant when discussing the 'expansion' of sectors where part-time work has formed an increasingly large proportion of all work. Very often the increase in part-time work is explained as if it were the *result* of the 'vast expansion' of the service sector rather than being the reason why the expansion seems to be so vast. Two women who work 20 hours a week theoretically do at least as much work as one woman working a conventional 40 hour week, and they probably do more. We should be cautious, therefore, of accepting explanations which attribute the rise in part-time work to the expansion of the service sector at face value.[10] We should be cautious, too, of government claims that the increase in jobs is *per se* evidence of an economic recovery. In some sectors the expansion is likely to be more 'real' than in others.

Reasons for the Growth of Part-time Work

The question of *why* part-time employment has continued to rise is a critically important one, and two different kinds of explanation have been offered. According to one line of argument employers create part-time jobs when there is a shortage of labour; according to the other, part-time jobs are created for reasons connected to the organization of the labour process – because employers substitute part-time jobs for full-time ones, or because they need a flexible labour force.

In the 1970s there were clearly many full-time workers (both men and women) who had lost their jobs in manufacturing industry, many of whom would (theoretically at least) have been available to work in the service industries on a full-time basis. In Coventry, 12,954 women (40 per cent of the female manufacturing labour force) lost their jobs between 1961 and 1976 because the decline in women's employment in manufacturing industry started earlier there than in many other places. Many men too lost their jobs in Coventry's manufacturing industry during the 1960s and 1970s. Coventry is thus a good example of a phenomenon which became more general during the 1970s, thousands of full-time jobs in manufacturing industry were lost in the same period that the service sector was expanding. This suggests that the widescale development of part-time jobs in the service sector in the 1970s cannot be explained in terms of a shortage of labour (although there is some evidence that a labour shortage may have played a part in the continuing employment of part-time workers in a few manufacturing industries, clothing and footwear and electrical engineering, for instance). Other factors, it seems, must have been more important.

It is sometimes suggested that the increase in part-time work during the 1970s can be explained in terms of the substitution of part-time workers for full-time ones. The question of substitution is a complex one, and the evidence on the extent of substitution is not entirely clear. Rubery and Tarling (1986) have suggested that between 1971 and 1974 some substitution of part-time workers for full-time ones occurred but that, unlike the 1980s when substitution principally occurred in the service sector of the economy, this was concentrated in manufacturing industries. Dex and Perry (1984) also suggest that there may have been some substitution of part-time jobs for full-time ones in the 1970s. They found evidence of substitution in the early 1970s in the textiles, clothing and food and drink industries, all industries in which part-time employment continued to rise while total employment fell. Dex and Perry (1984) also found that whereas full-time jobs were lost to a greater extent than part-time jobs in manufacturing industry as a whole, part-time employment experienced greater proportional decreases than full-time employment in downswings in the economy, which suggests that part-time work is particularly vulnerable to cyclical fluctuations (cf. Bruegel, 1979)[11]

Dex and Perry (1984) suggest that women have been relatively well protected from the effects of the recession because of their concentration in the service sector of the economy, and that there is little evidence of substitution having occurred in this sector during the 1970s. It has recently been suggested, however, that the substantial growth in women's part-time working has been more rapid in sectors like distribution and other services which might in other circumstances have been expected to provide jobs for young workers.[12] The various employment protection laws which were passed in the 1970s, the introduction of a graduated system of employer's national insurance contributions, and the income tax system (in which married women have an earned income allowance), it is suggested, may all have contributed to a preference on the part of employers for married women part-timers over full-time young workers during this period.

Whether married women have been employed in jobs which might otherwise have gone to young workers is a very important question which has considerable political implications, but as yet the evidence on this is inconclusive. Indeed, it is difficult to discover definite evidence about substitution from analyses of aggregate statistics like those discussed above because these do not provide information about the kinds of full-time jobs which have been lost and the kinds of part-time ones which have been created. It is thus impossible to discern whether the jobs are commensurable. In their workplace studies, Robinson and Wallace (1984) found some instances of part-time workers being substituted for full-time ones, but these were generally cases of part-time women workers being substituted for full-time women. This suggests that at the level of the enterprise substitution has taken place within an already existing system of job segregation. As yet there is little hard evidence of part-time women workers being substituted for adult full-time men.

Studies by Hunt (1975) and McIntosh (1980) and our own research suggest that flexibility may be more important than substitution as an explanation for the growth of part-time work. Both Hunt and McIntosh suggest that flexibility, and the fact that the work to be done was not sufficient to warrant full-time cover, were among the reasons most often given by employers as to why they employed part-time workers. The National Federation of Self-employed and Small Businesses also emphasized the importance of flexibility in its evidence to the House of Lords Select Committee (House of Lords, 1981–2).

Our own research also underlined the importance of flexibility in explaining the growth of part-time employment but we concluded that this did not provide a *sufficient* explanation of why so many jobs (especially in the service sector) were organized on a part-time basis. We found that employers had devised different means of attaining flexibility when they employed women from those which they used when they employed men. Part-time jobs were created in areas of women's work, especially manual work, and in domestic and caring occupations. In areas of men's employment, in contrast, employers used other means of obtaining flexibility (e.g. overtime and short-time working). Thus, while it is undoubtedly true, as Robinson and Wallace (1984) have argued, that employers derive many economic advantages from employing part-time workers, our own research suggests that this cannot be explained solely in economic terms. Gender enters into the picture. It is because they are 'women's jobs' that so many of the jobs in the service sectors of the economy are part-time. And because they are women's jobs flexibility takes a particular form.

A Note on the 1980s

The trends of the 1970s have continued into the 1980s, with a further 579,000 part-time jobs for women being created between December 1981 and December 1985. At present, just over one in five jobs are done by part-time women workers, and nearly half of all women's jobs are part-time. The trend for women's part-time jobs in manufacturing industry to be lost has continued, with 52,000 part-time jobs disappearing between December 1981 and December 1985, and the loss of women's part-time jobs has been proportionally slightly higher than the loss of women's full-time jobs and considerably higher than the proportion of men's full-time jobs which were lost over the same period.[13]

The number of part-time women workers employed in manufacturing industry fades into relative insignificance when compared with the number employed in the service sector, however. The total number of women's part-time jobs in services increased by just over 600,000 between 1981 and 1985, while the number of women's full-time jobs declined by just over 100,000 and the number of men's jobs increased by 222,000 (table 1.9).

Table 1.9 Employment in the service sectors, 1981 and 1985 (thousands)

| | Men | Women | | |
		Full-time	Part-time	Total
1981	6,029	3,691	3,376	13,096
1985	6,251	3,585	4,003	13,839
	+222	−10	+627	+743

Source: Calculated from *Employment Gazette, Historical Supplement no. 1,* August 1984, and *Employment Gazette*, May 1986, Table 1.4.

Since the figures do not distinguish between men's full-time and part-time jobs, it is not clear how far the increase in men's jobs is also an increase in part-time employment. What is clear, however, is that women's part-time work has become an increasingly important form of service work, and that women's full-time work

Table 1.10 Part-time women workers in the service sectors, 1981 and 1985 (thousands)

	1981	1985
Retail distribution	728.6	895.5
Education	601.1	670.8
Hotels and catering	434.1	489.6
Medical and other health services	451.7	536.2
Other services	246.5	311.6

Source: Calculated from *Employment Gazette, Historical Supplement no. 1*, August 1984, and *Employment Gazette*, May 1986, table 1.4.

in services has declined. In 1985 just over half the women working in the service sector worked part-time, and just over a quarter of all service sector jobs were part-time. With the exception of public administration and defence, which saw a very slight fall in the numbers of women employed part-time, the number of women's part-time jobs increased in every major service industry in the early 1980s. Table 1.10 shows the largest concentrations of women working part-time in service industries.

In several of these industries the expansion of part-time employment occurred while full-time employment was contracting. The changes within education are the most startling, with a staggering 60,000 women's full-time jobs and 1,800 men's jobs being lost between 1981 and 1985, and 69,700 new women's part-time jobs being created. Retailing and public administration also saw some loss of women's full-time jobs, although (as discussed above) it is difficult to tell how much substitution has taken place in the expansion of part-time working. Rubery and Tarling (1986) have suggested that in the early 1980s substitution was concentrated in the service industries, and certainly the loss of full-time jobs in retailing and education does suggest that some measure of substitution may have occurred. However, other changes – for example, the extension of shop opening hours in retailing – have also played a part in the growth of part-time employment, as Robinson and Wallace (1984) point out.

Looking to the future, the number of part-time jobs is projected to go on rising throughout the 1980s to reach 5.7 million in 1990 (Elias and Wilson, 1985). These jobs will mostly be concentrated in the service sector of the economy, although there may be some increase in part-time working in manufacturing industries as employers attempt to create a more flexible labour force. It must be emphasized, however, that calculations of job losses and gains, so favoured by economists, do not begin to capture the variety of ways in which work is being restructured. Part-time jobs may not have disappeared as fast as full-time ones but there is a variety of other ways in which they have been adversely affected by the recession and the restructuring of work: the cutting and reorganization of hours, part-timers being sent to work in other workplaces, the abolition of retainers paid during the school holidays and the deregulation of employment contracts through privatization, for instance.

If current trends persist, the hours of many part-timers are likely to go on decreasing, pay rates will be subject to less regulation as Wages Councils are weakened, and more and more part-time workers will find that their earnings are beneath the threshold for paying national insurance contributions. Moreover, part-timers employed by sub-contracted firms in privatized sectors of the economy may well find themselves getting lower rates of pay than they received for doing equivalent work within the public sector, with worse terms and conditions of employment.

International Variations

It is often assumed that the pattern experienced in Britain – a steep increase in married women's employment and a large growth in the number of part-time jobs – is typical of the general direction of change in modern capitalist countries in the post-war world. However, although many countries have experienced a rise in the rate of women's employment since the war, the levels of women's participation in the labour market have varied markedly, as has the extent and pattern of part-time working. An analysis of women's activity rates across the countries in the Organization for Economic Cooperation and Development (OECD) reveals several different patterns.

A few countries (e.g. Australia and Canada) started from a relatively low baseline in 1950, with less than a third of women of working age in the labour force, and experienced a large increase in women's participation rate (to around 50 per cent) by 1977. In a second (and much larger) group of countries – Belgium, Finland, Spain, Sweden, the United Kingdom and the United States – women's participation rate increased significantly between 1950 and 1977. In Sweden, which today has the highest female activity rate of any OECD country, the rate doubled, from 35.1 per cent in 1970 to 70 per cent in 1977. A third group of countries – France, Iceland and The Netherlands – experienced only slight increases in women's participation in the labour market (less than 5 per cent), while a final group – Austria, Greece, Ireland, Japan, Luxemburg and Turkey – experienced a decline in women's participation rate between 1950 and 1977.

Today, OECD countries can be divided into three groups: a

group of Nordic nations which have the highest participation rates for women, a middle group of countries in which the female participation rate averages between 50 and 60 per cent (the United Kingdom among them), and a final group in which participation rates are significantly lower (table 1.11). Women are much more likely than men to work part-time in all the OECD countries for which statistics are available, and the incidence of recorded part-time work varies between countries from less than 10 per cent of the female labour force (in Ireland and Italy) to over 40 per cent (in Denmark, Sweden and the United Kingdom). Women are prominent among part-time workers in all OECD countries, although the ratio of female to male part-timers varies considerably (table 1.12). At 94.3 per cent, the United Kingdom had the highest proportion of women part-timers of any country in 1981, followed closely by Germany and Denmark, while Greece had the lowest, in close company with Italy, Japan and The Netherlands. OECD data show that women's share of part-time employment grew in Britain between 1973 and 1981 by 2.2 per cent, and that the ratio of female to male part-timers also increased in most OECD countries (Paukert, 1984). Over nine million people in the European Community had a part-time job as their principal occupation in 1981, while a further two million did part-time work on a casual basis. In the United Kingdom, like Denmark, France, The Netherlands and Belgium, the vast majority of the part-time workers had a main occupation which was part-time, whereas in Greece and Italy the extent of part-time casual work was far higher.

Crossnational evidence makes clear that there is no simple correlation between female activity rates and part-time working, as is commonly supposed.[14] Finland, for instance, has a very high female activity rate but a low level of part-time working among women, whereas the United Kingdom has a female activity rate which is closer to the OECD average and a high level of part-time working. France and Japan have female activity rates similar to that of the United Kingdom, but significantly lower levels of part-time working among women, although the extent of part-time working is growing in both countries. There are undoubtedly a variety of reasons for this. Part of the difference between France and Britain, for instance, can be accounted for by the greater importance of the agricultural sector in the French economy and,

Table 1.11 Labour Force participation rates[a] and the female share of the labour force (%)

	1950			1977			1983[b]		1982
	Men	Women	Female share	Men	Women	Female share	Men	Women	Female share
Australia	99.7	29.6	22.4	89.6	51.7	35.8	87.0	52.4	37.0
Austria	97.4	51.1	38.5	82.4	48.1	38.5	82.7	50.3	38.7
Belgium	86.3	32.8	27.9	82.1	45.6	35.6	79.4	49.4	37.7c
Canada	94.2	26.2	21.3	85.3	51.9	37.8	85.0	60.3	40.9
Denmark	100.4	49.6	33.6	91.0	67.3	42.2	89.2	72.5	44.4d
Finland	97.9	59.9	40.6	78.3	64.7	45.8	82.7	73.5	47.1
France	93.0	49.5	35.9	84.4e	50.1	37.6	79.4	52.1	38.6
Germany	98.0	44.3	35.1	83.5	48.4	37.6	80.0	49.6	38.2
Greece	94.1	41.4	32.1	82.7c	31.2	27.7f	78.8	36.1	32.0d
Iceland	100.0	40.9	28.5	93.9c	45.1c	31.6	–	–	31.1c
Ireland	102.9	36.9	25.5	92.1c	33.3	27.5e	86.5	36.2	27.7c
Italy	99.0	32.0	25.4	82.9	37.1	31.9	81.0	40.8	33.8
Japan	97.5	57.6	38.4	89.3	53.1	40.0	89.1	57.2	39.0
Luxemburg	92.5	37.6	29.2	85.5e	31.1e	26.2	–	–	29.7
Netherlands	95.1	28.5	23.4	81.9e	32.0e	28.0	80.3	38.7	30.5
NewZealand	95.9	30.0	23.5	86.2	40.4	31.5	85.8	45.4	34.6e
Norway	99.7	36.6	27.1	87.4	58.5	39.6	86.1	67.0	42.2
Portugal	99.6	26.3	22.4	87.2	50.4	39.1	89.5	55.8	40.4
Spain	101.1	17.6	15.8	87.6e	32.5e	28.6	79.3	33.1	29.5
Sweden	98.6	35.1	26.3	88.1	70.0	43.7	85.9	76.6	46.2
Switzerland	100.3	39.1	29.7	92.2e	51.7e	34.1	90.0	48.6	35.3
Turkey	112.7	86.7	44.4	92.8e	53.2e	38.4	–	–	–
United Kingdom	97.2	40.7	30.7	91.3	57.3	38.2	87.9	57.5	39.1
United States	92.5	37.2	28.9	85.2	55.7	40.3	84.7	61.9	42.8

[a] Defined as labour force of all ages divided by population aged 15–64
[b] Estimates by the secretariat.
[c] 1981   [e] 1975
[d] 1980   [f] 1971

Source: OECD (1980, 1985).

Table 1.12 Overall size and structure of part-time employment (%)

	Both sexes		Men		Women		Female share	
	1973	1981	1973	1981	1973	1981	1973	1981
Australia	11.4	15.9	3.4	5.2	27.3	34.6	79.6	79.0
Belgium	2.8	6.4	0.4	1.3	8.2	16.4	89.8	86.2
Canada[a]	10.6	13.5	5.1	6.8	20.3	31.8	69.5	72.0
Denmark	17.0	20.8	1.9	3.0	40.3	43.6	93.4	92.0
Finland[b]	3.9	4.5	1.4	1.7	6.7	7.6	81.0	80.2
France	5.1	7.4	1.4	1.9	11.2	15.9	82.1	84.6
Germany	7.7	10.2	1.0	1.0	20.0	25.7	92.4	93.8
Greece	–	2.1	–	1.1	–	4.3	–	63.0
Ireland[c]	4.0	3.1	1.8	1.3	10.1	8.0	67.5	68.6
Italy	3.9	2.7	2.3	1.4	8.5	5.8	55.4	64.1
Japan	7.9	10.0	4.8	4.9	17.3	19.6	60.9	67.3
Luxemburg[c]	4.5	5.8	1.0	1.0	13.9	17.1	83.3	87.5
Netherlands[d]	4.4	19.4	1.1	8.4	15.5	45.2	80.4	67.6
New Zealand	10.8	13.9	4.7	5.0	22.0	27.4	71.3	78.7
Norway[a]	23.5	28.3	8.7	10.6	47.6	53.6	77.0	77.9
Sweden	18.0	25.2	3.7	7.2	38.8	46.4	88.0	84.5
United Kingdom	15.3	15.4	1.8	1.4	38.3	37.1	92.1	94.3
United States	13.9	14.4	7.2	7.5	23.8	23.7	68.4	70.3

[a] 1975 and 1981
[b] 1976 and 1981
[c] 1973 and 1979
[d] 1981 data are not comparable with 1973 data because of a change in the definition of part-time workers.

Source: OECD (1985).

until recently, the lesser development of the service sector (cf. Garnsey, 1984). However, state policies can also have a significant impact on the patterns of women's participation in the labour market, and the higher level of full-time working among women in France can partly be explained in terms of the better provision for working mothers of childcare facilities and maternity leave. The figures cited here should caution us against making the assumption that high female activity rates are inevitably associated with high levels of part-time working. They suggest that the different levels of part-time work in different countries is a complex phenomenon which requires explanation. An analysis of state policies (not only concerning childcare provision but also state benefits and employment legislation), trade union practices, ideological assumptions and cultural norms, as well as the changing industrial structure, are all critical factors in explaining the different patterns.

In the 40 years since the end of the Second World War, part-time work in Britain has developed as a particular form of work organized on the assumption that it will be done by women with domestic responsibilities. But it is important to recognize the variety of ways in which part-time work has been used in other countries and the different ways in which it is related to the dominant form of full-time work. Our own research into women's part-time employment, described in the next three chapters, concentrated on discovering how part-time labour was used in the overall organization of work. In the next two chapters we look at the different ways in which part-time workers were employed in some of Coventry's manufacturing industries and in three of its public service industries.

2

Manufacturing Industry

An important aim of our research was to explain the growth in part-time employment. We also wanted to see how far the patterns of part-time employment in Coventry conformed to the patterns proposed by the 'deskilling thesis' and the 'industrial reserve army thesis', especially in the light of claims like Bruegel's (1979) that part-time women workers in manufacturing industry were particularly disposable in periods of recession.

Coventry is a city which has been dominated by manufacturing, and this domination has been reflected in the patterns of employment for both sexes, though to a greater extent for men than for women. Men's employment in manufacturing grew steadily after the war, and by the mid-1970s nearly three-quarters of Coventry's male employees worked in manufacturing, a figure nearly double that for Great Britain as a whole. Women's employment in manufacturing also grew in the post-war years, when proportionately more Coventry women were employed in manufacturing industry than was the case nationally. By the mid-1970s, however, the pattern of women's employment in Coventry was much closer to the national pattern, with around two-thirds of the female workforce employed in the service sector of the economy. Indeed, in the 20 years between 1951 and 1971 there was a complete reversal in the proportions of women employed in the manufacturing and service sectors. Part-time work, too, increased in the post-war years. In 1961 it was proportionately more important in Coventry than it was nationally, and between 1950 and 1970 it became an increasingly important form of women's employment in manufacturing. By 1971, however, part-time employment had become much less important in Coventry's manufacturing industry and more important in the service sector of the economy.

In this chapter we discuss how part-time work has been cons-

Table 2.1   Women's part-time employment in Coventry's manufacturing industries 1976

| Industry | Women | | Men |
	Part-time	Full-time	
Food, drink and tobacco	144	150	808
Coal	1	14	454
Chemical	4	32	152
Metal manufacturing	43	110	912
Mechanical engineering	411	2,961	14,779
Instrument engineering	16	73	112
Electrical engineering	397	4,157	10,924
Shipbuilding	49	338	1,443
Vehicles	343	4,924	49,403
Metal goods n.e.s.	183	942	3,749
Textiles	123	690	2,655
Leather goods	2	30	3
Clothing	31	301	13
Bricks, pottery glass	29	52	365
Timber furniture	49	136	661
Paper, printing etc.	128	383	914
Other manufacturing	65	565	1,734
All manufacturing industries	2,018	15,858	89,081

n.e.s. – not elsewhere specified

Source: Census of Employment (1976).

tructed and organized within some of Coventry's manufacturing industries, looking both at production occupations and at clerical and administrative work, and we show how gender has played a part in the construction of part-time jobs.[1] Our project concentrated on those industries in Coventry with the largest concentrations of women working part-time in 1976: mechanical engineering, electrical engineering, vehicles, and food, drink and tobacco[2] although, as will become evident in the course of discussion, part-time workers were few and far between in mechanical engineering and vehicles by the time of our fieldwork.[3] We also discuss part-time work in Coventry's textiles industry.

Table 2.1 shows the distribution of women's and men's employment in Coventry's manufacturing industry in 1976 (the latest year for which Census of Employment Statistics were available at the time of our research). While the industries we studied all employed relatively large numbers of women part-time, there was considerable variation in their overall dependence on part-time female labour (table 2.2). The 343 part-time women workers in the

Table 2.2 Part-time women workers in selected manufacturing industries, Coventry, 1971 and 1976

	1971			1976		
	No.	As % of all women workers	As % of total workforce	No.	As % of all women workers	As % of total workforce
Food, drink and tobacco	160	43.12	11.34	144	48.97	13.06
Mechanical engineering	373	10.21	2.19	411	12.18	2.26
Electrical engineering	1,708	23.80	9.27	397	8.71	2.56
Vehicles	576	7.29	0.83	343	6.51	0.62
Textiles	232	19.49	5.38	123	15.12	3.54

Source: *Census of Employment* (1971 and 1976).

vehicles industry represented a mere 0.6 per cent of the total workforce and 6.5 per cent of the female workforce. By contrast, the 144 women working part-time in the food and drink industry represented 13.1 per cent of the industry's entire workforce and just under 50 per cent of its female workforce. The five industries we studied also revealed different patterns of part-time employment between 1971 and 1976. Two of them – food, drink and tobacco and mechanical engineering – employed an increasing proportion of part-time women workers, while the other three reduced their proportions of part-time women workers.

Electrical Engineering: Telecommunications

In 1971 electrical engineering was the largest manufacturing employer of part-time female labour in Coventry, accounting for 1,708 part-time women workers. By 1976 the number of women employed part-time in electrical engineering had declined to 397, or 2.6 per cent of the total labour force.[4]

Electrical engineering in Coventry is almost entirely dominated by one telecommunications company. In 1976 telecommunications comprised 97 per cent of total employment in electrical engineering, and 90 per cent of this was accounted for by this one company.[5] To understand the substantial use and dramatic decline of part-time work in electrical engineering in Coventry is, in this instance, to understand the employment policies of a single, multinational firm. This firm has been the largest employer of women, and of women working part-time, in Coventry's manufacturing industry since the Second World War. In 1970 it employed 1,990 women part-time in its Coventry factories, comprising 14 per cent of the total workforce. By 1980, there were only 355 women employed part-time in the company's Coventry factories, comprising 3.5 per cent of the workforce.[6]

The large amount of part-time work in the company in the 1950s and 1960s had been a response to the labour shortage which existed in Coventry during this period, although it is important to emphasize that the fact that the company responded to a labour shortage by creating part-time jobs, rather than by adopting some other solution, requires explanation. Among the important factors which led the company to employ women on a part-time basis were that it already employed women full-time in manual jobs and that the labour process was organized in such a way that people could work on a variety of different shifts. Since 1970, in contrast, the trend within the company has been for total employment to fall and for manual labour in particular to be disposed of, as the organization of production has drastically changed. The labour process has become much more capital intensive, and new technology has been extensively introduced as the company has shifted to producing more electronic kinds of telephone exchange equipment.

The telecommunications company is part of a large, multinational corporation, and Coventry is the head of its telecommunications division. At the time of our fieldwork it had five factories in Coventry, producing telephone exchange apparatus and equipment, mainly for the Post Office; Coventry is also the centre of the company's telecommunications research and development work. In the ten years before our fieldwork the company had been reorganizing its production dramatically for several reasons. First, from the 1920s to the mid-1960s the company had enjoyed favourable market conditions, mainly as a result of being a major supplier of telephone exchange apparatus to the Post Office. However, these favourable conditions began to change in the mid-1960s. The oligopolistic relationship with the Post Office was undermined, and the company was threatened by increased international competition. Secondly, in an endeavour to counter the increased competition, the company embarked on fundamental restructuring. It was involved in two large mergers in 1968 and 1969 which made it the largest electrical company in the United Kingdom and gave it a monopolistic position in telecommunications. It reorganized its capital structure, and closed several plants. In the field of telecommunications it decided to move into producing electronic telephone exchange equipment. By the mid-1970s the company had begun to produce new kinds of intermediate telephone exchange equipment and to engage in intensive research and development of electronic exchange equipment. It made extensive use of new technology in this and developed new forms of labour process which have fundamentally changed the structure of its labour force. The changing fate of female labour and part-time labour within the company has to be understood within this context.

Throughout the 1950s and 1960s the company produced electromechanical telephone exchange apparatus and equipment. The major tasks on the shop floor were assembly work, wiring, relay adjusting and skilled work in the machine shop. Women were extensively employed on the shop floor. They worked entirely on jobs which were classified as semi-skilled, and the major form of women's work was wiring. When a shop steward was asked what women had done, he said simply 'wiring, wiring, wiring'. The labour process was highly labour intensive and loosely organized. Wiring work was highly competitive and individualized, with each worker wiring one kind of board. All work was paid on a piecework basis, and wages were low in comparison with wages in other sections of Coventry engineering industry. The variable demand for telephone apparatus and equipment meant that there were many peaks and troughs in production and the workforce spent much of its time on waiting time, waiting for work. When work came in, it had to be performed at great speed, and competition to build up piece rates was intense. Being organized and paid on an individual and piecework basis, work could easily be picked up and put down.

With the exception of brief periods of decline, total employment in the industry rose steadily from 1948 to 1970. The male employment rate broadly followed the total employment rate, with a progressive trend upwards, but declines in the level of employment were less sharp for men than for the total workforce. The female employment rate also followed the total rate but periods of cyclical unemployment were felt more severely by women and when total employment peaked (1963 and 1970), rises in female employment were particularly sharp.[7] Unfortunately, the statistics available to us do not distinguish between full-time and part-time work, so it is impossible to discern the extent to which it is part-timers who account for the greater peaks and troughs in the rate of female employment. However, what they do show is that women in general suffered more severely from redundancies and/or lay-offs in periods of low employment (especially 1953 and 1959) than men, and were brought into employment in large numbers when the scale of production expanded (in 1962–3 and 1969–70).[8]

It was in the context of a general shortage of labour throughout most of this period that large numbers of married women went to work for the company which had problems in recruiting male labour, probably because of its low wage rates in comparison with the car industry and the poor conditions in which its workforce laboured. This had certain advantages for women wishing to work. During this period it was possible for women to specify the hours they wished to work. For most women work was organized from 9.00 a.m. to 3.30 p.m., or from 5.00 p.m. to 9.30 p.m. (the twilight shift) but some women worked mornings only, and others afternoons only. The company was willing to make concessions to maintain contact with married women who had family responsibilities and who might be persuaded to come to work for it on a part-time basis. In the early 1960s discussions took place about converting three houses owned by the company near its largest factory into a nursery, but this never materialized (cf. Chesterman, 1978). In February 1968 the company started an advertising campaign to recruit 300 extra women workers, whom it wooed with the following Valentine in the local paper:

> Though major export jobs are planned
> There's just one thing we lack.
> We really miss your helping hand
> We'd love to have you back;
> There's full-time work five days a week
> On jobs that you know well.
> So now your services we seek
> Much more than words can tell.
> And on this rather special day
> The time seems opportune
> To send this Valentine, to say
> 'Do come and see us soon'.[9]

Until around 1970, the company was obliged to organize its labour process so that it could attract labour, and it encouraged women to work for it either full-time or part-time. Since 1970, the general trend has been for total employment in the company to decline, although the decline levelled off again after 1978. This decline can be explained in terms of the changes in the organization of production which the company has been introducing since the early 1970s. There has been a shift away from loosely organized, labour-intensive forms of production towards highly rationalized, capital-intensive forms, and in particular there have been moves away from wiring and soldering tasks towards the use of printed circuit boards, from manual assembly towards the use of component insert machines, from manual testing towards computer-aided testing, and from research and development based on the drawing office towards computer-aided design. There has also been a shift towards the use of plastic parts (which has involved the construction of a large new plastic moulding area and the contraction of the paintshop and painting processes).

At the time of our research, the company was not yet fully producing electronic exchange equipment, and was still manufacturing parts for electromechanical telephone exchange equipment used extensively throughout the British telephone system. Thus the changes in the labour force which were being brought about by the transformation of the labour process had not yet been fully effected. The general direction of change, however, was absolutely clear. The changes in the organization of the labour process have already led to significant job loss, and are likely to lead to further loss of jobs in the future. In the 1970s it was predominantly manual workers' jobs which disappeared. In 1970 there were 9,400 manual workers in the company, but in 1978 the number had decreased to 4,600 rising again to 5,000 by 1980. The number of employees classified as staff remained virtually constant over this period, and the ratio of male to female staff remained roughly the same, at 2 : 1.[10] The decline in the number of manual employees meant that in 1980 staff constituted about 5 per cent of the company's labour force. Among manual workers it was direct production workers who sustained the most severe job losses. At first men and women direct production workers lost their jobs in roughly the same proportions. However, between 1977 (when the decline in direct employment levelled off) and 1980, male employment increased while female employment continued to decrease.

A closer look at the figures on job loss among female manual workers shows that it was part-timers who suffered disproportionate job losses. Between 1970 and 1980 the numbers of part-timers employed by the company declined from 1,991 to 355. Part-time employment fell particularly sharply between 1974 and 1976, comprising a fairly large proportion of the total drop in direct employment in that period. Within this general decline in part-time direct employment, it was part-timers on the day shift rather than on the evening shift whose jobs declined most drastically between 1974 and 1977. Among indirect employees, too, part-timers on the day shift were most severely affected.

We tried to discover why it was part-timers who were the first to go, and how the process of disposing of them was effected. It seems that in the 1970s management had a definite policy of phasing out part-time work on the day shift. At the time of our research there were only a few women working part-time on the day shift, 'doing their time' before retirement. One of the managers interviewed gave three reasons for the phasing out of part-time work: (a) because part-time workers were too expensive; (b) because management wished to simplify and rationalize the grading structure; and (c) because it was difficult to have part-timers on the line.

It is virtually impossible to weigh up these different factors in the decision to phase out part-time work. However, the main reason seems to be connected with the fact that part-time work did not fit into the new form of labour process being developed, rather than being simply a matter of cost. Since the new labour process was much less labour intensive, the company was no longer obliged to develop flexible working arrangements in order to satisfy its requirements for manual labour.

In 1974 the company called for massive redundancies because it was starting to produce an intermediate type of telephone exchange apparatus and equipment, which needed less manual labour, and in particular was able to dispense with much of the wiring work which had been an integral part of the process of producing electromechanical exchanges. It was inevitable that a lot of women would lose their jobs because their work was disappearing with the changing labour process. However, a policy was agreed between management and trade unions that part-timers (and the disabled) should be the first to be made redundant. Many part-timers lost their jobs overnight. Others were given the opportunity to work full-time, and if they refused were made redundant. Faced with the managerial demand that large numbers of jobs should go, the trade unions accepted the widely held assumption that part-timers are not principal wage-earners and are not fully committed to paid work. The personnel manager and the shop stewards who had been involved in negotiating the redundancies commented that 'part-timers aren't proper wage-earners', that 'part-timers aren't usually breadwinners', and that 'part-timers' work is only marginal' when asked to justify the agreement that part-timers should be the first to go. Nobody whom we interviewed among management, trade union officials or shop stewards dissented from the view that part-timers *were* the first to go in 1974, and that they *should have been* the first to go. Such action against part-timers would now probably be deemed illegal under the Sex Discrimination Act of 1975 on the grounds of indirect discrimination since the Employment Appeals Tribunal has stated that taking part-timers first is 'grossly discriminatory' (in the case of *Clarke* v. *Eley (IMI) Kynoch Ltd*). There are, however, still a wide variety of circumstances in which employers can justify making part-timers redundant first and, as Robinson and Wallace (1984) point out, occupational segregation may render part-time women workers particularly vulnerable to redundancy.

Some part-timers continued to be employed on the evening shift in the company. Such shifts have come and gone over the years, varying with the state of demand for telephone exchange equipment. Management was more open about the possibilities of maintaining a part-time evening shift than it was about having part-timers on the day shift. A part-time evening shift had a clear advantage in enabling the machinery to be run for 20 hours a week more, and was more profitable to the company. It was mainly women with children under school age who worked the evening shifts, and as the *Women and Employment* survey (Martin and Roberts, 1984) has shown, this is also true at a national level.

Our company had no maternity leave provisions beyond the statutory minimum, so many women left work when they had children, and the company appears to have been able to entice them back to work on an evening shift as and when it wished. In 1977 a special order for a small receiver had to be processed quickly. The company decided to resurrect a twilight shift which had been terminated 18 months earlier at one of its factories. It had no difficulty in recruiting 100 women who had previously worked on this twilight shift, nor in getting them to sign a contract accepting that they would only work for 6 months, but that they would be flexible enough to go on working if the firm wished to extend the period of work. Since the shift was staffed by people who had previously worked on the twilight shift, they did not need any training, but could go straight into work (cf. Chesterman, 1978). This is an important advantage which frequently accrues to managements who have women returning to paid employment on a part-time basis, and means that they do not have to foot the bill for training. Management seemed confident that it could continue to recruit ex-employees who had left work to have children for part-time work, a belief which was undoubtedly justified, given the high rate of female unemployment in Coventry. The fact that part-timers have continued to be employed intermittently on evening shifts suggests that cost *per se* does not prohibit their use, and that when a flexible workforce is needed to extend the length of the working day, part-time women workers are employed.

The part-timers employed in the company all received the same basic rates of pay as full-timers, and they received a premium (time and one-fifth) for working on the evening shift. They were all employed on piecework. They worked 20 hours a week and did not receive overtime pay unless they worked more than the normal 40 hour week. Part-timers were formally excluded from the company's pension scheme (although exceptions could be considered on an individual basis) and from the company's sick pay plan. This is very common practice in companies employing part-time women (see chapter 6). The part-timers were all union members as an informal closed shop operated on the shop floor, something which is by no means universal practice.

There appeared to be no part-time female clerical workers employed by the telecommunications company (a fact we found a little hard to believe). One of the people interviewed, who had worked as a clerical worker in the company from 1966 to 1974, described the conditions in which he started work. His description paralleled accounts of the organization of wiring in the company in the same period: there were no salary scales, wages were low, methods of payment were individualized, and people could virtually specify the hours they wished to work. Around the time of the mergers, the company wanted to rationalize the grading system for clerical workers, as it had for shop-floor workers (although, in fact, it had great difficulty completing a job-evaluation study to accomplish this). It seems, therefore, that the disappearance of part-time labour from clerical work was associated with management endeavours to rationalize its labour processes and that it paralleled the rationalization of the shop-floor labour process already discussed.

The company had computerized certain office functions: for example, stock control and wages. And, more recently, it had introduced a series of terminals running off its main computer which were used to edit documents and to store and retrieve information. The training department had just had a new word processor installed which it used to process applications for apprenticeships, which were dealt with far more swiftly than they had been by clerk typists operating ordinary typewriters.

At the time of our fieldwork the company's demand for clerical workers was static. It seemed likely, however, that the long-run trend would be for the number of clerical workers to diminish as the new technology was more fully integrated into the office labour process (although, as the training officer pointed out, there were a lot of tasks which would continue to be performed by secretaries and clerk typists – not least that of making the coffee!) It seemed unlikely that the company would consider reintroducing part-time clerical work.

In many respects the telecommunications company provides a classic instance of part-time workers being used as an industrial reserve army of labour, brought into production when there was a labour shortage, and disposed of again when the company no longer required the same level and kind of manual labour. A close look at this case reveals, however, that both the introduction and disposing of part-time labour needs to be understood within the context of the existing structure of job segregation in the workforce. Part-timers were only employed in particular manual and routine clerical operations, and they were only employed on jobs which were already undertaken by women. The employment of part-time labour both mirrored, and reinforced, the existing patterns of job segregation.

The Textile Industry

In textiles, the pattern of part-time employment was fairly similar to that in electrical engineering. Women worked part-time in jobs which were segregated and these jobs largely disappeared as the labour processes were restructured and new technology was introduced. In 1976, 23 per cent of Coventry's textiles labour force were women, and 15 per cent of these women worked part-time (Census of Employment, 1976). Textiles manufacturing in Coventry was far from typical of the industry nationally. It was dominated by two firms; one was part of a large, multinational corporation which specialized in synthetic fibres, and the other was the sole survivor of Coventry's ribbon-weaving industry which had been important in the nineteenth century.

Before the Second World War, the multinational company was a large employer of female labour, mainly in weaving occupations. During the war the weaving sections were bombed, and after the war the Coventry workplace became the company's main experimental site. It developed a highly capital-intensive form of labour process, and introduced a continental three-shift system, which included a night shift. Women were precluded from working on the nightshift by protective legislation, and in 1978 women were restricted to day shift work in only three of the workplace's seven workshops.

The other textiles firm has had a very different history. In the nineteenth century it was a major manufacturer of ribbons, but in the twentieth century it has diversified into manufacturing name tapes and woven labels, and more recently woven pictures, printed labels and luggage name tapes. Until the late 1960s the company was relatively prosperous. It had benefited from government contracts during the Second World War, and from the monopolistic position it enjoyed for 25 years after the war. It employed a large female workforce in its weaving workshops, some of whom worked part-time. Weaving required a highly skilled workforce. Weavers were trained for four months at the firm's training school, after which they spent another year 'sitting with Nellie' in the traditional way, learning from a more experienced weaver how to build up speed.

Before the war the firm had always drawn its workforce from the immediate locality, but the bombing of Coventry and the post-war redevelopment of the city centre led many of its workforce to move away. Colleen Chesterman (1978) suggests that this dilution of the firm's 'pool of skill' forced the firm to devise new ways of retaining its skilled workforce. Among these were the employment of married women weavers with family responsibilities at hours which were compatible with their domestic commitments. The personnel officer described the organization of work in this period as 'a veritable warren of part-time hours'. It seems that women worked during school hours, or in the mornings only, or in the afternoons only, or from 11 a.m. to 3 p.m. Since weaving was individualized, with each worker working her own loom, and payment was on a piecework bonus system, work could be organized on an individual basis, and picked up and put down at variable times. It was when the firm was short of trained workers that these variable shifts were established, and in 1968 the company ran large advertisements for an evening shift to run from 6 p.m. to 10 p.m. in its trimming section:

> We hope a number of our female employees will return. A large number leave us when they get married, and this new

shift is an ideal opportunity for them to earn some extra money now. (Quoted in Chesterman, 1978)

The similarities between this industry's use of and need for part-time labour and that of the electrical engineering industry are striking. However, by the end of the 1960s the firm's market position had changed. It was weakened by imports of Eastern ready-made clothing, which undercut British firms, and by the introduction of printed labels. In addition, a power struggle among the firm's managers and chief shareholders led to its takeover by a large company which was looking for new fields into which to diversify. These changes, together with the firm's vulnerable market position which affected its profitability, led to moves to rationalize its production and restructure its labour force. The rationalization began with the closure of various weaving workshops, and the removal of machines from old ribbon weaving firms which the company had taken over to the firm's main Coventry site. The company began to diversify into such fields as woven pictures and printed labels, thereby becoming less reliant on the woven label market. Most important for the workforce, and for the fate of the women part-time workers, was the establishment of a double day shift system, with one shift running from 6 a.m. to 2 p.m. and a second from 2 p.m. to 10 p.m. With the union's agreement, a vote to move to the new shift system was taken, and workers who were unwilling to make the change were moved to shops which still operated on the old system. By 1975 all shops worked a double day shift system, with the exception of the name tapes section. The changes were accompanied by improved productivity and cutbacks in staffing levels, and pressure was brought to bear on part-timers to leave. The personnel officer justified this in the following terms:

They would not make the change: we were part of their life rather than them of ours. They would use the excuse of domestic commitments long after their families had left home. (Quoted in Chesterman, 1978)

In the course of the 1960s management had a new source of labour – immigrants from Asia who settled in the area around the factory. This, together with the changes in the organization of the shift system, meant that the company no longer needed to hire part-time women workers. The rates of pay in the company were so low that it is said that women who could find work elsewhere in Coventry did so, and white men generally found much more highly paid work in the city's engineering industries. The firm thus increasingly came to rely upon Asian labour. Asian women usually worked full-time. The close-knit extended family in which many Asian women lived enabled women to work full-time because their children could be cared for by other members of the family. Thus, despite its low wages, and despite the shortage of labour, management no longer devised part-time working arrangements to attract people to work for it.

Colleen Chesterman (1978) suggests that there was now some erosion of job segregation in the industry with the movement of Asian men (who found it hard to get work in the better-paid engineering industries which were dominated by white male workers) into weaving occupations. At one time during this period Asian men staffed an entire weaving shop. Apparently the company segregated Asian men from women on the grounds that the men had refused to perform what was described as the 'housekeeping side' of the weavers' work (keeping the area around their own looms free of dirt and threads) when they worked alongside women, because they felt that this would lower their status. This was an interesting case of jobs having gender-related aspects which only became problematic when men and women worked alongside each other. It seems likely that the move to the new double day shift system became acceptable to the workforce because the composition of the workforce had changed and included more men than previously.

Over the past few years weaving within the workplace has been revolutionized. a *Venture* programme shown on Central Television in January 1982 portrayed one lone woman working in the company's weaving workshop, surrounded by electronic machinery. Apparently she was the sole survivor of the company's female workforce, the remainder having been made redundant as the system of weaving using cards (which had remained virtually unchanged since the mid-nineteenth century) had been computerized. In both companies women's jobs disappeared as the labour process was changed. Part-time working, in particular, was done away with, or else reduced when work begun to be organized on a more capital-intensive basis and more complex shift systems were introduced.

As in telecommunications, part-time working developed in the context of job segregation. Interestingly, in the ribbon-weaving firm, the division between women's and men's jobs changed as Asian men began to be employed to do work which previously was done by women, and this appears to have hastened the decline in part-time work. In the textile industry it seems to have been a case first of white women and later of Asian women and men (who found it difficult to enter the better-paying jobs in Coventry's engineering industry) forming alternative sources of labour. Only the white women were employed on a part-time basis, however.

Baking

Our next case study, baking, shows a markedly different and more complicated pattern of part-time working. Job segregation is again an important part of the story, in that women are mainly employed part-time on the confectionery side of the industry and in clerical and ancillary work where full-time women workers are employed, but here we find part-time working becoming increasingly import-ant. National employment statistics show that between 1950 and 1968 the food, drink and tobacco industry employed a higher proportion of its female workforce on a part-time basis than any other manufacturing industry. While all manufacturing industries showed a marked increase in the proportion of women they employed part-time, the proportion in the food industry increased more rapidly than other industries. In 1959, 21.7 per cent of this industry's female labour force were employed part-time. By 1968, it had increased to 30.6 per cent. Between 1971 and 1976 the numbers employed in the baking industry declined, although the decline was less marked in Coventry than it was nationally. What is particularly interesting about the baking industry, however, is that the decline in part-time employment was much less than the decline in full-time employment (both male and female), so that part-time women workers became a larger proportion of the industry's workforce. Since 1973, part-time have constituted over 50 per cent of the industry's total female workforce, and in 1976 they comprised 16 per cent of the total workforce in Coventry.[11]

The industry is intensely competitive, with low profit margins, and is beset with problems which stem from the nature of its major product, bread. There has been a decline in the demand for bread since the war, and successive governments have brought pressure on the industry to keep the price of bread down. The demand for confectionery has declined too, but not as substantially as the demand for bread. Competition (e.g. from in-store bakeries in supermarkets) and the declining demand for their products have prompted the bakeries to rationalize production and diversify their products.

Bread and confectionery are highly perishable products and have to be produced daily. Demand varies considerably over the week, and increases substantially at certain times of the year (e.g. Christmas and Easter). These variations are, however, fairly predictable. Successful firms have developed forms of labour process which enable them to survive in a highly competitive market and to meet variations in demand.

Our fieldwork in baking was primarily concentrated in two workplaces, one plant bakery and one master bakery, and was supplemented by information from a second plant bakery and a second master bakery to which we gained limited access.[12] An analysis of the firm's employment statistics show that male employment declined annually in each firm, with the largest firm shedding 25 per cent of its male workforce between 1971 and 1976.[13] The pattern for female employment, however, was more varied, with decreases in one year being partially offset by increases in the following year. The downward trend in full-time male employment reflected two major changes in the industry. The phasing out of door-to-door sales led to distribution workers (mostly men) being disposed of, while the introduction of a more highly automated bread-making plant and a decline in the amount of bread produced by master bakers led to a drop in the number of bread production workers. Since the organization of clerical work in the industry was closely tied to the organization of distribution, the decline of door-to-door sales also had an impact on clerical work and led to a drop in the number of part-time clerical workers on the evening and weekend shifts.

Bread production is almost totally dominated by men. A survey conducted by the Prices and Incomes Board in March 1970 found that men formed 90 per cent of bread production workers but only

48 per cent of confectionery production workers. This was true of both the bakeries we studied. In the plant bakery bread production was 100 per cent male, although there were a few part-time women employed as roll-packers, working Sunday and evening shifts. It was strictly demarcated from confectionery production, which was female. Most of the bread production workers were of Asian origin, as is quite common in the baking industry. The division of labour in the master bakery appeared to be much less strictly demarcated as between jobs, with workers covering a broader range of jobs in a normal working day, but here again bread production was undertaken by men.

All operations in the baking industry were organized around the daily despatch of the day's production, and peaks in bread production were met by men working overtime. The plant bakery regularly employed men on a casual basis to cope with sickness, holidays or absenteeism in the area of bread production. 'Casuals' were dismissed after ten weeks and taken on again two weeks later in order that management could avoid 'being lumbered with them permanently', as one of our respondents put it. This meant that they had no legal protection. There was a local agreement that bread production vacancies would be filled by long-term casual labour, which was always male. Additional casual labour – usually male students – were taken on in holiday periods.

We were consistently given three reasons why women were not employed in bread production: (a) because a lot of overtime is required, and there are statutory restrictions on the amount of overtime which women are allowed to do; (b) because there is nightwork and work which is done very early in the morning: (c) because the work is hot, heavy and dirty. We were not convinced that the last of these reasons could explain the absence of women from bread production. The labour process was highly mechanized in the firms we studied, and in the plant bakery most of the bread was produced by machinery which was automated from the moment the ingredients entered the dough mixer until the baked bread emerged to be sliced and wrapped. All that was required were people to supervise the machines at various points, to take lids off the tins and to check the weight of the products or the quality of the dough. The number of heavy jobs which remained in the production of bread were very few. The master bakery had also subdivided some occupations in bread production, although some 'skilled' jobs, for which an apprenticeship was normally required, remained.

It seems that women's continued absence from bread production is related to the long hours of work and the rotating shift system necessitated by the Baking Hours of Work Act which requires people to work 2 weeks of nights and 2 weeks of days. Hours of work in the industry are long, and a substantial amount of overtime is worked. Men frequently work 11- hour shifts. In the plant bakery, weekly hours of work were typically from 53 to 56, while in the master bakery they were between 45 and 50. Bread production in the plant bakery also involved a substantial amount of nightwork. The hours of work are limited by the Baking Hours of Work Act, which lays down regulation for nightwork in the industry which apply to men, and forbids permanent nightwork. Wages are low, so that the male workers have come to rely on overtime to make up their wages.[14] A man's wages could be virtually doubled by overtime and nightwork premiums. This has made attempts to lessen the number of hours of overtime worked ineffective. Increases in roll-packing necessitated by higher demand were met by part-timers working an hour longer, by extra women working only on Fridays or by increasing the pace of work. Both bakeries said how intense the work pitch became at Easter with the production of Hot Cross Buns. The Easter 'crisis' was represented as a 'Dunkirk-like' event when everyone pulled together and did their best.

Confectionery production in these companies was less highly mechanized than bread production, especially in its latter stages. In the plant bakery tartlets and pies were produced mechanically and only required finishing by workers at a conveyor belt with mechanical aids. Other pastry products, such as sausage rolls, involved a combination of manual and mechanical production. The master bakery produced similar products with less advanced technology. There were no conveyor belts in the master bakery and women moved trays of confectionery by hand. There was a greater range of semi-skilled occupations associated with confectionery production, and confectionery finishing was done by hand. Most of the work on the confectionery side was classified as unskilled or semi-skilled, but in both firms there was one skilled confectionery occupation, fancy cake decoration. All workers on the confectionery side were women (with the exception of two or three young men serving apprenticeships in the plant bakery) and there were considerable numbers of part-time women workers in both firms: 19 in the plant bakery and 16 in the master bakery.[15] Mobility of labour is considered extremely important in the industry. In the plant bakery the union agreement contained a 'mobility of labour' clause which enabled management to transfer a roll-packer to the pastry belt and even a decorator to roll-packing (without, as an ex-cake decorator told us, 'a by-your-leave or any question as to whether you can spare the time from your own work'). The union agreement specified that workers would be paid at the higher rate (when appropriate). However, there was some dispute within the company about whether the rate would apply for just the hours worked or for the whole day on which the job was done. One aspect of the mobility was that most women were employed in the least skilled jobs (e.g. packing) and learned other tasks when they were temporarily asked to do them. When vacancies occurred they were filled from workers lower down the hierarchy and the less skilled jobs became vacant.

Pay on the confectionery side of the industry was lower than on the bread side. There was a single grading structure for the industry, which reflected the segregation of women's and men's jobs. This grading structure was introduced as a consequence of the 1970 Equal Pay Act, and was said by a Baker's Union official to have increased the segregation of women's and men's jobs. Analysis of wages data for the master bakery showed that every women's hourly rate, unlike the men's, was below the union rate for the job. The men also all had substantial bonuses (at least double the average women's bonuses) as well as premiums for working overtime. The women were heavily concentrated in the bottom three grades, the only exception being the fancy cake decorator. Some of the women received bonuses, but mostly they were lower than the men's.[16]

Like bread, confectionery has to be swiftly despatched, and there are peaks in the weekly production cycle. Whereas in our firms bread production peaks were met mainly by an increase in male overtime, and to some extent by the use of casual male labour, in confectionery production women were employed on a part-time basis to cope with peaks in demand, to cover for meal breaks and to stand in when there was sickness, leave or absentee-ism. Part-time workers were used to provide maximum flexibility.

They were expected to fill in for any job and to do additional hours, and occasionally days, as necessary. If the machinery broke down it was expected that part-timers would be able, and willing, to wait until it was mended rather than go home when their time was up.

In the plant bakery part-timers were hired very specifically in relation to perceived need. An exercise had been carried out to establish precisely how many hours cover were needed for each job in the bakery. On examining the documents connected with this exercise, it became clear that where a typically male job was only estimated to require 60 per cent of full-time coverage the actual cover proposed was one full-timer. However, where the job was typically female, the cover was strictly limited and the job was constructed as a part-time one. This is a clear instance of the question of gender entering into the construction of jobs as full-time or part-time.

Flexibility is also the key to understanding the organization of clerical work in the baking industry. The majority of office/clerical work was part-time. Once again the necessity to keep abreast of work every day was evident. The routine clerical work involved the daily recording of orders despatched and of sales made. In addition, both bakeries tried to respond to changes in orders coming in from the shops and to correct orders on the same day so as not to lose sales. All such changes added to the paperwork. Some of the clerical work was time-specific in that it was related to the period of the day when vans were leaving the factory to deliver goods or returning to the factory after selling them. In the plant bakery a further factor determining the pattern of part-time work was the need to produce a report of the week's production for submission to the regional office on a Wednesday. It was evident in the plant bakery that women were employed to work for precisely as many hours as was necessary to get the work done, and there was no slack in the system as there would have been if full-time workers had been employed. If and when a job was not finished by the end of the day, the woman involved was expected to stay on until it was finished.

Ancillary work in the baking industry bears a slightly different relationship to production than in other industries and is classified as 'hygiene'. In the plant bakery the 11 part-timers employed were all women, and all but one of the full-timers were men. There were three sorts of jobs involved. The first was tray-washing, which seemed to be one of the most unpleasant, hot and dirty jobs in the bakery. The women stood at either end of an enormous machine which belched out steam every time they opened it to put in or take out an oven tray. They worked in heavy waterproof overalls and Wellington boots. The machine was situated in the loading section of the bakery which meant that the women were exposed to lorry fumes as well as continually changing temperatures as the doors were opened and closed. There was no possibility of talking while they worked since the machines hissed constantly. Unlike men's jobs, which were more highly paid because they were supposedly more physically stressful than women's jobs, tray-washing was amongst the lowest paid work in the bakery. It seems likely that this was a job which was hard to fill (certainly at existing wage levels), and that having part-timers doing it reflected this. In the master bakery it was said to be difficult to find people to do tray-washing which was done by part-time women and 'Saturday boys'.

The second type of ancillary job was a cloakroom/laundry person. In the plant bakery, all the workers wore clean white hats and coats every day and these were issued to women by a female part-timer, and to men by a male part-timer. These people were also responsible for keeping toilets and washrooms clean. One difference between the men and women in this job was that the women were also responsible for repairing laundry (although they did not receive extra pay for this). In the master bakery, the workers (or their wives or mothers) had to wash and mend the overalls. The male attendants, by contrast, were paid at a higher rate than the women on the grounds that they could clean walls up to a height of 8ft while the women were only expected to clean up to 6ft. The third type of job was a more conventional cleaning (sweeping-up) job, which was done by part-time women workers in both bakeries.

Flexibility was the keynote in the employment of part-time workers in the baking industry, an advantage greatly emphasized in the evidence presented to the House of Lords Select Committee hearings on part-time work by the National Federation of Self-employed and Small Businesses (House of Lords, 1981–2). Indeed, the National Federation stated quite categorically that whatever additional costs are incurred in employing part-time workers are compensated for by their flexibility.[17] What has not been recognized in discussions of flexibility, however, is the extent to which managements use different strategies to attain flexibility when their labour force is female from those used when the labour force is male. Our research in the baking industry showed these different strategies quite clearly: where men were employed, flexibility was attained through overtime working and the use of temporary labour, whereas where women were employed, flexibility was achieved through part-time employment.

Although flexibility is usually discussed in terms of its advantages for management, it is possible for part-time workers to turn it to their own advantage when they have a sufficient power base within the workplace. In baking, the willingness of part-timers to do additional hours (which, as in the telecommunications company, were not paid at an overtime rate unless they went above the normal full-time working week) was close to being a formal obligation without actually being specified in the women's contracts. And the women saw it as an obligation both to their fellow workers and to their employers. Since they sometimes needed this flexibility themselves (for instance, when their children were ill), they would provide it for their fellow workers. The women were also conscious of the extent to which their employers needed flexibility and at times had used this as a weapon in negotiations with management. Several years ago, for instance, when the plant bakery's management refused to start talks about equal pay, the clerical workers refused to do extra time and fill-in work until talks began, a refusal which led to the immediate commencement of talks. More recently, the company tried to change the sick pay arrangements in a way which would have been particularly prejudicial to those part-timers who did not pay a full national insurance stamp. When a trade union representative told management that the part-timers would stop being so conscientious about filling in if such measures were introduced, the new sick pay arrangements were withdrawn.

Mechanical Engineering and Vehicles

Coventry is a city which has been heavily dominated by engineering, and particularly by the car industry. Not surprisingly, therefore, a considerably higher proportion of women's employment in the city is in metal-based manufacturing than is the case in Great Britain as a whole. However, in Coventry women form a smaller proportion of the engineering workforce than they do nationally. In 1976, there were 5,269 women employed full-time and 343 part-time in the car industry; women comprised 10 per cent of the total workforce, and 7 per cent of these worked part-time. And 2,961 women worked full-time and 411 worked part-time in mechanical engineering. Here women comprised 19 per cent of the total workforce and 12 per cent of these worked part-time (table 2.2).

Since fairly large numbers of women were employed in both industries in 1976, we had planned to study part-time work in them using similar methods to those used in the other firms under consideration. However, the recession affected Coventry's engineering industries so heavily in the late 1970s that by the time of our fieldwork there were very few women working part-time in either industry. We found ourselves in the curious position of having to research an 'absence', trying to find out what had happened to the part-timers who had been employed in 1976 and why so few women were employed (either full-time or part-time) in production occupations.

It is customary to explain the relative absence of women from production occupations in engineering in terms of 'tradition' or by asserting that engineering is a 'male domain'. Such explanations do, of course, contain an element of truth. However, they tend to imply that women have *always* been absent from the engineering industry and we found in our fieldwork that many interviewees chose initially to answer questions about women as if this were the case – as if women had *never* worked in the production side of the industry and as if this was what needed explaining. In fact, significant numbers of women worked in the engineering industries during the war, and women continued to be employed in some areas of engineering subsequently. This suggests that explanations in terms of 'tradition' are unsatisfactory. We therefore tried to find out what had happened to the women who had worked on the production side of the industries and where the part-timers had worked.

We discovered that where women had been employed in engineering it was nearly always in jobs which were segregated from men's jobs, and in jobs which were defined as unskilled. Two of the machine tools firms we studied had employed women full-time on 'unskilled' or 'semi-skilled' jobs in the 1950s and 1960s. One firm had employed women as machinists on small machines and as crane drivers and wirers.[18] Another firm had also employed women as machinists on small machines. In the four machine tool firms we studied it was virtually impossible, however, for the women to attain skilled status even when the work they did was as skilled as that performed by men whose jobs were defined as skilled. Although many of the women were actually able to 'set' their own machines, since this was defined as the task of a 'skilled' worker they *had* to (officially at least) ask a setter to do it. Both men and women we talked to acknowledged this. Two processes prevented women from achieving skilled status in these Coventry firms. The majority of skilled workers had served apprenticeships from which women had been barred. Interestingly, however, some men who had not served apprenticeships were eventually able to gain skilled status after years of service by being promoted into one of the skilled grades. This never happened to women. There was a completely separate grading structure for women which simply did not allow this. By the time of our research the small machines on which many of the women had worked had disappeared and the women were no longer employed. The women in these firms had not been discriminated against (as the part-timers in the telecommunications firm had been) but the jobs which they had been doing had simply disappeared.

Although the machine tool industry had in the past employed a small number of women in manufacturing occupations, we found no evidence that the firms which produced heavy machine tools had employed part-timers in production jobs. Part of the explanation for this was that the industry was not subject to short-term fluctuations in demand. In the firms we studied male overtime was also a rarity and had been for years, and there was little variation in the working week. Colleen Chesterman (1978), however, found that some women had been employed part-time in a machine tools firm which had produced chains. This firm had employed small twilight shifts of women twice in the 1960s to catch up on a backlog of inspection work. These shifts came to an end in the early 1970s as the company lowered its inspection standards in response to intense international competition, and the company closed down in the first four months of our project.

The firms we studied were keen to emphasize that they had had no problem in getting women to work on a full-time basis, but in the machine tool industry we came across the most open prejudice against employing part-timers. The prejudice was expressed in extremely moralistic tones, and it was suggested that part-time work was a form of skiving. The machine tool firms appear to have experienced few of the advantages of employing part-timers which the telecommunications and textiles firms had enjoyed in an earlier period and which the baking industry was continuing to exploit.

In vehicles the story was somewhat different. Much of the assembly work in the vehicles industry was of a semi-skilled kind. Shiftwork was considerable, and the demand for the product much more variable. In principle, the labour process seemed much closer to telecommunications than to machine tools but, unlike telecommunications, only men were employed on the shop floor. However, Colleen Chesterman in the late 1970s found that one of the vehicles firms she studied had employed women on particular tasks, for example, cleaning the glass areas of cars, and machining (in the trim shop). The latter is still a female occupation at Fords, as recent industrial action by women over a discriminatory grading structure has highlighted. Colleen Chesterman (1978) also found that young men were being employed in preference to women in some of the occupations which had previously been designated as female.

Perhaps the most interesting piece of evidence discovered by Colleen Chesterman comes from this same large car firm. During the 1960s management needed to build up production of some components, and took on a twilight shift of male workers. This used the plant between 4.15 p.m. and 8 p.m., that is, between normal shifts. This twilight shift was constructed on quite different terms from women's twilight shifts, however. Management assumed that, being male, the labour force would need to earn a full-time 'family wage'. The men were therefore kept on to work on other machines from 8 p.m. to midnight, working alongside the night shift workers. The twilight shift was therefore effectively a full-time shift and the men were paid as such, with generous bonuses.

Having discovered that there were no part-timers employed in production occupations, we expected to find a concentration of them in clerical jobs. However, in both industries part-time clerical workers, too, were few and far between. A number of the firms had employed part-time clerical workers in the 1950s and 1960s when they had been short of full-time labour. However, for a variety of reasons – declining profitability, management endeavours to rationalize the labour process in the face of increased competition and the development of new forms of grading structures – part-time clerical jobs had generally been disposed of. The occasional part-time clerical worker who remained worked as a telephone receptionist and in a handful of administrative jobs. One of the personnel managers whom we interviewed said that his company used part-time telephonists and receptionists in part because the job needed doing for longer than the 'normal' working day (coverage being needed over lunchtime) and in part because it was a public relations job which required someone who was charming and friendly, adding that it was not possible for someone to smile for 8 hours a day. Other part-time clerical workers were scattered through the administrative side of the firms, and very often a woman was the only part-timer in her department. In the 1950s and 1960s it had frequently been possible for an individual woman to arrange to reduce her hours of work if her circumstances changed, for instance, a favoured elderly woman with failing health could go part-time, as could a younger woman who acquired new domestic responsibilities, but this was no longer allowed. Managements argued that part-time workers cost more to employ since administrative costs, pension contributions etc. were increased, and that part-timers would only be employed where there was a specifically part-time requirement.

It was in the computing sections that we found women employed on a part-time basis. This mainly occurred in the evenings, although two of the firms we studied also employed part-time punchroom operators during the day. The explanation given by management in one of the machine tool companies for employing women part-time in the evenings was an economic one: 'Computers are a very expensive installation and if you've not got one working for a large portion of the possible hours then it's uneconomic.' In this firm the systems and computer area was the only area to operate flexitime. Other companies, however, were less flexible. In one of the large car firms a crisis was looming because a woman who had been employed as a programmer in the computer section wanted to return to work on a part-time basis. This woman was said to be a highly productive whiz-kid, whom the department desperately wanted back. However, the directors were resisting this on the grounds that 'it would open the flood-gates'. 'Let one in and they'll all want to go part-time' was a theme commonly expressed by management. Nowhere was this more vehemently expressed than in the engineering industry.

It is remarkable that in a city which is so heavily dependent on engineering, we found so few women employed on the shop floor. As mentioned above, women form a smaller proportion of employees in the engineering industries in Coventry than they do nationally, and in a sense it is even truer to say that the engineering industry in Coventry is a 'male domain'. To understand why this is so would require another rather different research project. Part of the explanation may lie in the fact that Coventry's engineering industry is less varied than is the case nationally and is dominated by a few large firms specializing in the manufacture of heavy machine tools rather than in light engineering. Furthermore, in the years preceding our research the engineering industry in Coventry underwent numerous mergers and rationalization exercises in a generally unsuccessful attempt to ward off the effects of the recession. At the time of our research all the firms we studied were undergoing major upheavals and one of them closed in the course of our fieldwork. Since then, two more of the machine tool companies have closed. The absence of women, full or part-time, from production occupations in the firms we studied may reflect not only the particular composition of the industry but also the fact that these large firms are particularly severely affected by the crisis.

The fact remains, however, that employment statistics record that a large number of part-timers have worked in the industry and yet we could only account for a handful. The explanation for this is, we think, twofold. Employers sometimes forgot about part-timers. They would claim that they employed none, but after some prodding would remember half a dozen in an office here, and another one there. It seemed as if, despite the relatively large number of part-timers in the industry as a whole, they were such a small proportion of the workforce in any particular workplace that they seemed to be invisible. Even with consistent prodding, however, we could never account for as many part-timers as employment statistics suggested had existed.

In the end we concluded that the discrepancy between what we were told about part-time employment and the numbers revealed by the statistics was probably due to changes in the organization of ancillary work, namely cleaning and catering. Virtually all the engineering firms had contracted out their cleaning and catering work fairly recently so that many of the workers who used to be employed directly by the company (and therefore had been recorded as employees in official statistics) were now employed by a specialist cleaning or catering firm and were thus counted as employees in the service industries, even though they were often cleaning the same factory or working in the same canteen as they had done for years. Such changes in the organization of cleaning and catering work are highly significant. The reorganization of this work has made part-time cleaning and catering workers particularly vulnerable. They have frequently found that along with a change in employer they have lost hard won improvements in pay and conditions and also the possibility of support from other workers and trade unions in the factory. In one of Coventry's larger car factories catering work has recently been reorganized in this way, and workers have lost bonuses and holiday entitlements, and also suffered a cut in pay of £30 per week. Such reorganization also has implications for the applicability of equal pay legislation since, under the law, comparisons are allowable only with people working for the same employer. In Coventry at the moment a woman is attempting to prove that the car factory where she works as a sub-contracted catering worker (and has done for years) is in fact her employer in order to pursue a claim for equal pay.

Patterns of Part-time Employment

The most common explanation offered for the rapid growth in the employment of women on both a full-time and part-time basis in the 1950s and 1960s is that it was a response to a shortage of labour during this long period of boom. There is clear evidence that women were employed on a part-time basis at this time in a number of the manufacturing industries we studied. It was then that the telecommunications firm made extensive use of part-time female labour on the day shift, as did one of the textile firms which Colleen Chesterman (1978) studied. It was also in this period that a number of firms hired part-time women on twilight shifts to cope with fluctuations in demand or backlogs of work. Women were also employed as part-time clerical workers in a whole range of industries, and as cleaning and catering workers.

Our research suggests that there were in fact three basic patterns of part-time employment during this period of economic expansion. First, managements employed women on a part-time basis during the day if they could not attract women to work full-time in manufacturing and clerical occupations. The precise reasons why they were unable to attract full-time labour are not clear, but the argument which is couched purely in terms of labour shortage would seem to be an over-simplification. The evidence from telecommunications and textiles suggests that there was a labour shortage relative to wages, and that part of the reason why these employers could not attract full-time labour was because they paid too little. Firms were thus forced to make certain jobs part-time in order to get women to work in them. We can only speculate that higher pay might have made these unpopular occupations more attractive and that they might therefore have remained full-time.

The second major pattern of use of part-time female labour during this period was on twilight shifts. These were devised as a means of extending the length of the working day or week to meet short-term increases in demand for the product. Personnel managers reported that they had had to make some concessions to accommodate women's own needs in order to encourage them into paid employment, for instance, by organizing twilight shifts at hours at which women could leave children at home with their husbands. These shifts often lasted only a few months.

The third use of part-time workers was in cleaning and catering jobs. We will discuss the reasons why these jobs, which are essentially domestic ones, are part-time in the following chapter.

The period from 1970 to 1980, in contrast, was a period of deepening recession for British manufacturing industry, and there was no longer a labour shortage. The general trend was for part-time employment to decline in manufacturing industry. Part-time women workers disappeared from production occupations in telecommunications and textiles, both industries which had made extensive use of them on both day and evening shifts in the 1950s and 1960s. The few women who had been employed on the shop floor in Coventry's other engineering industries had disappeared by this time too and there were far fewer part-time women clerical workers than in the earlier period. The numbers of cleaning and catering workers had declined, too, as these jobs were sub-contracted to specialist firms.

There seem to be several reasons for the decline in women's part-time employment in manufacturing industry. Certainly the fact that firms no longer have difficulty in recruiting labour is significant. So too are three factors to do with the actual organization of work. First, part-time work declined because the jobs on which part-timers had been concentrated were cut back with the introduction of new technology and changes in the labour process. In some cases (telecommunications, for instance) the reason why it was part-timers (rather than full-time women workers) who lost their jobs was that management and trade unions reached an agreement that part-timers should take a disproportionate share of this job loss. Secondly, part-time employment declined when a new shift system was introduced. This happened in one of the textile firms where part-time workers were displaced by full-time workers, many of them immigrants. Thirdly, part-time jobs disappeared in the engineering industry because managements engaged in large-scale rationalization of their labour forces when faced with increasing competition, and part-time work did not fit into the new forms of labour process.

Part-time employment has not, however, disappeared completely from Coventry's manufacturing industry, as the evidence discussed in this chapter shows. Since this has been a period of deepening recession, with a steady increase in the level of unemployment, the presence of part-time workers – in the baking industry, and in computing, for instance – cannot be explained in terms of a shortage of labour. Our research points to three main reasons why part-time workers are still employed. First, they are still used to extend the length of time over which production is carried out, working on a Saturday, Sunday, or twilight shift. Secondly, part-time workers have been used to provide a flexible labour force to cover peaks and troughs in production over the working week. The clearest instance of this was in the baking industry which made extensive use of part-time workers both in clerical work and in confectionery production. Thirdly, part-time workers have been employed as telephonists and receptionists, in jobs where there was a specific part-time requirement, and as ancillary workers.

There was (and undoubtedly still is) a high degree of job segregation of women's and men's work throughout Coventry's manufacturing industry. In all industries clerical work was done by women. In some industries (e.g. vehicles, mechanical engineering), the labour force in production occupations was exclusively or overwhelmingly male. In others (e.g. baking and telecommunications), there was a definite pattern of segregation between men's and women's jobs *within* production occupations.

Throughout the industries we studied, the employment of women on a part-time basis was related to job segregation. Where the full-time labour force was female, managements generally used part-time women to attain flexibility, whereas where the full-time labour force was male, other means of attaining flexibility had been devised. The case of the large car firm which hired men to work a twilight shift but made their hours up to a full-time shift and remunerated them with generous shiftwork bonuses illustrates our central argument very well. Employers use gender-differentiated ways of meeting a labour shortage or attaining flexibility. Where men are employed, jobs are invariably full-time and flexibility is gained through overtime and short-time working, and sometimes through the employment of temporary workers. Where women are employed, on the other hand, flexibility is attained through the creation of part-time jobs.

3
The Welfare State

The state is the largest employer of women workers, and these are particularly concentrated in its welfare services – health, education and social services. Our research focused on these three areas of welfare service employment in Coventry.[1] We approached the public sector services with similar questions to those we posed in manufacturing industry. We wanted to find out how part-time women workers were used in the public sector, how these uses had changed over time, and how they were being affected by cutbacks in public expenditure. We were also interested in job segregation. We wanted to know what kinds of jobs the women who worked part-time were doing, the extent to which they were employed throughout the occupational hierarchy and how full-time and part-time work were differentiated.

Analyses of employment in the service sector of the economy are far less theoretically developed than analyses of manual work in manufacturing industry, and there is also less reliable statistical evidence to draw upon. To a large extent, therefore, one has to develop an appropriate framework and set of concepts as one goes along, and to map out the patterns of employment with far less a priori assistance from other studies and official statistics. Furthermore, the scale of employment in the welfare services, the way in which it is administered and organized and its dispersal among many different kinds of workplace makes it difficult to research. It is far easier to analyse the labour process in a factory than to understand how work is organized in a social services department, where the work is scattered across residential establishments, hospitals, social work teams, and a whole range of domiciliary services. Yet it is often in these scattered and ever-changing workplaces that part-time workers are to be found.

Although much work in the public sector is, broadly speaking, caring work, and is rather different from production work in manufacturing industry, we found that similar factors governed the employment of part-time workers in both sectors. To a large extent these had to do with management's need for flexibility. A good deal of part-time work was used to extend the length of the working day or working week, either because continuous care was needed (as in hospitals or residential establishments) or because care was needed for more than a 'normal' working day or week. Part-time workers were also employed when work was needed for *less* than a 'normal' working day, week or year. In the education sector, for instance, teachers and clerical assistants were often employed part-time on a sessional basis and did not receive pay during the school holidays. Part-timers in the public sector were also frequently employed on a temporary basis which deprived them of employment protection and gave employers additional flexibility in coping with year-by-year changes in public expenditure. Furthermore, many part-timers in the welfare services were employed to do jobs which were only needed at a particular time or times of the day (for example, school meals workers, children's crossing wardens, hospital kitchen and mobile meals staff).

There were, however, two factors which affected the employment of part-time women workers in the public sector which made it rather different from manufacturing industry. The first is that managements employed professional women on a part-time basis in order to attract women who were already trained and experienced back into employment when their skills were in short supply. Whereas in the manufacturing sector it was extremely rare to find women doing professional or administrative jobs part-time, in the public sector there was a considerable number of part-time professionals and paraprofessionals. None the less, part-time work has tended to be treated as the exception rather than the rule within these occupations, and part-timers have often been employed to do work which full-timers were unable or unwilling to do (for example, working nights) or to do special jobs (for example, remedial teaching or providing special care for the elderly and the disabled).

At the other end of the scale, almost all women's manual work and much unqualified caring work in the welfare state (like cleaning and catering work in manufacturing industry) has been organized on a part-time basis. 'Home helping' and cleaning, for instance, have developed as part-time jobs. Although factors to do with the need for a flexible labour force are clearly important in explaining why these have become part-time, it seems unlikely that these provide a *sufficient* explanation. The division of labour within the family, and the gender ideology based upon this, are also part of the explanation, for employers regard women, and especially wives and mothers, as ideal employees to work in domestic and caring occupations because these are similar to women's unpaid domestic work in the home. And since wives and mothers, who are the preferred source of labour, generally have domestic responsibilities, given the lack of public facilities for child care, they are often only able to work part-time.

Employers thus make use of skills which women have learned informally within the family, yet the women's jobs are not generally classified as skilled. It would be wrong to conclude from this that women are 'naturally' suited to such jobs, but more accurate to say that domestic work and much unqualified caring work have been constructed in such a way that they repicate women's domestic role within the home. Gender ideology has an important role to play in the construction of these unqualified caring and domestic jobs. It also contributes to a process in which the jobs tend to be low paid and defined as unskilled, and more recently have become a target of the government's privatization strategy (cf. Coyle, 1985).

The Health Service

The health service has always been an important employer of female labour, and in recent years the growth of the health service and changes in its structure have led to a vast increase in its labour force. During the 1970s part-time employment became not only an increasingly important part of health service work but also an increasingly typical form of women's work in the sector. Part-time women workers increased as a proportion of the total workforce from 30 per cent in 1971 to 41 per cent in 1977 and part-timers increased as a proportion of the total female workforce from 35 per cent in 1971 to 49 per cent in 1977.[2] Whereas in 1971 one in 13 of Coventry's part-time women workers worked in the health service, by 1977 the figure was one in nine.

Employment in Coventry's health sector increased by a third between 1971 and 1977. In 1971, 4,990 people were employed in the health service; by 1977 the total had risen to 6,680.[3] This expansion in the total labour force was to a large extent accounted for by a large increase in the numbers of part-time workers. Of the 1,690 employees added to the payroll, 1,333 were part-timers. The increase in part-time jobs was overwhelmingly an increase in jobs for women. Of the 1,333 new part-timers, 1,270 were women. The increase in full-time jobs, in contrast, was mainly an increase in jobs for men: 205 of the 357 new full-time jobs created between 1971 and 1977 were occupied by men. In January 1981, 85 per cent of Coventry Area Health Authority workforce were women, and nearly half of these (47 per cent) worked part-time; 96 per cent of the part-time workforce were female.

The Coventry Area Health Authority covers a large number and a wide variety of workplaces, ranging from the city's two large general hospitals to a number of smaller specialist hospitals, clinics and doctors' surgeries. Since 87 per cent of the part-time women workers were employed in the hospital sector, we focused our fieldwork on Coventry's two main hospitals. The first was Coventry's major residential hospital, which is one of the new large district hospitals built as a result of the 1962 Hospitals Plan and situated on the edge of the city. The second, in contrast, is situated near the city centre. It houses the Authority's major outpatient clinics and laboratories, as well as some residential wards, and is the centre at which all Coventry's medical records are kept. In January 1981, 740 (33 per cent) of the Authority's part-time women workers were employed at the district hospital, while 456 (20 per cent) worked at the central hospital. Most of the remainder of the part-time women workers were fairly evenly spread among Coventry's other hospitals (with the exception of The Peabody), each of which accounted for between 6 and 8 per cent of the total part-time female workforce.

Women's work in the health service is heavily concentrated in two occupational groups: nursing and ancillary staff, which together in our study accounted for 76 per cent of women's employment and 82 per cent of women's part-time employment. Despite this heavy concentration of part-timers among nurses and ancillary staff, considerable numbers of women were also employed part-time throughout the occupational hierarchy. They comprised 61 per cent of ancillary staff, 40 per cent of clerical and administrative staff, 40 per cent of medical and dental staff, 37 per cent of nursing staff, and 25 per cent of professional and technical staff in 1981.

In the late nineteenth century there existed a fairly simple division of labour within the voluntary hospitals between doctors and nurses. Doctors had ultimate control over the organization of health care in the hospital, and were principally concerned with the diagnostic and curative aspects of health care, while nurses specialized in the caring aspects. They had their own sphere of competence, but this existed within a hierarchy of responsibility and control in which doctors had the ultimate authority. This division between medicine and nursing, cure and care, embodied a strict form of sexual division of labour, with doctors being almost exclusively male and nurses almost exclusively female. Since the nineteenth century the organization of health care within hospitals has been fundamentally transformed, especially with the development of the National Health Service. Our project was concerned with looking at changes which have occurred within the caring occupations which were once the sole province of nurses, and a central argument is that the increasing reliance on part-time women workers must be understood in terms of the extensive subdivision and fragmentation of caring tasks within the hospital system.

Nursing care within much of the hospital sector involves continuous work. It also requires a good deal of nightwork. Although some parts of the hospital (for example, the theatre and surgical wards) have much of their work concentrated during the 'normal' working day and week, a substantial amount of nursing care has to be provided continuously, 24 hours a day, 7 days a week. The nursing administrator at the district hospital said, when interviewed, that she preferred not to employ part-time trained staff if this could be avoided, and that the only reason she did so was because it was difficult otherwise to get trained cover at nights. She said that she preferred full-time trained staff because part-timers could not have the same knowledge and understanding of patients' needs when they did not provide continuous care. Continuity, she said, is especially important when nursing care is organized as a team caring for all the needs of a small group of patients. The aim of team care is to improve overall care by enhancing the relationship between the nurse and the groups of patients whom she is caring for. When work is organized in this way (as it was at her own hospital) there is less scope for employing part-timers:

> In awareness of the patients' needs, a full-timer is likely to have more awareness and get to know the patient. You think, if you were an SRN [State Registered Nurse] and you were working, say, two mornings and two evenings. So today you might be working from 8 till 1 and you come in tomorrow from 5 till 9.30 and you're in charge of that ward. So you're walking in on 26 patients, you have a report, but you don't *really* know what's been happening. You haven't been there for over 24 hours. But if it was a full-timer who would have worked from 8 till 5, and tomorrow she's going in at a quarter to one, she's got time in the afternoon to get to know those patients while the SRN from the morning is on, and surely she's going to provide a better standard of care tomorrow night than you will when you walk in fresh to take over. . . .
>
> Let's look, then, at night duty which is perhaps easier. If I've got one full-timer working four nights, surely she is going to provide a better standard of care, in that she will know her patients pretty well from four nights. I could employ two people doing two nights, but the odds are that when they come on duty they have been away for at least five nights, and it could be one week. They [could] work Monday and Tuesday and the next Thursday and Friday, so they could come back and not know any patients out of the whole lot which could have changed over. But the odds are that with a full-timer working four nights, she's going to know half her ward when she comes in, in the evening, at least. It's the element of people, patients, not factory or things.

Trained staff at the district hospital were expected to become specialists in a particular field of nursing, to do courses in their particular field and to work on wards related to this specialism. However, part-time trained nurses were not sent on courses to further their training, something which one of the unions, The Confederation of Health Service Employees (COHSE), had identified more generally as a problem for part-time nurses.

Despite the fact that part-time nurses did not receive further training, it was evident that the training which they had received when working full-time was of immense benefit to the hospital. The hospital thus gained from the fact that part-time nurses had generally received training in a specialism when they were full-timers, and it did not have to provide them with opportunities for, or pay for them to receive, further training. In this respect nursing is like so many other part-time occupations. Employers benefit from the women's training, but this is seldom recognized and the women are rarely paid for it or promoted, nor are they formally encouraged to extend it.

The hospital's policy was to try to use full-time trained staff to cover the day, and part-time trained staff to cover nights. Full-time staff worked a rotating shift system, with two early shifts from 8 a.m. to 5 p.m., two late shifts from 1.45 p.m. to 9.30 p.m., and another half-day, a shift system which, as we pointed out in our discussion of baking, is difficult to combine with childcare responsibilities. Part-time nurses worked on the night shift, doing two or three nights a week. Weekend work was shared out between staff at the hospital, although some other hospitals employed part-timers specifically to cover weekends. Weekend work was said to be popular among the nurses because of the bonuses it carried. Either way, part-timers were used to provide 'off-peak' cover. They were guaranteed one weekend off in four, and often got more than this, but their contracts explicitly specified that they must be prepared to work flexible hours. In the first year after being trained all staff were expected to do three months' night duty, often described as the 'Cinderella' of nursing work. This arrangement increased the trained staff available to do night duty.

Despite the nursing administrator's preference for employing full-time nursing staff, the district hospital did in fact employ many part-timers, virtually all of them women. Indeed, 44 per cent of the trained nurses at this hospital worked part-time. However, there were fewer part-timers at the more senior levels. Only 4 per cent of the sisters worked part-time. There were also some temporary part-time nurses, taken from the nursing bank, who were generally used to cover for holidays and sickness.

A good deal of nursing work in hospitals is done by untrained nursing auxiliaries, and 89 per cent of the auxiliaries at the district hospital were women working part-time. The full-time nursing auxiliaries were generally young women who were waiting to start their training. Nursing auxiliaries within geriatrics were all women working part-time. The nursing auxiliaries were employed in such a way that they provided a flexible labour force to cover peaks of work over the working day and week, especially when there were fewer trained nurses on duty. The part-time auxiliaries were employed on particular shifts and, unlike full-timers, their shifts did not rotate. They worked either from 8 a.m. to 1 p.m. or from 5 p.m. to 9.30 p.m. Despite attempts to smooth out the workload over the day, by bathing patients in the afternoon rather than in the morning, for instance, much nursing care was still concentrated in the mornings. The part-time auxiliaries were employed either to cover these morning peaks in workload or to cover evenings, when there were fewer full-time staff on duty. Very similar patterns of part-time employment existed at the central hospital, although there was a higher proportion of full-time auxiliary nurses there. This was due to the fact that most of the city's outpatient clinics were housed at this hospital, so there was more work in the 'normal' working day.

Paramedical occupations are generally more highly skilled and better paid than many women's jobs. Like nursing, they provide some opportunity for part-time employment. Twenty-five per cent of the paramedical workforce in the Coventry Area Health Authority worked part-time. The part-time jobs were mainly routine, often quasi-domestic jobs, but in a few cases qualified women were employed on a part-time basis to work in weekly clinics. At the district hospital part-timers were not employed in the whole range of occupations, nor even in the whole range of occupations in which full-time women could be found.[4] Mostly they worked in the medical laboratory and the pharmacy, and they were consistently concentrated in the least skilled and lowest paid jobs. In the pharmacy, for instance, men occupied all but one of the senior positions, full-time women were mainly concentrated in the technician grades, and the ten part-timers all worked as pharmacy assistants (the only ancillary grade in the pharmacy), a largely domestic occupation in which no full-timer was employed.

At the central hospital there were more full-time women workers in professional jobs and part-time work was less segregated from full-time women's employment. There were also a few women employed part-time as opticians, dietitians and orthoptists who worked in the weekly outpatient clinics.

Women working part-time were also concentrated in the lower-level jobs in the administrative and clerical areas. At the district hospital, while most of the men and some of the full-time women worked in general administration, the lower-level clerical, secretarial and typing jobs were invariably done by women, many of whom worked part-time. Medical records and ward clerks were largely part-time jobs. The concentration of part-timers in medical records was in part a consequence of the fact that the work was concentrated in the mornings, when the clinics were held. Like so much part-time work, it was a product of a need to have cover at peak times. However, a trade union representative commented that he thought another reason for part-time employment in this area was that the work was extemely strenuous:

> As I say, the filing generally is done by part-timers, that is all part-timers. I think that it is often done because of the pressure on women, and it is a very heavy job filing, particularly if you have a look at the racks. You know, there is not enough room up there for the X-rays and notes and consequently you really have to jam them into these racks to get them in. There is very little space between these racks as well. Literally some of them are like that and you have files and case notes which have to go sideways, and I think it is quite a heavy job. So I think what has happened is that they have part-timers because people could probably put up with 4 hours of it but probably not 8. Not day in and day out.

This is an interesting comment on a job which is conventionally regarded as a clean and sedentary 'feminine' job.

The other main group of part-time clerical workers comprised ward clerks, most of whom worked at weekends. Although the jc' was done in regular office hours it needed cover 7 days a week. The ward clerk's job involved dealing with doctors' notes, menus, filing and typing, arranging transport for patients, checking patients in and out, and so on, tasks which used to be done by nurses. One clerk was attached to each ward, although busy wards sometimes had more. We were interested to discover that whereas the nursing administrator did not use part-timers to cover weekends but instead employed a combination of full-time and part-time nurses, a different administrator in the same hospital used full-time ward clerks during the week and part-timers at the weekend. This shows that there is no single pattern of employment in a given institution, but that different patterns of work organization may be devised for different groups of workers.

The general process of fragmenting care has led to much of the routine caring work in the hospital system being done by ancillary workers. The size of the ancillary workforce has grown enormously since the inception of the National Health Service (NHS), increasing nationally by 53 per cent between 1949 and 1974. Ancillary workers constitute about 30 per cent of the hospital labour force, and in many places a large proportion of them are black, or immigrant or migrant workers from the New Commonwealth and from Ireland (cf. Doyal et al., 1981). There is a strict form of job segregation between male and female ancillary workers with men working as porters and women doing domestic work. In Coventry 61 per cent of the ancillary workers were women working part-time. The women doing full-time ancillary work tended to be concentrated in the higher supervisory positions, while the part-timers were to be found in the lower grade occupations. Sixty-eight per cent of the part-time female ancillary workers fell into three occupational groups. The vast majority of these (over 600) were cleaners, and 71 were catering assistants. The district hospital was the largest single employer of these part-timers, accounting for 266 of them, while the central hospital employed 116. There were extremely few full-timers in these occupations, and most hospitals did not employ any full-time cleaning staff in these pay groups. Most of the hospitals had some full-time catering assistants, but the proportions varied. At the central hospital there were four part-timers to each full-timer, whereas at the district hospital the ratio was one to one. The part-time ancillary workers worked on average slightly more than half-time: generally around 20 hours a week. The preponderance of part-time women in these occupations makes them *de facto* part-time jobs.

Four occupational groups at the district hospital contained no part-timers (catering-managerial and supervisory; stores; portering-supervisory; operating department). There were no part-time cooks. Thus any women who worked as a cook was employed full-time. Part-timers were invariably concentrated within the lowest grades of ancillary workers. The lowest pay grade, group 1, contained only two occupations, catering assistant and cleaner/domestic assistant, which were entirely female occupations and mainly part-time. Together they accounted for 68 per cent of all part-time ancillary workers at the hospital. There were no men in group 1. The male jobs of cleaning windows, for instance, were classified in group 3. A further 18 per cent of part-time women workers were found in group 2 jobs, which were also entirely female occupations. Thus 84 per cent of the part-time women workers were concentrated in the bottom two pay grades in which there were no men. A similar pattern of employment could be found at the central hospital.

Part-time women domestic workers were employed as a very flexible labour force to work for periods of the day when there was specific work to be done. Cleaning, for instance, mainly took place in the morning, and serving food was concentrated over meal times, both periods which were covered by part-time shifts. Part-timers were also employed to provide cover outside the normal daytime hours of work. At the district hospital, for instance, part-timers were employed on an evening shift to work in the staff dining room and to serve meals, working from 5.00 or 6.00 p.m. to 9.30 p.m. It seems fairly clear that women ancillary workers in the hospital sector were employed on a part-time basis for similar reasons to those which prevailed in the baking industry, to cope with peaks of work in the normal working week. As in manufacturing industry, however, where men were employed their work was organized on a full-time basis. Portering, for instance, was undertaken entirely by men, who worked full-time and flexibility was attained through overtime; porters at the district hospital regularly worked a 49-hour week.

Since the mid-1960s ancillary work in the hospital sector has been subject to large-scale rationalization, and bonus schemes have been introduced following two reports by the National Board for Prices and Incomes which examined low pay among ancillary workers, and suggested that improvements in pay should be tied to higher levels of productivity. Ancillary workers were removed from the control of the ward sister to a separate system of managerial control. The bonus schemes appear to have led to an increase in the number of part-time ancillary workers employed.

Jobs have been subjected to a high level of managerial control, and also to work-study techniques. A major form of reorganization suggested by the management consultants brought into the district hospital has been to increase the number of part-time workers to cover peak hours. A shop steward outlined the effects of the bonus schemes at this hospital in the following terms:

> In the health service another way that we end up with a lot of part-time staff is because of the productivity schemes which were introduced in 1976. Any extra payments that they make they have to make from within the department and that meant job reductions. But what we've found is that the actual amount of people employed has stayed stagnant but the hours have been reduced because what the time and motion people do – they'll come in and look at the peaks of work, and they'll take part-timers on just for those peak hours. What happened was that whereas we probably had about 40 full-time workers at one time in the Central Sterile Supplies Department, supplying the operating theatres, this is quite skilled work, you have to learn what packs to make for what operations, etc. It's not classed as a skilled job, but it does take a certain amount of skill and there are different grades within the department, depending on ability. What happened was – I think there are only two full-timers left in there now and all the rest are part-timers. So where bonus schemes have been introduced, there has been a drift towards part-timers. One of the effects is that the ratio of male employees has changed – we've got more females than before.

At the central hospital, the hours had also been reorganized as a result of the introduction of work-study techniques. The domestic department, for instance, had begun to appoint people in the afternoons, to cover the gap between the morning staff and the evening shift. Trade union representatives at both hospitals told us that one of the consequences of the introduction of work study had been an increase in managerial control over the organization of domestic work; thus the women had very little control over their hours or conditions of work. Cleaners, for instance, had been moved from cleaning wards to cleaning offices without management taking into account whether they liked the contact with patients which working on the wards gave them. And hours of work had been changed at little or no notice. One consequence of this, according to trade union representatives whom we interviewed, was that it had become hard for them to keep tabs on how ancillary work was being reorganized, such was the variety of hours of work and the number of locations at which domestic work in particular was performed. Portering, however, had not been reorganized. This continued to be organized on a full-time basis, with regular shifts covering the 24-hour working day. The porters all worked the same rota, and the union representatives (who were often porters anyway) said they found it easier to keep tabs on any reorganization. One of the porters commented that management was anyway less likely to try to reorganize their work – a consequence, one might assume, of the fact that they were men, working full-time, who were also more vocal in the union.

Our research took place before the Secretary of State at the Department of Health and Social Security (DHSS), Norman Fowler, instructed hospitals to put contracts for cleaning work out to tender, and the consequent privatization of services in many areas. Privatization has undoubtedly intensified the pressures placed on part-time workers with staffing levels being cut, contracts being modified, hours being reduced, rates of pay lowered and people being moved from department to department (cf. Coyle, 1985). In some cases, too, contract cleaning firms have used under-aged workers. In many respects this looks like an extreme case of the subdivision and routinization of hospital work which has made it more like cleaning work in other situations. However, the privatization of services has had unintended consequences and doctors and other medical staff, as well as trade unions, have publicly criticized sub-contractors for providing inadequate standards of cleaning and for failing to recognize the specific requirements of hospital cleaning. Despite some speculation in the press that the standards of cleaning have been so poor that the Secretary of State may be forced to withdraw his instruction that cleaning services must be put out to tender, the 1980s have seen a new offensive in privatization. Sub-contracting of hospital services is part of a much larger offensive to lower wages, reduce benefits, and deregulate the contract between employer and employee, as Angela Coyle (1985) points out.

Quite clearly the health service relies for its very survival on the work of its part-time women employees. They were found in all the main occupational groups, although invariably in the lower grade jobs, and were disproportionately concentrated in the unqualified nursing and manual occupations. Part-time nurses were employed when there was a shortage of trained staff to work on the night shift, but women working part-time were mainly employed as a flexible form of workforce to provide 24 hour cover and to cover peaks and troughs of work over the working day and week. Women working part-time were also employed to do domestic jobs which in many ways replicated their household roles. Far from being marginal to the hospital workforce, part-time women workers were indispensable to its operation.

Social Services

The social services is another major employer of part-time women workers. Of the 2,360 people employed by Coventry Social Services Department in September 1979, 1,474 worked part-time. Thus, nearly 63 per cent of the workforce worked part-time and most of these part-time workers were women.[5] The general trend was for the number of part-time manual workers employed by Coventry Social Services Department to increase between 1975 and 1979, although there were some fluctuations over this period. Management interviewees suggested that this increase was primarily due to the fact that Coventry's demographic structure had been changing with the result that the numbers of elderly people requiring care had increased.

Social services departments have an extremly broad range of activities and include a wide variety of occupational groups. They provide care for four main client groups: children, the mentally ill and mentally handicapped, the physically handicapped and the physically ill and the elderly. There is no dominant type of employment in social services, nor is there a dominant locus of employment (such as the hospital or school). Care is provided in a number of different ways in a variety of locations. In 1977 Coventry Social Services Department had 73 residential and day-care establishments. These varied in size from 50 to 9 places and catered for a variety of client groups. The department was also responsible for 9 day nurseries, 4 hospital social work services, 16 district social work teams based in local communities, a home care service, street wardens, children's supervisors, a fostering and adoption unit, a mobile meals service and miscellaneous other services.

Part-time women workers were heavily concentrated in residential care and supportive services for the elderly, although, as in the health service, they were also to be found in a variety of other occupations. All types of residential care depended to a considerable extent on part-time staff, mainly to do domestic work (for instance, preparing and serving meals, cleaning, maintaining clothes and linen) and to provide secretarial and clerical help. In 1977 there were 246 such staff (87 per cent of the total in Coventry's residential establishments), all working on a part-time basis. Part-timers were not, however, uniformly distributed across the different types of residential establishment. They were heavily concentrated in homes for the elderly. There were only four trained full-time workers in these and a large number of unqualified assistants who worked part-time, many working at particular times of the day (e.g. at meal times and bedtimes) when the workload was heaviest. This was in sharp contrast to children's homes, whose care staff were all trained and most worked full-time. The care of children has been defined as a professional task requiring social work training, whereas caring for the elderly has been defined as non-professional, as work which can be carried out by unqualified but caring women. The part-time childcare staff were used in a similar way to part-time trained nurses; providing cover in the evenings, at nights and in the early mornings. There has recently been a shift within the profession towards a redefinition of what constitutes appropriate care for the elderly, and the development of this as a specialism may ultimately lead to the professionalization of such care. At the time of our research, however, the employment of substantial numbers of women part-time providing care for the elderly in residential establishments was linked to the fact that this was regarded as 'unqualified' work.

Women were also heavily employed part-time in supportive services for the elderly, particularly as home helps. Home help organizers' jobs were full-time, but there were only four full-time home helps in Coventry. In contrast, there were 714 part-time home helps or assistant home help organizers in 1979. The home helps worked a regular 20½-hour week, consisting of 20 hours of direct care and half an hour 'reporting back' time on Fridays. Many also did unpaid work – shopping, for instance, or checking up that a housebound client was all right at other times.

Social work was the mode of care in which part-timers were employed the least, although the number of part-time social workers has increased in recent years. Although social work is a profession in which women form the majority of the workforce, as in nursing they are concentrated in the lower positions in the occupational hierarchy. Men are over-represented among senior directing, managing, professional and advisory staffs, and also among the more senior social work jobs.

In 1979 there were only 19 part-time social workers (compared with 131 full-time) and three part-time welfare assistants (compared with 33 full-time in Coventry). The increase in part-time social work was mainly a response to a shortage of qualified social workers. However, management would sometimes employ a woman part-time if her department wanted to keep her and she did not want to work full-time (when she had young children, for example). This was reminiscent of the situation in telecommunications in the 1950s and 1960s when women seemed able to exercise some power in determining their hours of work. Managements would accommodate them because they experienced a shortage of labour. The part-time social workers were mainly ex-employees of the department or had otherwise learned about the job through the grapevine. They had a variety of different kinds of job (attached to GPs, or hospitals, or the adoption and fostering unit for instance), and only one of those who answered our questionnaire had a caseload involving mainline family and childcare work.

Education

The education service was the single largest employer of women part-time in Coventry. It had an enormous array of temporary, intermittent and part-time workers, and in Coventry women mainly worked part-time as teachers, clerical assistants and in catering and cleaning jobs. We were not able to obtain such comprehensive information about part-time employment in education as we were for the health service. However, it is clear from the limited evidence available to us that similar patterns of job segregation and part-time employment existed here to those in other areas. Part-time women workers were concentrated in lower-grade teaching jobs and in clerical and manual occupations.

In March 1981 part-time teachers accounted for 22 per cent of all lecturers and teachers in England.[6] In the school sector there had been a vast increase in the number of part-time teachers in maintained schools during the 1960s and early 1970s when there was an acute shortage of teachers. Between 1965 and 1975 the number of part-time teachers increased by 37 per cent as a result of a recruitment drive to encourage married women to return to teaching part-time. The mid-1970s, however, was a period of falling school rolls and government cutbacks which, combined with a large number of newly trained teachers, meant that there was no longer a shortage of labour.

Since 1975 the number of part-time teachers has fallen and part-timers have formed a decreasing proportion of the teaching profession (Trown and Needham, 1980). Virtually all the part-time teachers in Coventry schools at the time of our fieldwork were on scale 1 posts (the lowest grade) as a consequence of the provisions of the Burnham agreement. Furthermore, education was the one sector we studied in which women employed in teaching and in clerical work part-time were explicitly restricted to the lowest grade by agreement. In other sectors part-timers were formally paid on the same rates as full-timers, even if they were *de facto* concentrated in the lower grades. Although there is provision for part-timers to be appointed above scale 1 in exceptional cases (such as when two part-timers are temporarily filling in for a full-timer in a scale 2, 3 or 4 post), it seems that in practice this rarely happens. In Trown and Needham's (1980) national survey of teachers, 53 part-timers were on scale 1 posts, two were on scale 2 posts and two were on scale 3 posts or higher. All the part-time teachers we talked to in Coventry were on scale 1 posts. One of these had previously been head of department (on scale 3) and had left to have a baby. When she returned part-time after a term's absence, she taught the same pupils, but on a scale 1 post. Two others were 'exceptions' in terms of the Burnham agreement (that is, they were filling scale 2 posts because no full-timer could be found and were therefore eligible for scale 2 pay) but both were paid on scale 1 despite the fact that they had previously held scale 2 posts full-time before leaving to have children.

Part-timers in the school system are often employed to perform specialist teaching roles. In this respect they are employed in similar ways to part-time social workers. Trown and Needham (1980) found 58 per cent of part-timers working in primary schools and 92 per cent in secondary schools performing specialist tasks, while only 24 per cent of primary and 4 per cent of secondary part-timers were primarily working as class teachers. In primary schools over 75 per cent of the part-timers' specialist roles were in either the remedial/reading/language area or the art/music area.

The reason given by the local authority why information on the number of part-time teachers in Coventry was not available was that the numbers are subject to wide variation. This was because a high proportion of part-time teachers were employed on a temporary basis. Often they were not paid during the school holidays. Temporary teachers were also used to cover for illness. There was a variety of temporary arrangements within teaching, of which supply teaching and fixed-term contracts were the most typical. In Trown and Needham's (1980) study over half the part-time teachers were on fixed-term contracts which meant that they had no security of employment. It is not surprising, therefore, that many part-timers have been the first to lose their jobs when staff numbers have been cut, although sometimes their hours have been cut instead. In Coventry, all the part-timers in primary schools who had been teaching six sessions a week had their hours cut to five sessions a week at the time of our research. In a few cases, however, the cuts had created new opportunities for part-timers, as full-timers had left their posts and been replaced by part-timers. Most of these part-timers were appointed on a temporary basis and had no job security. The introduction of part-time workers in this way represented a form of casualization of the workforce. In further and higher education, part-timers were even more likely to be temporary. If they were lucky they would be employed on a yearly basis, but many were employed on a term-by-term or sessional basis. Most part-timers are employed and paid on an hourly basis, a single pay rate applying to all regardless of experience or length of service. They are also excluded from all benefits (sickness, holidays, pensions etc.).

Many schools relied heavily on part-time clerical assistants. In July 1981 there were 190 part-time clerical assistants employed in Coventry schools, compared with 56 full-time. The full-time clerical assistants were all employed in secondary schools, while the primary schools were entirely staffed by part-timers. The number of hours worked by the part-timers depended on the size of the school, and schools in social priority areas were awarded additional hours. Most clerical assistants were on the clerical 1 scale, although senior clerks in secondary schools were on the clerical 2 scale. All the part-time clerical assistants were on clerical 1. The practice of paying retainer fees to school secretaries during the school holidays was discontinued several years ago. Clerical workers who worked over 30 hours a week were allowed to join the superannuation scheme, but most part-timers worked fewer than 25 hours a week and were therefore ineligible. If they paid the full national insurance stamp they were entitled to sickness benefit in certain conditions, for instance if they had worked for the local authority for more than six months. The length of time for which they received payments depended on their length of service.

The main area of part-time employment in education was in manual work.[7] As in other areas of the welfare services there was a strict division between men's and women's occupations, with men working predominantly as caretakers. Although we did come across a few women caretakers, women were principally employed in catering and cleaning. In March 1981 there were 3,979 manual workers employed by Coventry's Educational Department, only 407 of whom worked full-time. Of the 3,572 part-timers, 1,948 worked in catering and 1,378 in cleaning. There was a substantial decline in the numbers of cleaners and catering workers employed in Coventry schools between 1975 and 1980, although the proportions of full-time and part-time job loss differed for the different groups. Of the 615 catering jobs which were lost, 66 per cent were part-time, while only 34 per cent of the cleaning jobs lost were part-time.[8]

The school meals service is by far the largest employer of catering personnel in local government; a survey undertaken in January 1977 showed that 86.4 per cent of all catering staff in local government in England and Wales worked in schools. The service is staffed almost entirely by women, the great majority of whom work part-time. In March 1981, there were 2,102 people employed in Coventry's school meals service, 93 per cent of whom worked part-time. As in the national survey, part-timers were concentrated in two occupations: as general assistants and supervisory assistants, the latter being an occupational category which was entirely part-time.

Staff in the kitchens can broadly be divided into 'skilled' and 'unskilled'; the skilled staff include supervisors (in the larger kitchens), cooks in charge, cooks and assistant cooks. They generally worked full-time, while general assistants worked a mixture of full-time and varied part-time hours, with the great majority employed only over the lunchtime period. Similarly, dining room and supervisory assistants worked only at lunch time. Very small numbers of men were employed in the school meals service, principally in central administration and in transport. Sometimes men were also employed on boiler and stoking duties (the latter being graded as skilled work). As may be imagined, the most intensive part of what is a hot, demanding and in many respects extraordinarily skilful job is through the period of final preparation, serving and washing and cleaning up after meals. So intensive is this work that it has rarely been found possible to apply bonus schemes to it. For those in charge of kitchens, the tasks are varied and cover wide responsibilities, including the organization of the establishment, supervision of all the workers engaged to prepare, cook and serve meals, ordering supplies and keeping stock information and other records, planning menus and monitoring nutritional standards, and controlling wages and time sheets. The introduction of cafeteria services, progressively introduced in Coventry since the autumn of 1980, gave rise to additional responsibilities. Cafeteria services have also modified the responsibilities of other staff.

The work of the school meals service is closely tied to the school day, week and year. This means that the work is heavily concentrated at particular times and this is reflected in the workers' contracts. In particular, school meals staff are obliged to take their own holidays during school holidays or public holidays; they do not have all the year employment but are subject to 'retention fees' of half wages during the holidays, subject to them giving an undertaking to return to work, if required, at the end of the school holidays.[9]

The school meals service has been under considerable pressure in recent years, especially in the context of cuts in public expenditure. The number of children eating school meals has been falling fast, while those taking their own food has increased. Between October 1976 and October 1977 in England the proportion having school dinners fell from 69.4 per cent to 61.7 per cent, while those taking their own food increased by two-thirds to over one million pupils. In Coventry the numbers having school meals fell by 7 per cent in the summer term of 1980 and total staffing hours were reduced by 6.5 per cent. Although there were no redundancies, 16 kitchens were closed and the staff were redeployed. An attempt to introduce a 'cook-freeze' system into Coventry, based upon a model operated in Leeds, was successfully resisted by the local trade union, the National Union of Public Employees (NUPE).

Although the education sector is different from the other two sectors discussed in this chapter in that the hours of work in schools and colleges are very different from those in hospitals and residential establishments, there are nevertheless time requirements which are different from the 'normal' working day and which play an important part in determining the ways in which work is organized. Teaching and clerical work and also domestic work are required for less than a 'normal' working day, and indeed, less than a 'normal' working year. As in the other sectors, we found women were employed part-time to do work which was required only at certain times of the day, week or year. There were large differences between professional work in education and clerical and manual work. Most teachers were employed full-time, and part-time work which had been quite common when there was a labour shortage was the exception rather than the rule. This was not true of the other kinds of women's jobs, however. Most of the clerical work in schools was part-time, and much of it was classified as temporary, especially in primary schools. Furthermore, most women's manual work was part-time. Once again we found an extreme form of job segregation between men and women manual workers, with men's jobs (e.g. caretaking) being full-time, and women's (e.g. cleaning and catering) generally being part-time. As in the health and social services, women manual workers were generally employed in the education service on a part-time basis to do work which they customarily did at home. With the exception of a few cooks, who had training and formal qualifications, the jobs involved skills which are learned and practised at home but which are not granted formal recognition when they are incorporated within public non-familial forms of labour process.

Patterns of Part-time Employment

A major difference between the welfare services and manufacturing industry (discussed in chapter 2) was that in the former large numbers of women professionals were employed, and women were absolutely central to the labour process in all areas. Whereas in manufacturing women tended to work almost exclusively in manual and clerical and, to a limited extent catering and cleaning jobs, in the welfare services they were employed throughout the occupational structure. This did not mean, however, that job segregation was non-existent in the public sector. Far from it. Despite the fact that the workforce in each of the sectors we studied was predominantly female, the men were disproportionately represented in senior jobs while women were in lower-level jobs, and especially in clerical and manual occupations. The number of women working part-time in professional jobs varied. Quite a large number worked as registered nurses, virtually all on night duty, but there were only a small number of part-time social workers and teachers. Where they were employed in professional occupations the part-time women were on the lower grades (for instance, they were staff nurses rather than sisters, and social workers rather than senior social workers). In both social work and nursing, however, the majority of part-time workers were found in unqualified positions, working as care assistants in social services and as nursing auxiliaries in the health service. Part-timers provided the bulk of labour in both of these areas. Similar patterns prevailed within paramedical occupations in the health service. Men were generally found in the senior positions, although occasionally a woman working full-time was in a senior position, especially in 'feminine' occupations such as radiography or physiotherapy. Women working part-time, on the other hand, were systematically concentrated in the lowest grades.

As in manufacturing industry, clerical and administrative work relied heavily on women, especially at the lower levels. Women working part-time were generally employed on the most routine tasks (for example, copy-typing), and in the health service many worked in medical records and as ward clerks. In social services part-timers were scattered throughout the many different types of workplace, as were school secretaries in education. Manual workers in the welfare services were almost completely segregated by gender.

Men worked as porters, caretakers and drivers, while women worked as cleaners, home helps and catering assistants. In the sole occupation in which men and women both worked, cooking in hospital kitchens, the men worked as trained cooks, while the large number of women worked as kitchen and dining-room assistants. In the school meals service, in contrast, only women were employed to prepare, cook and serve food. With the exception of a few skilled jobs like cooking, women working in manual occupations in the welfare services always worked part-time.

As the analysis of manufacturing industry suggested (chapter 2), it seems likely that different factors operate to create a demand for part-time labour in a period of economic expansion from those which operate in a period of recession. Thus, until the mid-1970s the shortage of labour undoubtedly contributed to the demand for part-time labour in the welfare services. In Coventry, in particular, there was a sudden and very rapid need for labour in the mid-1960s with the more or less simultaneous opening of a large new hospital, a polytechnic, a college of education and a university. To state that a labour shortage existed, however, does not, in our view, constitute an adequate explanation as to why so many of the new jobs were part-time, as discussed in chapter 2. Since full-time employment in manufacturing industry was on the decline, there should have been plenty of people available (both women and men) who wanted, or would have expected to get, full-time jobs. The reason why the new jobs were part-time thus requires further explanation.

The evidence presented in this chapter points to four main reasons for the organization of so many jobs in the welfare services on a part-time basis. First, there has been a continuing shortage of labour in professional occupations like teaching and nursing (or in sub-specialisms within these). In the absence of adequate childcare facilities, allowing married women to re-enter the profession on a part-time basis was one immediate way of enticing them back into employment. Other strategies which might have persuaded women with children to stay on at work or attracted more men into the professions – improving pay or professional status or terms and conditions of employment, especially those affecting working mothers – could only be pursued in the longer term (as they have to a certain extent in nursing and social work).

In the short-term, part-time working was the only way of meeting a labour shortage. Part-time workers, however, have always been a minority within the professions.

A second reason for the growth of part-time employment is that employers needed a particularly flexible form of workforce which could work beyond the 'normal' working day or week. Whereas many employers in manufacturing industries undoubtedly wanted to extend the length of the working day in order to use the plant for longer or extend the scope of production, they always had some choice over whether to do this or to increase profitability through other means. Furthermore, manufacturing employers are precluded, formally at least, from employing women at night. In the welfare services, however, many employers have no such choice. In the health and social service sectors, for instance, residential care has to be provided throughout the day, week and year (even though attempts are often made to try to limit the amount of work done outside the 'normal' working day and week). Part-time workers are extensively employed, in this context, to enable continuous care to be provided in the residential sector. Time constraints also affect the organization of work in the education service, but in rather a different way. Hence work is organized on a periodic basis, and a variety of patterns of part-time employment have been evolved to cope with the vagaries of the school year. Although teachers have successfully negotiated full-time status, school secretaries and clerical and manual workers are only employed in the school term, and many of them work part-time (although some of them work quite long hours).

The third reason why part-time workers have been employed so extensively within the service sector is that they can cover peaks of work during the working day or week, or do tasks which are only needed at a particular time of the day, for example, school meals workers, and children's crossing wardens. In many respects they are similar to the confectionery and clerical workers who are employed on busy days in the baking industry.

The final reason that almost all the domestic and unqualified caring work in the welfare state has been organized on a part-time basis, is that this work is as quintessentially women's work, which require the skills which women have learned in the home as wives and mothers. Since older married women are seen as the ideal employees for these jobs, they have been organized, at least in part, to dovetail with women's domestic commitments.

A major theme running through both this and the previous chapter is that it is almost always women who work part-time and women's jobs which have been constructed as part-time jobs. Thus, even if men's and women's jobs are governed by broadly similar requirements (for instance, by similar needs for flexibility) it is generally only the women's jobs which are organized on a part-time basis. Manual work in hospitals illustrates this point well. Within the hospital sector there was total segregation between portering, which was done exclusively by men, and domestic manual work which was done by women. Arguments could easily be advanced for organizing portering on a part-time basis which are similar to those which we have advanced for women's manual occupations: 24-hour coverage is needed, there are peaks and troughs of work during the normal working day, etc. Yet portering was done by men working on a three-shift system while women's manual work was all part-time. It is hard to escape the conclusion that gender is a significant element of the difference between the two occupations and moreover that it enters into the construction of women's jobs (and especially manual jobs) as part-time.

4
Attitudes of Employers

The pros and cons of part-time employment have been the subject of considerable controversy in post-war Britain, among employers, trade unionists and, to a certain extent, feminists, although the economic climate in which these have been debated has changed over the years. In the 1960s part-time workers were generally regarded by managements as something of a 'necessary evil', as a 'shifting unreliable section of the labour force, presenting all kinds of difficulties, and not really belonging to the regular establishment', as Viola Klein (1965, p. 127) put it.

In a study of personnel managers in manufacturing industry conducted in 1961, Klein (1965) found that the most common objections made to employing part-time workers were that it was difficult to maintain continuity of employment and that the costs of employing them (especially their national insurance contributions) were too high. The managers interviewed also mentioned that part-timers were irregular attenders at work and had high turnover rates, and were thought likely to engender unwelcome demands from full-time workers, who might, for instance, want their hours of work reduced. Klein points out, however, that only 14 firms of the 120 who replied to her survey failed to employ any part-time workers, which suggests that, despite these objections, many managers did in fact find them advantageous. The most important advantages of employing part-timers cited were that they provided a source of labour in times of scarcity, that they were a labour force which was flexible enough to enable managements to meet fluctuations in demand, and that they could easily be disposed of.

In our interviews with employers in Coventry we were able to discover a good deal about the attitudes of management to employing women in general and part-time women workers in particular. In many respects similar views to those described by

Klein prevailed, although how employers regarded women workers and part-time workers varied considerably with the extent to
which these workers were central or marginal to their production
processes. In sectors where women were extensively employed
part-time, like the health service, employers' attitudes were rather
different from sectors like heavy engineering where very few
women were employed.

Our concern in this chapter is not to document employers'
attitudes in any systematic way, as sociologists or market resear-
chers studying attitudes often do, but rather to try to convey some
sense of the ideological mechanisms at work in their statements.

Women and Men Workers

In the manufacturing sector we encountered arguments which
explained women's exclusion from particular jobs (often the
better-paying 'skilled' jobs) by reference to some inherent characteristic which the women were said to lack – like strength,
technical competence or skill – and their concentration in other
occupations, (like wiring or packing) by reference to some
inherent characteristic which the women were said to possess – like
a proclivity for doing boring work. What is interesting is the way in
which the arguments for and against employing women are similar
in form. They identify some attribute of a particular job (for
instance, a need to manipulate heavy loads), they assume that all
women are inherently incapable of doing this, and they then assert
that their inability to manipulate heavy loads is a sufficient reason
to exclude women not just from one particular job but from all
jobs done by men. The attribute becomes a criterion of differentiation and exclusion.

A common argument we encountered is that women cannot do
certain jobs because of their lack of strength. It is perhaps worth
mentioning that although we sometimes felt that employers were
simply trying to evade awkward questions by recourse to ste-
reotypes, we were generally surprised by their apparent conviction
in the validity of the explanations they offered us. They were quite
often confused if we asked precisely what sort of strength was
involved in a particular men's job or whether something needing
to be carried weighed any more than a bag of shopping or a baby.

If such points about women's everyday lives are now a common part of the rhetoric of feminists, they appear not to have impinged on the consciousness of many of those responsible for recruiting workers. One of the employers in the baking industry outlined the reasons why women could not work on bread manufacture (as distinct from confectionery manufacture) in the following terms:

> We don't have women on oven work, we don't have women on heavy mixing, although we give equal pay we still think there are some jobs within an industry like ours that are not the type of thing women should do . . .
>
> We don't like to see women lugging round great 70lb bags of flour, for instance, when men should be doing it . . . The oven work is very hot, it's heavy and it's hazardous . . . Heavy mixing is not women's work, even in this enlightened day and age . . .
>
> I don't like to see women lifting 100lb of dough from the mixing bowl to the table. . . .

Leaving aside for the moment the question of whether differences in physical strength, whatever their origins, can ever be valid explanations of women's absence from men's jobs, it was clear that this explanation could not account for the extreme job segregation in the baking industry where many men were doing much less strenuous jobs than some of the women. Women lifting trays of cakes out of the ovens were handling very heavy loads, for instance. Furthermore, when women were doing jobs which were heavy, or hot, or dirty, as tray-washing was, the jobs were never described in this way, and the fact that they were heavy, hot or dirty was never used as an explanation of why women were doing them. It is as if 'heavy' or 'dirty' work is so bound up with conceptions of masculinity and is so antithetical to definitions of femininity that it is completely overlooked in jobs which women do. It is also not generally recognized in pay and grading systems.

It was interesting to discover that it is only relatively recently that 'heavy' work has become a significant category for determining pay in the baking industry. The bottom pay group, in which the majority of women were concentrated, was group F which according to the National Agreement, covered:

all other workers not specifically covered elsewhere . . . who
are principally employed on *light or simple repetitive duties*,
packing and despatch and other *light or simple duties* in and
around the bakery, including *the handling of light materials*
(our emphasis).[1]

Group E workers, in contrast, who were mainly men, were
employed on repetitive tasks which were said to involve 'sustained
physical effort'. Likewise, a distinction was drawn in cleaning
between light cleaners (group F) who were all women, and
high/heavy cleaners (group E) who were all men. Group D work
also included a reference to 'heavy' work. The inclusion of
'heaviness' into the grading system categories appears to have
occurred after the Equal Pay Act had been passed and the
previous 'male' and 'female' rates of pay were abolished
(somewhat tardily in 1977). In the 1970 and 1972 National
Agreements, when there were still separate male and female pay
rates in existence, there were no references to 'light' or 'heavy'
work as a characteristic distinguishing between different pay
groups. It appears, then, that the distinction between 'light' and
'heavy' work was not a 'traditional' distinction, but was one which
has recently been introduced, presumably as a means of avoiding
giving women equal pay. This is by no means an unusual
phenomenon, as a study of the implementation of the 1970 Equal
Pay Act and the 1975 Sex Discrimination Act conducted for the
Department of Employment has shown. This study identifies a
number of 'minimizing strategies' by which employers evaded the
requirements of the Equal Pay Act, among them the separation of
grades by reference to 'heavy', 'light' and 'unskilled' work (see
Snell et al., 1981, esp. chapter 3).

Similar arguments were frequently used to explain women's
absence from many engineering jobs, with one employer making
the additional observation that 'it's dirty, greasy work and women
don't like it . . . they break their nails and their hair-do's get
messed up.' If this was a common argument, however, it was by no
means omnipresent, even in heavy engineering. An employer in
one of the machine tools companies said that women did not drive
cranes because 'that was hot, heavy, dirty work and women didn't
do that sort of work', but in a different machine tool company
where women had been employed as crane drivers appeals to

'feminine' rather than 'masculine' characteristics were made in describing the job and explaining why women did it.

> we do have people in the cranes in the shop, the overhead travelling cranes. Traditionally, we have had men and women in there, there's no distinction whatever. In fact, I think the fitting foreman preferred to have ladies up there because if they weren't busy all the time they could do a bit of knitting if they wanted to. Quite frankly, he wasn't bothered, and he said he used to find they'd got a more sensitive touch with the raising and lowering work. They've got machine control mechanisms at their fingertips to control the crane unit and he said he thought their fingers on the actual buttons which only reacted in the units were more sensitive somehow. So they got paid the same rates and everything . . . there was no argument about that.

Thus, a job which was thought to be unsuitable for women because it fell into the 'heavy and dirty work' category in one firm was suitable for them, in another, because it required a 'sensitive touch', something which women had learned through knitting. Here again the form of argument is similar, even if it is used to draw radically different conclusions so far as gender divisions within employment are concerned. In this case crucial characteristics of the job are associated with femininity, with attributes which all women are assumed to share. Similar kinds of parallels between characteristics of the tasks to be performed and 'feminine' skills like knitting have been drawn to try to persuade women to enter into non-traditional jobs when labour is scarce, and are highly reminiscent of wartime attempts to persuade women to enter engineering. In 1943 the Ministry of Labour issued a pamphlet entitled 'Women in Shipbuilding' which attempted to persuade employers to extend their use of female labour. It commented:

> It is no exaggeration to say that the average woman takes to welding as readily as she takes to knitting, once she has overcome any initial nervousness due to the sparks. Indeed, the two occupations have much in common, since they both require a small, fairly complex manipulative movement which is repeated many times, combined with a kind of

subconscious concentration at which women excel . . .
(Quoted in Riley, 1984)

Similar themes are echoed in the film, *Rosie the Rivetter*, which
discusses women's experiences of wartime work in the USA.

Another argument we encountered for the exclusion of women
from skilled jobs was that the women lacked the requisite skills. A
manager in one of the machine tools firms said that 'they never had
women as machine operators because the degree of skill is so
high'. Initially we accepted the 'skill' argument at face value,
thinking that women's exclusion from apprenticeships was a major
factor explaining their absence from jobs which were classified as
'skilled'. It became apparent, however, that things were not in fact
quite so simple. In the machine tools industry, for instance, while
it was true that most skilled engineering workers had served an
apprenticeship, this was not the only route by which men became
classified and paid as 'skilled' workers. In many companies it was
possible for a man to be defined as a 'skilled' worker after he had
worked on the shop floor for some years. Women, on the other
hand, had their own quite separate pay scale which did not allow
them to become 'skilled' workers in the same way. Any skills
learned by women on the shop floor were not given formal
recognition. This is a good example of the process described by
Phillips and Taylor (1980, p. 53) who suggest that 'far from being
an objective economic fact, skill is often an ideological category
imposed on certain types of work by virtue of the sex and power of
the workers who perform it.'

This pattern was repeated on the administrative and clerical side
of engineering. Here women's exclusion from apprenticeships was
an important reason given for their absence from administrative
and higher clerical jobs. But once again while most of the men in
these jobs had served an apprenticeship or had an engineering
degree, this was not always the case. One employer told us that
there was a woman in his department who knew more about the
business than any of the men in the department, and everyone
went to her for advice, but that she would never get promoted
because she had no formal qualifications.

One thing which was very noticeable in the accounts given as to
why women were not employed in particular jobs was how easily
they slipped from being accounts offered in terms of some

supposedly 'objective' facts, for instance, differences between men's and women's strength, women's lack of technical 'know-how', or their lack of 'skills' into accounts about the social inappropriateness of certain kinds of jobs for women. This slippage is very clearly illustrated in the comments from the baking manager quoted on page 104 who used phrases like 'I don't like to see . . .', it's 'not the type of thing women should do. . .', and 'men should be doing it . . .'

So far we have discussed the explanations we encountered as to why women were absent from certain jobs. A very similar form of argument was also used to explain the prevalence of women in routine unskilled jobs like wiring and packing. In telecommunications, all those we interviewed on the management side told us that the reasons why women were employed on wiring and relays were that they liked doing boring, repetitive work and were much better at it than men. One of the managers went on to stress that the reasons for this had nothing to do with physical differences, but with emotional differences. 'It is because they are emotionally different from men that women are willing to do fiddly, boring, frustrating work', he said. Women's suitability for packing in the baking industry was explained in similar terms: 'Women are much neater than men, they've got more patience . . . they like making things look nice . . . None of the men in my family can pack up a Christmas present', we were told. A careers officer working for the local council had developed this argument with special reference to working mothers. After saying that he thought it 'a jolly good thing for women to work, I'm all for it', he went on to say that the jobs done by women should not be too interesting because: 'you can't have both parents coming home still thinking about their jobs. When a woman gets home she's got to start thinking about the kids and if she's got an interesting job she won't want to do that. A man's got to have an interesting job because that's his life, you see.'

Such arguments identify characteristics of particular jobs – for instance, that they are boring or fiddly – and then assume that all women have attributes which make them particularly well suited to performing such jobs because of their emotional or physiological make-up. Such generalizing and reductionist forms of argument play an important role in perpetuating the patterns of occupational segregation in which women are generally excluded from better-paying 'skilled' jobs in manufacturing industry and concentrated in routine jobs which are classified as unskilled.

The attitudes of training officers who were responsible for recruiting young people onto training schemes provided some interesting insights into how young men and women were regarded in different kinds of company. The telecommunications firm was undergoing very rapid changes in technology and in the reorganization of its labour process, and one of the problems it faced was the need to recruit large numbers of people into jobs associated with the new technology used to produce electronic telephone exchange equipment. The training officer said that he was not particularly concerned whether he recruited men or women into the new technical jobs, although quite a strict form of sexual division of labour did seem to be emerging within the occupations associated with the new technology. He said he wished to recruit more young women, and advanced several positive reasons for doing so. First, they were a reserve of labour which could be drawn into occupations associated with the new technology and, secondly, they had had to overcome so many barriers in order to enter engineering in the first place that 'they have got something from a drive point of view.' The training officer also thought that women would have a 'feminizing' influence on the company which was trying to counter the 'dirty' and 'unglamorous' image of engineering and to substitute a conception of telecommunications as clean and antiseptic, more like a laboratory than a 'metal-bashing factory'. Young women, he felt, were a potentially 'cleansing' and 'humanizing' force who could assist in this cultural battle. They were also a humanizing force with regard to men: 'I think boys of that age seem to behave in a slightly more mature fashion when there's one or two girls around. Boys will be boys but when there's a girl around they are simply a bit more sensitive.' In addition, he said, young women tended to have a different kind of insight: 'The insight which a girl has is a little different from the insight a boy has, so it becomes complementary when they are on a project'. Here, again, stereotypical views as to what constitutes 'masculine' and 'feminine' characteristics were in operation but, unlike the vehicles and heavy engineering industries, which seemed happy with their 'masculine' images, telecommunications was trying to change to a more 'feminine' perception.

The machine tools industry, in contrast, was in crisis, and was generally getting rid of existing workers rather than recruiting new ones in Coventry. Nevertheless, we discussed with the training officer in one company the processes by which he recruited apprentices, when he did so. Rather than seeing young women as a humanizing force, this training officer argued that any young women who worked on the shop floor had to be tough. She must not mind rough or sexy talk: 'If you're a girl and you've got to walk through here with all these men around, it's no good whining if they whistle at you and pinch your backside. You've got to be able to hold your own . . . it's very tough for a girl.'

There was clearly no desire in this 'metal-bashing factory' to effect any change in its image. This training officer also lamented the lack of women in engineering and declared that he thought it an appalling waste of skill and talent. However, skill and talent were apparently not enough to get a young woman an apprenticeship in this firm when one had applied the previous year. The training officer recounted how withdrawn she had seemed when she came for the day of interviews and tests, at which she had been the only woman. Her marks were, the training officer said, 'on the good side of average', and better than the marks of some of the young men who were taken on. The young woman was not admitted to an apprenticeship, however, since she was thought to be withdrawn, had apparently not looked at people during the interview and this was interpreted as a lack of commitment. In this firm personal attributes were given high priority in determining whether or not a candidate was accepted. The training officer described his system of ticking off names when the candidates arrived in the morning (before any conversation, interview or test) on a three-point grading of what might be described as their 'social attributes'. The training officer claimed proudly that these ticks hardly ever let him down. Where young men with similar marks on their tests had been rejected this was on the grounds of untidiness, lateness, slovenliness, insolence and, in one case, was due to the fact that the candidate had pink and green hair (despite the fact that he had got excellent marks on his tests). In the young woman's case, however, shyness and lack of confidence constituted grounds for rejection since they were interpreted as reflecting her attitude to work. This machine tools firm showed no desire to change the masculine image of engineering, which was undoubtedly detrimental to women seeking work within it.

Two omissions from our discussion of employers' attitudes should be conspicuous. We have so far said nothing about why domestic occupations in all sectors (e.g. cleaning, catering, home helps) were done by women nor why secretarial work and shorthand -typing were almost always women's jobs. This is partly because the evidence we collected arose in the context of discussions about why men or women were employed in particular occupations. Our discussions were inevitably most illuminating when the question 'why?' related to problems which employers had encountered or to practices which they felt they had to justify. Some questions seemed ludicrous because they did not relate to problems which the employers had experienced. To enquire why women were invariably hired to do domestic or secretarial work was one such question, the answer to which seemed blindingly obvious: these were 'naturally' or 'traditionally' women's jobs.

Domestic work, it was commonly believed, was 'naturally' women's work because it is a form of work which women have traditionally undertaken, whether unpaid within the family or for a wage outside the family. Secretarial work and shorthand-typing seem equally obviously to be 'traditional' women's work, despite the fact that clerical work in the nineteenth century was generally performed by men, and has only become women's work in the twentieth century.

There is little explicit evidence about employers' attitudes in these areas because these are questions on which conceptions of gender are deeply held; so deeply held, in fact, that employers did not feel they had to produce any explanations of, or justifications for, their practices. But perhaps more significant is the fact that employers generally found it easier to answer, and more comprehensible to be asked, questions about women's absence from 'male' jobs than they did questions about men's absence from 'women's' jobs. Of course, many women's jobs were part-time jobs, especially in the public sector, and this was an additional reason why the employers did not consider them to be appropriate jobs for men, for it was generally assumed that men had wives and families to support and needed, therefore, a full-time job paying a 'family wage'. Furthermore, many women's jobs in the public sector are caring and domestic jobs and these are held to be inappropriate jobs for men. Home helps, for instance, were frequently described as 'motherly women' who were 'qualified' for the job because they had learned the appropriate skills in their own families. It seemed inconceivable to those responsible for hiring home helps that men might start doing cleaning and shopping.

Clearly it is those areas in which conceptions of gender are so deeply held that are the most difficult to prize open, and they are also some of the most important for feminists to open up. At least if conceptions are made explicit, one can begin to challenge them. But if they are so implicit that they are never recognized, let alone discussed, the task of breaking down job segregation and changing gender relations at work becomes exceedingly difficult. The evidence discussed so far shows that the distinctions made between men's and women's attributes are quite variable, though by no means random. There is no single attribute which is held to explain the differences between women and men, but employers make reference to different attributes (for instance, skill, strength, technical 'know-how', ability to tolerate boring work) in different contexts (cf. Game and Pringle, 1984). The discourse within which these references are made is always a dichotomous one. Masculinity is associated with skill, or technical 'know-how', femininity with domesticity or the capacity to do routine boring work. Such dichotomous formulations are inevitably limiting, particularly for women. They are part of the process whereby gender is constructed within the labour market, and they also play an important part in the creation and perpetration of job segregation (cf. Scott, 1985; Reskin and Hartmann, 1986).

Attitudes to Part-time Workers

Part-time women workers were always seen in terms of their domestic and family responsibilities. Although the assumption was commonly made that part-time workers were married, it was not primarily marriage *per se* (i.e. responsibility for a house and a husband) but responsibilities for children (or occasionally some other dependent) which were proposed as an explanation as to why it was women who worked part-time. Employers generally specified quite clearly who they expected to recruit as part-time workers, in terms of their age, their marital status and the age of their children, and sometimes their proximity to the location of their workplace. A number of employers expected to hire their part-time workers from the immediate vicinity, thus saving them from expending time and money in travelling to and from work. Furthermore, they often had clear views about what kinds of women they could hope to employ at particular times of the day. One of the bakeries and one of the mechanical engineering firms said that their full-time daytime workers all had older children who could fend for themselves when their mothers were out at work, or children who had grown up. Another baker who employed women part-time on a variety of different shifts said that the women's finishing times depended on whether or not they had someone for the children to come home from school to. The part-time day shift (running from 9 a.m. to 3.30 p.m.) in the telecommunications firm had been devised for mothers who had children at school, while the evening shift (from 6 p.m. to 10 p.m.) was designed to attract mothers with children under five.

The employers were generally concerned about the childcare arrangements that their part-time women workers had made, and whether these were reliable. One mechanical engineering manager said that: 'If they work part-time or full time and if they have got young children they have got to make arrangements for them. They have got to be reliable arrangements'. The managers definitely saw the question of childcare as being within their sphere of concern, especially when employing women part-time, and frequently questioned women wishing to work part-time about their childcare arrangements. The following statement made by an employer in the baking industry sums up the sentiments of many of the employers we spoke to:

> We like them to have set hours so they know what they're doing . . . to get the children organized. Because I know, I've had children when I was at work and I understand how difficult it can be . . . They always say, well, I've got someone to look after them, but I say yes, but there is always the holidays. I mean it's O.K. now but when the holidays come up have you got someone?

In the period after the war employers devised a whole variety of arrangements in order to accommodate women's 'need' to organize their paid work around their domestic responsibilities. According to Hallaire (1968, p. 18) 'firms . . . adapt[ed] their timetables to allow part-time employment for a substantial proportion of married women and a substantial minority of older workers', particularly in the Civil Service and the nursing and teaching professions. In recent years, however, employers have not devised flexible time-tables to anything like the same extent. In some sectors, however, where there was still a labour shortage in particular occupations, flexible arrangements have been organized. The nursing adminis-trator at the district hospital had devised patterns of part-time working either two nights a week or two evenings a week from 5 p.m. to 9.30 p.m. in order to attract nurses back into the profession after they had had children. Her assumption was that their husbands could care for the children at those times. Fur-thermore, the plant bakery, like a number of Coventry factories, employed women part-time in the computer room in the evenings. We were told that:

> They work staggered patterns . . . and we established the working pattern of two evenings and alternate Saturdays because we thought that gave a certain flexibility to people . . . It's more costly by doing this but it did look more attractive for a lady who's got young children, her husband has to look after them if she's coming out to work in the evening, but periodically certain things crop up which they want to do together from a domestic or social point of view and if they have flexibility in that they know they have got Thursday night and Monday night off this week, it's a more attractive proposition . . . We found that we could attract people and some of them worked for us over 20 odd years just doing two evenings and alternate Saturdays.

Our respondent pointed out that the flexibility benefited both the bakery and the women themselves.

> It works both ways, you have flexibility within that set up but you can say to girls in those circumstances, 'would you mind working three evenings this week to cover for holidays or sickness?' We do allow them flexibility within their own circumstances as well and if, say, a girl works regular Wednesday evenings and something happens and her hus-band comes home and says he has got to go out on Wednesday this week, she has the option of coming in and

saying 'would you mind swapping my Wednesday for your Monday?' sort of thing. So we try to be a little bit reasonable where that is concerned because we realize that looking after husband, kids, family etc. does cause its problems. But we expect them to be reasonably responsible from a working point of view.

She concluded that: 'we've made the time to fit the people, what we thought would be more conducive to attracting people, people with children who want to work in the evening if their husband will look after the kids.' This view was echoed by other employers who wished to attract women part-time into occupations in which they were short-staffed.

Both the nursing administrator and the social services administrator also spoke of the importance of devising arrangements which would enable women to return to work part-time after having children, although such arrangements seemed generally to be worked out on an individual basis. The possibilities for negotiation seem to be strongest in the women's professions (nursing and social work) because of their reliance on female labour. The social services administrator spoke of two cases where the department had tried to accommodate women returning to work part-time:

A female social worker who has had a family and wants to come back into employment but not full-time, somebody probably the department knows, worked with us before she had a family. *The department don't want to lose her experience* and are willing to shape our establishment around it (our emphasis).

A clerk who has actually gone off on maternity leave having worked in the department for 11 years as a full-timer. During that time she has married and is now expecting a child, she has gone off on leave and when she comes back she will come back as a part-timer. Because we have changed the establishment around her in effect. *It happened to fit in with other considerations* but one of the guiding factors that led to that decision was the fact *that we didn't want to lose her* and she wanted to come back but only as a part-timer (our emphasis).

The fact that part-time women workers generally have responsibility for children did not always mean that managers made attempts to accommodate them. One vehicles firm which used full-time female labour on the shop floor saw the fact that part-timers might have problems connected with childcare as a reason not to hire them: 'Women who are eligible for part-time work have families and young children and the disadvantages would be holidays, school holidays. And sickness of course . . . if the children are sick?' Futhermore, several of the employers told us that women with young babies should not work. For instance, at the plant bakery:

> One anticipates that if somebody comes back with perhaps a small baby. . . that to me raises all sorts of problems because I wouldn't think that that is something which people ought to do. I would have thought that it was necessary to stay at home and look after a young baby, but that's probably old fashioned, I don't know.

And at the master bakery: 'I don't like employing people with small children. I do, I have to, but I know their loyalty lies with their family and when you've got a job your loyalty is to them, you're their servant, aren't you?'

The motivations of women working were also discussed. Most employers talked about the financial considerations which lead women to seek paid employment, especially in the recession. It was assumed that most women now have to work. One of the employers in the baking industry thought that the fact that most women now go out to work for money gives them the motivation to work well. In addition, the plant bakery manager thought many women wished to work for 'therapeutic' reasons:

> Well, as I say, some of them have worked for us for quite a long time. We do have some younger people and it is I suppose initially the people with young children that look for this kind of evening work. Apart from the financial consideration there could be some therapeutic side to it, coming out in the evening, having a chance of a natter with somebody about this, that and the other. They are kept fairly busy, they don't just sit there all evening, but it does give them a chance to see other people which they wouldn't do. It's probably a fifty-fifty thing.

Clearly, financial arguments can be double-edged. One of the people giving evidence to the House of Lords Select Committee suggested that since the decision to work part-time was 'a domestic arrangement', women may wish to keep their earnings down. The reason for this, she suggested, was that 'I think the husbands are a little bit concerned that, if they [the wives] start earning too much, he will lose some of his allowances and things like that' (House of Lords, 1981–2, p. 48).

Although the typical part-timer was undoubtedly a married woman with young children, we were told of women who did not fit into this category. One of the baking employers spoke of an unmarried part-timer, explaining that she used to work full-time until her mother died: 'There's her and her brother. I think she went part-time after her mother died to look after the house as well as her brother.' She also said that the company employed one or two young single women on a part-time basis in its shops: 'I've got one [unmarried single girl] just started on Monday in this shop here attached to the bakery: 27, she took the part-time vacancy because she was unable to get full-time work. And she had previously only worked part-time as well.' This was not an isolated incident. Several people whom we interviewed remarked that they had had people applying for part-time jobs because they were unable to get full-time jobs. They clearly found this confusing since, as one baking employer commented, they thought 'young girls *should* work full-time . . . but if they can't get full-time jobs. . .'. As yet, however, these were still regarded as exceptional cases. In the rare instances where respondents had any experience of employing part-time men, they usually said that the men worked part-time either because they were retired or because it was a second job. As the personnel manager at the plant bakery put it:

At the moment I am trying to push through a policy of retirement age which will involve the retirement of our internal van drivers who are all over 65. In which case we would have to replace them certainly with women because you are not going to get a man under retirement age who wants to work 4 hours a day.

It is this need for flexibility which seems to be most central to people's conceptions of part-time workers. The part-timer is seen to be a woman with young children, who does not want full-time work but wants a job which gives her a bit of money, gets her out of the house and which is compatible with her maternal/wifely role. The managers whom we interviewed talked at length about part-timers as if they were representative of *all* women. They spoke of women as having divided loyalties, requiring flexible hours, needing to take time off work if the children were sick and therefore being prepared to fill in for each other when needed. When part-timers were employed during the day they were seen as needing hours which fitted in with school times. When they were employed in the evenings or at weekends they were thought to need hours which enabled their husbands to look after the children. And the employers often implied that they were doing women a favour by giving them part-time work.

The domestic responsibilities of women who were employed on a full-time basis were, in contrast, rarely mentioned. When asked about full-time women workers employers generally replied that they were extremely reliable and stable workers. Most of them had been with the firm or organization for years. The possibility that these women might like more flexible or shorter hours was never countenanced. However, in one firm a trade union representative for engineering clerical workers told us that she had been trying to persuade the firm to create more part-time jobs and to consider job-sharing. She said that of the 17 married full-timers in her office 11 would prefer part-time employment, but the firm would not consider it at all. (This firm has been getting rid of its part-time clerical workers over the past few years, and considered part-timers to be more expensive.)

The point to emphasize is that part-time women workers are defined by their domestic responsibilities. Thus, when their labour is needed, employers seem prepared to recognize these and sometimes even to accommodate them. In other circumstances, however, their domestic circumstances become a reason not to employ women on a part-time basis, and at times not to employ them at all. Either way, part-timers are not generally seen as wishing to do interesting work, or as wanting training or promotion, and certainly there are very few opportunities for this. We found virtually no part-time jobs from which part-timers could be promoted into other part-time jobs. Promotion invariably entailed becoming full-time. And when women work full-time, the recognition of their domestic responsibilities, and their need for flexibility, seems to disappear.

In a period in which employers' desires for flexibility, government policies of deregulation and privatization and cuts in public expenditure dominate the agenda, it will not be easy for women to assert both their rights to equality and their own needs for flexibility, their equality with men and also their difference. However, that in some sectors employers have had to devise practices and hours of work which take women's own needs for flexibility into account shows that there is some room for manoeuvre, especially where part-time workers are central to the labour process.

5
Theoretical Perspectives

Part-time work has not as yet been a central object of discussion in theoretical analyses of work, although it has received more attention recently as its importance within the economy has begun to be appreciated and people have become more interested in 'non-standard' forms of work and new forms of flexibility. Generally, however, the prevailing assumption that part-time workers are marginal to the world of work has been unquestionably reflected within discourses on work.

Women's Two Roles

Writing in the period of economic expansion of the 1950s and 1960s, when Britain experienced a continuing labour shortage in the long post-war boom, writers like Myrdal and Klein (Myrdal and Klein, 1956; Klein, 1965) argued that married women were an untapped labour reserve, and they heralded part-time work as an important means of enabling married women to participate in the labour market. This theme was echoed in Jean Hallaire's study of part-time work, undertaken for the OECD in 1968. Klein wrote in 1965 that married women comprised the sole untapped labour reserve since single women were already employed at nearly the same high rate as men, and she argued that the principal way in which this reserve of married women workers could be activated was by creating more part-time jobs. Like others writing within this framework, Klein unquestioningly accepted the association of women with maternal and domestic responsibilities. She quoted favourably a statement by the National Manpower Council of Columbia University that 'women constitute not only an essential, but also a distinctive, part of our manpower resources . . .

distinctive . . . because the structure and the substance of the lives of most women are fundamentally determined by their function as wives, mothers and homemakers' (Klein, 1965, p. 83). Part-time work was thus represented as an ideal means of enabling women to combine their domestic responsibilities with paid work and of creating, in Hallaire's words, (1965, p. 37), an 'equilibrium between the duties of a wife and mother and economic necessity'. The construction of certain jobs as part-time was unquestioningly associated, within these theories, with the assumption that women are *naturally* wives, mothers and homemakers.

Myrdal and Klein further suggested that 'some types of work lend themselves *by their nature* to part-time employment' (Myrdal and Klein, 1956, p. 113, our emphasis), and cited as examples domestic work, catering, social services and childminding. They argued that apart from these primarily domestic occupations and a few 'special cases', employers were largely disinclined to employ people on a part-time basis except when driven to by acute labour shortage or by a temporary need for extra shifts. Hallaire (1968, p. 33) commented that 'part-time jobs may be regarded as adapting work to the man', and his analysis made clear that he regarded part-time work as one solution to the problem of marginal groups who want to work. Although married women were the largest 'marginal' group when Hallaire was writing, he suggested that part-time work should be adopted not only for women, but for all workers subject to 'limiting conditions'. Among the other groups for whom he considered part-time work a possibility were retired people and students.

Myrdal and Klein were clearly worried lest part-time employment became associated solely with women and showed considerable insight into the consequences of this happening. They suggested that part-time employment may be a good *temporary* solution for women wanting to resume their careers later, a kind of 'refresher course', but that it was neither practicable nor desirable as a more permanent pattern of work for married women. And they argued that women needed to be regarded as full workers and not as 'helping hands' if the difficulties married women faced in attempting to reconcile a career with family life were not to be perpetuated. It was in this context that they advocated a whole series of policy changes, some of them very radical – for example, extended maternity leave, training for the over forties, houses built for working women, better planned distribution, rationalized housework, public services, school meals, day nurseries, nursery schools and domestic help. Their policy proposals show that even 30 years ago the more radical 'women's two roles' theorists were aware of tensions between women's domestic and wage-earning roles, and believed that social policies could make it easier for women to combine these roles.

Despite the fact that these analyses undoubtedly were radical in the 1950s and 1960s, they now seem much more limited (cf. Beechey, 1978; Birmingham Feminist History Group, 1979). They are problematic in three crucial respects: in unquestioningly accepting the sexual division of labour within the family; for assuming that there are certain jobs which women are 'naturally' suited for; and for assuming that women's equality would automatically follow from the impact of industrialization and the long march towards democracy and progress. With hindsight it is evident that one of the main problems with these studies is that they adopted an extremely optimistic view of the future possibilities for women's employment, and they did not anticipate that, despite women's increasing participation in the labour market, most of them would remain at the bottom of the occupational hierarchy, in part-time, low-paid, unskilled, 'women's jobs'. Important observations were made (for instance, that domestic work, catering, social services and childminding were often undertaken by women working part-time) but the explanation offered – that these are jobs for which women are 'naturally' suited – is inadequate because of its biologically reductionist overtones.

A great strength of Myrdal and Klein's approach is that it pinpointed the importance of the family in defining women's participation in the labour market, and stressed women's desire to engage in paid work, both variables which have generally been absent from studies within industrial sociology and industrial relations and also from Marxist analyses of the labour process. Undoubtedly, the fact that in Britain most married women with dependent children work part-time cannot be explained without reference to the family, and to cultural norms and state policies surrounding it. What is crucial, however, is *how* the family is analysed, and today these studies seem inadequate in this respect. They did not question the sexual division of labour within the family which was assumed to have a 'natural' basis, and they were therefore unable to explain, in terms other than biologically deterministic ones, *why* women have primary duties as wives and mothers and why they have to fit their paid work around these.

Recent analyses have generally been much less optimistic than Myrdal and Klein about the possibility of women attaining equality with men in the labour market. The economy has changed dramatically since the 1960s and there is a much greater awareness today of the structural barriers to women's equality in the labour market. Feminists writing in the 1970s and 1980s have criticized not only the lack of public facilities for working mothers (as Myrdal and Klein did), but also the sexual division of labour within the family which places women at a disadvantage in the labour market, especially (but not only) when they are married and have young children, and which perpetuates their economic dependence on men. They have underlined the ways in which the state reinforces women's position in the family and the labour market. And they have shown how job segregation within the labour market itself severely limits women's opportunities. Paradoxically, this increasingly sophisticated analysis of the constraints under which women live and work has often resulted in a gloomy depiction of women, who appear as passive victims of a series of interconnected institutions – the family, the state and the labour market. Myrdal and Klein wrote about women as having much to offer in terms of skill, commitment and potential. By contrast, the woman who emerges between the lines of many of the more recent radical and feminist writings is a marginal worker who is often represented as dull, unskilled and uncommitted.

Marxist Approaches to the Labour Process

In recent years there has been a considerable revival of interest in analysing how the organization and structure of work is changing in modern capitalist societies. Many of the most stimulating and productive analyses (which became known as 'labour process theories') were inspired by Harry Braverman's seminal book *Labor and Monopoly Capital*, first published in 1974. In it Braverman applies Marx's theory to the mid-twentieth century in an attempt to analyse the ways in which the organization of monopoly capitalism has affected both the nature of work and the composition of the working class.

Marx's own work was very much concerned with analysing the changing forms of subordination of labour to capital and showing how transformations in the labour process affected the structure of the working class. Marx had very little to say specifically about women's employment, and those comments he did make tended to rest upon naturalistic assumptions about the different capabilities of men and women which were commonly held in Victorian Britain. However, his writings do contain two theses which have been widely used to explain the characteristics of women's employment in modern capitalist societies. The first is the 'industrial reserve army thesis', which asserts that as capitalism develops it draws more and more people into the system of wage labour and expels them again when they are surplus to production requirements. The second is the 'deskilling thesis', which asserts that as capitalism develops and employers seek to increase profitability they attempt to wrest control over the labour process from skilled workers and subdivide and simplify the labour process. Unskilled workers are thus increasingly employed in place of the skilled. Marx and Engels both believed that women would increasingly be drawn into the system of wage labour as a result of these processes and that in consequence the proletarian family would become more egalitarian.

In *Labor and Monopoly Capital* Braverman shows how these two key theoretical arguments are still relevant to an understanding of work in the mid-twentieth century. Braverman's main thesis is that work has become increasingly degraded in the twentieth century as a result of capital's relentless drive for higher profits. He sees the shifting gender composition of the working population as one expression of this. He argues that men have been 'sloughed off' from manufacturing industry as jobs have been deskilled and that the remaining manufacturing population is increasingly split between a small number of highly technical workers and a larger (but rapidly declining) number of unskilled manual workers. A similar process of deskilling has been taking place in service occupations, according to Braverman: once-skilled shop workers, clerical workers and secretaries are being replaced by unskilled operatives whose work is hardly distinguishable from factory labour. It is in these occupations, in particular, that women have been drawn into wage labour, according to Braverman – a tendency which reflects the general shift in the economy towards poorly paid manual occupations. Braverman argues that it is capital which created a supply of women to work on such jobs by penetrating the domestic economy and taking over the production of commodities previously produced within the family. Thus, women have become part of the industrial reserve army of labour, a position which they have continued to occupy because of the impossibility, in many families, of living on earnings which are less than a 'living wage'.

Labor and Monopoly Capital provides a graphic account of the processes of restructuring which have been occurring in Britain as well as in the United States. Perhaps more than any other writer on the labour process, Braverman has appreciated the extent of women's participation in paid employment since the war, and he shows how changes in the gender composition of the working population are linked to fundamental structural changes in the economy. His foresight in projecting future changes in the structure of the working population is particularly evident today, more than a decade after *Labor and Monopoly Capital* was first published. There are, however, a number of problems with the conceptual framework which Braverman uses to analyse the changes he describes.

The first problem is with Braverman's analysis of skill and deskilling. Braverman writes, implicitly, from the standpoint of the skilled male working class in manufacturing industry, the working class which was the reference point for Marx and Engels' writings in the nineteenth century (cf. Benenson, 1984). Braverman uses the term 'degradation' to encapsulate the processes he analyses, and is apparently mourning a world that is lost. As a number of his critics have pointed out, Braverman assumes that 'skill' is an unproblematic category, and ignores the fact that what counts as skill frequently involves social and ideological constructions which are related to gender (see, for example, Beechey, 1980; Phillips and Taylor, 1980; Cockburn, 1983). It is remarkable how systematically women's jobs, and part-time jobs in particular, are classified as unskilled or semi-skilled even when they involve complex competencies and even when the women doing them have responsibility at work and are central to the labour process. The unqualified caring jobs in many parts of the public sector discussed in chapter 3 are good examples of this. It is now more widely recognized that skills cannot be treated in an entirely positivistic fashion, and that they are, at least in part, ideologically and socially constructed. What is less widely acknowledged, however. are the implications of this observation for the deskilling thesis. Braverman's critics have generally focused on the fact that *Labor and Monopoly Capital* presents too unidirectional a view of the ways in which the working population has changed, and have pointed out that some 'reskilling' has also occurred (Wood, 1980). However, this modification fails to take adequate account of the complexity of the notion of skill. As Game and Pringle (1984) suggest, the 'deskilling' thesis is much more appropriate as a means of characterizing changes which have affected craft skills in some areas of manufacturing industry than it is for analysing women's work in the service sectors of the economy. Just as the concept of skill is 'gender biased', they argue, so the deskilling thesis is 'gender blind'. Most women work in jobs which have never been classified as skilled, and there is a good deal of evidence to suggest that this is often a consequence of the fact that these jobs have been defined as 'women's work'. Although one must be cautious about substituting one overly general explanation of women's employment (which gives priority to gender) for another (which gives priority to economic and technological factors) as this oversimplifies the complex ways in which skills have been constructed and reconstructed, gender does seem to have played a critical role in the construction of many women's jobs, and part-time jobs in particular, as unskilled.

A second and closely related problem is that Braverman does not satisfactorily explain why it is women are used as cheap and unskilled labour. He points to the fact that women are used by capital to perform tasks which they previously performed in the home, but the main thrust of his argument is economic: that women constitute a cheap and generally unskilled labour force which is being drawn into new spheres of production and substituted for men in the older spheres. Braverman does not, however, satisfactorily explain why women enter the labour market on different terms from men and he seems implicitly to accept Marx's naturalistic assumptions for this. In order to explain women's position in the labour market, it is necessary both to provide some analysis of the sexual division of labour in the family and the sphere of social reproduction, phenomena which lie outside the labour process as analysed by Braverman, and also to analyse the construction of jobs and recruitment within the labour process itself. Braverman is unable to do this because of the exclusively economic focus of his analysis (cf. Beechey, 1980).

A third point is that Braverman fails to consider the extent to which male workers and trade unions, as well as employers, are implicated in the processes he analyses (cf. Hartmann, 1976; Rubery, 1980). Many examples exist of the ways in which male workers, in many cases operating through trade unions but also more subtly through workplace cultures, have succeeded in getting certain jobs (usually their own) classified as skilled, and in blocking access to these jobs by women, whether by formal or informal means. Particularly good examples of this can be found in the run-up to the Equal Pay Act (between 1970, when the Act was passed, and 1975, the date of its implementation) when both employers and trade unions engaged in 'minimizing strategies' in order to evade the requirements of the Act that women should receive equal pay, and a whole host of other instances are documented in recent workplace studies (see Snell et al., 1981; Cockburn, 1983, 1985; Coyle, 1984).

Finally, although Braverman rightly points out that many women, in particular, are employed in poorly paid manual occupations, he ignores the fact that women's entry into the labour market may also be a source of social relationships outside the home and an independent income (cf. Coyle, 1984; Martin and Roberts, 1984). This oversight stems from his apparently completely uncritical acceptance of the notion of a 'family wage'.

Braverman comments that multiple job holding within the same family often leads to tensions and to discontent among workers and suggests that this is not a satisfactory alternative to the immense numbers of jobs which pay less than a living wage. While he is right to underline the fact that many jobs do not pay a living wage, Braverman's interpretation of multiple-earner families is problematic. As many feminists have pointed out, the 'family wage' is an ideological concept which accepts, indeed reinforces, women's dependence upon men in the family and their relatively low pay (cf. Barrett and McIntosh, 1980). Recent studies suggest that women are in the labour market to stay and that mostly they are economically dependent on their jobs (whether or not they live in households with male wage-earners and no matter whether they work full-time or part-time). Analyses like Braverman's, which uncritically accept the notion of 'the family wage', underestimate the economic importance of employment for women, and they judge it from a standpoint which has only a tangential connection to women's changing experience of work and family life. The concept of the 'family wage' is an ideological concept which involves considerable distortion.

Taken together, these criticisms reveal the weaknesses of a theory which focuses solely on the conflict between labour and capital at the point of production. Despite his very perceptive thoughts on the structure and organization of work in advanced capitalist countries, Braverman's conceptual framework is limiting. *Labor and Monopoly Capital* largely ignores the family and the state and the wider processes of social reproduction. Furthermore, Braverman's emphasis on economic factors at the expense of political and ideological ones and the wider ensemble of social relations renders *Labor and Monopoly Capital* incapable of adequately explaining the differences and inequalities between women and men as these are manifested within the world of paid employment. The division of full-time and part-time jobs has, in part, to be understood in terms of these differences.

Braverman's book, published in 1974, is primarily concerned with periods of economic expansion, whereas any analysis of the labour process in the 1980s will inevitably be preoccupied with recession and with the ways in which this has affected the organization of work. Discussing women's employment in the early days of the recession, Jean Gardiner (1976) pointed out that the two central Marxist theses, the 'deskilling thesis' and the 'industrial reserve army thesis', have radically different implications for how female labour will be used in periods of recession. The deskilling thesis asserts that women will be substituted for men because their labour is cheaper than men's, and women will therefore become more central to production processes. The industrial reserve army thesis, on the other hand, asserts that women are likely to be disposed of as production is cut back and labour processes are reorganized, and predicts therefore that they will become more marginal to production processes. Both theories have been used to analyse how part-time workers have fared in the recession.

In *The Part-time Trap*, a pamphlet written for the Low Pay Unit in 1978, Jennifer Hurstfield emphasizes the increasing employment of women part-time in the economy, especially in the service sector.

She argues that employers in industries like catering and retailing have experienced difficulties in attracting sufficient numbers of full-time workers, partly because of their low rates of pay. She suggests that they have therefore turned to part-time workers. These women have usually been employed on unskilled jobs and have often been introduced into the labour process in the context of deskilling. The question of how far part-time workers have been substituted for full-time workers is a very important one, and as yet the evidence on this is inconclusive. There is some evidence of substitution in certain industries in recent years but, as we suggested in chapter 1, this substitution has mainly been of part-time women workers for full-time women workers. Substitution, it appears, has generally taken place within a labour market which is already highly segregated by gender. If this is true, the substitution of part-time jobs for full-time ones cannot adequately be explained by reference to sex-blind concepts like deskilling. What is needed is a more sophisticated and detailed analysis of deskilling and other forms of industrial and organizational restructuring which takes gender into account.

In its simplest form the industrial reserve army thesis outlines a completely different situation. In a discussion of the different Marxist explanations of women's employment, Irene Bruegel (1979) attempts to render the industrial reserve army thesis open to empirical verification. She defines the industrial reserve army as a labour force which is brought into production when required and disposed of when conditions change and it is no longer needed. Analysing statistics of employment and unemployment she shows that between 1974 and 1978 unemployment among women rose faster than among men and that in every manufacturing industry which employed substantial numbers of women and where employment declined the proportional rate of decline was greater for women than for men. Furthermore, she argues, it was part-time women workers in manufacturing who were made to bear the brunt of the decline in employment over this period. Since part-time women workers were disposed of to a greater extent than men in the early years of the recession, she argues that they 'conformed most closely to the model of women as a disposable reserve army.'

Although this model is certainly applicable to some manufacturing industries, like electrical engineering and telecommunications, it does not apply universally. Generally speaking, part-time work has become an increasingly significant form of work, rather than declining in importance, as we demonstrated in chapter 1. Furthermore, Bruegel's exclusive focus on employment statistics to demonstrate disposability ironically has the effect of concealing some of the other ways in which restructuring has taken place in the recession, with specific consequences for part-time work.[1] For example, it was evident from our Coventry research, and also from Robinson and Wallace's (1984) case studies, that in many cases employers have reorganized and cut part-timers' hours of work rather than making the workers redundant. Indeed, Robinson and Wallace (1984, p. 33) suggest that reorganizing part-time hours may be regarded 'as providing an alternative to redundancy among full-time employees . . . [which] may well represent a more pervasive if less dramatic form of discrimination than dismissal'. Such employer's strategies are examples of a different and less visible form of 'disposability'. It is also evident that a major form of restructuring today is the privatization of services – a process in which women are often re-hired by new contractors to do the same jobs, but on new contracts with lower rates of pay and worse terms and conditions of employment (Coyle, 1985). An analysis of the adverse consequences of the recession needs to be sensitive to the different forms which cuts and restructuring can take, and to be open to the possibility that they may take different forms where workers of different sexes are concerned.

Other writers have defined the concept of the industrial reserve army more broadly than Bruegel, and have used it to characterize rather different features of part-time work. Writing about new forms of work organization in Canada, Pat and Hugh Armstrong (1986) argue that now that some women have attained a secure and permanent place in the labour force, it is principally as part-time workers that women will still provide a flexible labour reserve. They are a reserve because they are cheap, because their jobs are segregated from men's jobs, and because they are available to be called upon when there are fluctuations in demand (cf. Connelly, 1978). Part-time work thus appears as a principal means of ensuring that women remain available for work at peak periods of demand during the day, the week or the year. The Armstrongs argue that jobs in the tertiary sector are especially amenable to the intensification of labour through the use of part-time workers. By using part-timers, they argue, employers are able to increase productivity levels, to pay low wages, to increase their control over the workforce (because part-timers are less likely than full-time workers to be members of unions) and to use techniques and equipment which may well be unhealthy if used for longer periods of time.

In a paper entitled 'Recession, disablement and exploitation', Jane Humphries and Jill Rubery (1986) also give the industrial reserve army concept a broader meaning than Bruegel does and, like the Armstrongs, they focus on the exploitive conditions in which part-time workers are employed. They argue that part-time work was originally introduced as a labour reserve, as a supplement to full-time work when full-time labour was scarce in the post-war years, but that it is now used as a substitute for full-time labour. This transformation of part-time working from supplement to substitute, they argue, results from changes in employers' incentives to use part-time labour. In manufacturing industries part-timers are used to enable employers to maximize the use of capital equipment without incurring premium rates for overtime and shift working, while in services part-timers give managers greater freedom to fine-tune their manpower to patterns of operation and customer requirements. Humphries and Rubery (1986) underline the fact that the state plays a role in creating exploitive conditions of work, and they identify a series of disabling measures which the British state government implemented in recent years which have made it harder for women to combine their domestic responsibilities with paid work, and which have thus played a part in the increase in part-time working.

Humphries and Rubery (1986) appear to be arguing that the changing position of part-time workers can be understood in terms of a combination of the industrial reserve army thesis (what they call 'the buffer hypothesis') and the substitution hypothesis. In an earlier paper, however, Jane Humphries (1983) subsumes both hypotheses within a broader concept of the industrial reserve army. She suggests that existing formulations of the reserve army hypothesis have focused too narrowly on cyclical fluctuations and have thus overemphasized the ways in which women have been used as an employment buffer in the context of a sex-segregated employment market. If one moves beyond an analysis of cyclical fluctuations and considers instead the long-term processes of capital accumulation, Humphries argues, the role of the sexual division of labour as a barrier to substitution is lessened. Indeed, one can see more and more women joining the labour force. Since the war, according to Humphries, we have witnessed a tendency to convert women from being a secondary latent reserve into a primary reserve. The foundations of sex segregation, she suggests, lie in this process. According to Humphries (1983, p. 16) sex segregation and women's lower wages are not, in the main, effects of discrimination on the part of employers or male employees, but rather they 'reflect the historical assimilation of the latest latent reserve, which happens to be female, and whose initial experience in paid labour is in secondary employment'.

It is perhaps clear from this brief discussion that attempts to use the industrial reserve army thesis are fraught with problems. The analyses which use it range from the specific to the very general, from those which attempt to render it empirically verifiable to those which are far more wide-ranging. If defined in a narrow way, to refer to the kinds of situation outlined by Bruegel (1979) in which workers are brought into production and disposed of again, the concept does have a specific and identifiable meaning, but attempts to use it are problematic and there is a danger that it will endow job loss with more importance than other forms of restructuring. On the other hand, defining the industrial reserve army more broadly as the Armstrongs and Jane Humphries do, has the danger of being too all embracing. Clearly, the processes by which labour is becoming more and more intensified, and part-time workers are being used as a cheap and flexible form of labour, are very important. And in Britain today they are becoming more so as employers attempt to restructure labour in the interests of flexibility and as the effects of deregulation and privatization become more apparent. The process by which the labour force is becoming increasingly made up of women is also important, and this certainly requires explanation.

It is not clear that the industrial reserve army thesis provides an adequate explanation of these phenomena, and we have not managed to agree ourselves about the usefulness of the theory when defined in this broader way to analyse part-time work. In Tessa Perkins' view, the theory may have been inadequately conceptualized in previous formulations, but it none the less provides a useful way of thinking about the process of restructuring. Veronica Beechey, on the other hand, believes that the concept is too imprecise, and has become overloaded with too many different meanings to be particularly useful. What we would both stress is the importance of an analysis which focuses on the different forms which restructuring has taken in the past and which is sensitive to the role of gender in the process of restructuring. Where we disagree is on whether the reserve army of labour thesis has anything useful to contribute to this analysis.

We both agree, however, that the main problem with many recent Marxist analyses of the labour process is that they have followed too closely the letter of Marx's own writings rather than seeing these as a set of arguments and perceptive insights about the organization of work in the nineteenth century which require substantial reformation and empirical verification if they are to have any validity today. The great strength of both the deskilling thesis and the industrial reserve army thesis as they were formulated by Marx is that they provided a dynamic account of the organization of work, drawing attention to the ways in which both work and the working class were being restructured in the course of capital accumulation. Just as historians have had to develop new concepts which can analyse the specificity of these historical processes more adequately than Marx did, so we need new concepts which are applicable to today's labour market. These need to analyse the complex ways in which work is organized and is being restructured, to consider ideology and social relations as well as economic factors, and to be open to the ways in which gender enters into the organization of production processes, something which is ruled out of court by conventional versions of Marxism.

Dual and Segmented Labour Market Theories

The other main theoretical approach which has been used to analyse women's employment from the perspective of how the labour market is organized is that of labour market segmentation theories. These have recently become very popular among people concerned to analyse divisions (both ethnic and gender divisions) within the workforce, and they seem to have attained the status of a new orthodoxy among 'economically minded' sociologists and radical economists. Dual and segmented labour market theories are primarily concerned with explaining why there are divisions within the working population and with examining the functions such divisions have for employers. They were originally developed by economists as part of a critique of 'human capital' models of job differentiation. Human capital theories hold that the key fact which explains people's 'choice' of jobs and pay is the difference in individual human capital investment – that is, in the time individuals spend in education and training. They argue, for example, that women choose jobs which require less investment in education or training than typical male jobs, and that therefore women receive lower returns. By contrast, dual and segmented labour market theories approach segregation from the demand side. They argue that employers demand different types of workers, or a differentiated labour force, that people enter the labour market with different characteristics, and that the differentiation of occupations within the industrial structure causes, or reinforces, the division of the workforce into different types of worker, thus creating a vicious circle.

The first stage dual labour market theory, proposed by Doeringer and Piore (1971), argues that in contemporary production processes the skills and knowledge which are specific to one company have grown in importance relative to transferable (occupationally based) skills. This means that firms are eager to hold on to workers who have specific knowledge and skills. Consequently, firms develop strategies, such as paying higher wages and developing career ladders, for the workers whom they wish to tie into the firm. These workers are referred to by Doeringer and Piore (1971) as 'primary sector' workers. Primary sector workers are given privileges by employers and work in jobs with higher pay, better benefits and greater stability, while secondary sector workers, who employers do not mind losing, move between industries and occupations, often from one unskilled or semi-skilled, low-paying job to another. A dual labour market, according to this framework, is one which is subdivided into primary and secondary sectors. The division of the labour market has emerged from the strategies used by employers to retain the scarce labour of skilled and technical workers and to reduce employee solidarity by buying off the most militant and best-organized sectors of the workforce.

Applying the dual labour market model to Britain, Barron and Norris (1976) and a number of other writers have argued that the secondary labour market in Britain is pre-eminently female. According to Barron and Norris (1976), secondary sector workers are likely to be members of a social group or category which has five main attributes: dispensability, clearly visible social difference, little interest in acquiring training, low economism (i.e. low interest in economic rewards) and lack of solidarity. These are general characteristics of a secondary workforce and are able to account not only for the preponderance of women in the secondary sector but also for the men workers who are found there. Although Barron and Norris do not deal specifically with part-time work, they comment in a footnote that 'this important but neglected part of the economy strengthens the case for the dual labour market model, since its jobs are even less well paid and certainly an important source of work for women' (1976, p. 69). Part-time work would be explained within this framework as a consequence of employers' strategies in the labour market which confer privileges on skilled workers; the fact that it is mainly married women who do part-time work would be explained as a result of the fact that women have the typical characteristics of secondary sector workers.

Dual and segmented labour market analyses are an important advance over human capital models because they attempt to explain labour market behaviour in structural rather than individual terms, breaking the link between individual human capital investment and occupational position and pay. However, these early formulations of the model have been criticized for a variety of reasons: for explaining labour-market differentiation principally on the basis of tenure in an individual firm, for paying insufficient attention to industrial conditions (particularly product market and technological conditions), for ignoring class struggle and the power relations between workers and managements (especially trade unions) and for giving insufficient weight to supply-side factors.[2]

Opinions about the applicability of early dual labour market theories in explaining women's employment have been mixed. On the positive side, Irene Bruegel (1983) suggests that they provide some insight into the experience of women in the British labour market, particularly into the experiences of part-time women workers whose 'marginality [is] reinforced by their confinement to a secondary labour-market where, if anything, their *lack* of attachment is valued' (Bruegel, 1983, p. 159). Bruegel also suggests that dual labour market theories help to explain women's patterns of union membership which have 'more to do with the type of jobs they do than with any intrinsic antipathy to unions or inability to organise' (Bruegel, 1983, p. 160).

On the negative side, critics have pointed out that the image of women as 'secondary workers' can be contradicted by empirical evidence (Scott, 1986). Many of the jobs women do (for example, teaching and nursing) have career ladders (Grim and Stern, 1974), and in particular sectors of the labour market women have lower levels of job change than men and comparable levels of qualification and career commitment (Scott, 1986). Futhermore, recent research suggests that just under half the women working would like further training, which calls into question dual labour market theory's claim that women have a low intrinsic interest in training (Martin and Roberts, 1984).

These empirical criticisms underline some fairly fundamental problems with the way that dual labour market theory conceptualizes women's employment. A first problem is that, like the Marxist analyses discussed above, the theory has been formulated implicitly from the standpoint of the skilled male working class in manufacturing industry. It is thus better able to analyse production work in the manufacturing sector than work in the service sectors, which often involves competencies and responsibilities but which is not defined as skilled and is low paid. Even as an account of production work in manufacturing industry, however, the theory is problematic because of the way in which the distinction between primary and secondary sector workers is drawn. Primary sector workers form the focal point of the analysis, and the concept of the primary sector worker is fleshed out much more fully than the concept of the secondary sector worker. Secondary sector workers are generally poorly delineated and are defined negatively in terms of their difference from primary sector workers (cf. Kenrick, 1981).

A related point is that dual labour market theory is permeated by an uncritical acceptance of a masculine model of the labour market in which gender is both too present (although untheorized) and too absent. It is too present in so far as women are conceptualized simplistically – they are treated as if they were an undifferentiated group, as if all women were the same, with the same ethnic and class background, the same familial status, the same education and training, the same skills and so on. It would be unthinkable to analyse men's position in the labour market in such a simplistic way. It is significant in this context that the corollary of the fact that women are the main secondary sector workers – namely that men are the main primary sector workers – does not appear to warrant discussion. It is important to analyse why it is that primary sector workers are generally male, but this requires an analysis of the processes (both formal and informal) through which men have obtained, and maintained control over, primary sector jobs. An analysis of the processes of discrimination whereby many women have generally been excluded from primary sector jobs by employers, often with the consent or collusion of trade unions, would inevitably be part of the story.

Gender is absent from the model in other respects, however, because the characterization of the secondary sector generally implies that the attributes of secondary sector jobs are objective. So, for example, the notions of skill and training are absolutely central to the ways in which the distinction between primary and secondary sector workers is drawn, and the theory assumes that what counts as skilled work can be treated positivistically – as an objective phenomenon which is unaffected by employers' conceptions or by the bargaining power or social status of those who characteristically do it. It is quite clear, however, from recent empirical research (including our own) that gender enters into the definition of skilled work and that it also plays a part in what counts and does not count as training. That women's skills and training are systematically downgraded and undervalued is well documented. One has only to point to the large numbers of secretaries and clerks whose knowledge of the workings of their particular firms may be considerable, but for whom there is only at best a short career ladder, to realize that the definition of who does or does not constitute a primary sector worker is a reflection of ideological definitions and bargaining strength as much as (if not more than) objective skills and knowledge.

As soon as one begins to introduce an analysis of gender and of employers' attitudes and discriminatory practices into the framework of analysis, important new questions are raised, and ideological constructions and social processes have to be introduced into the theory whose predominantly economic foundations are thus called into question.

The Cambridge Labour Studies Group has recently formulated a 'second generation' labour segmentation theory which has refined and developed the analysis of labour markets in three main areas (Rubery et al. 1984). First, power relations, or class struggle, have been introduced into the analysis which now recognizes conflicts of interest among workers and managements and between them. Secondly, industrial conditions, specifically product market and technological conditions have been introduced into the theory. These, rather than divergent worker behaviour traits, are seen as the basis of labour market segmentation. Thus, 'the industrial structure . . . becomes the prime locus for analysis of employment structure but a locus in which social, political and institutional factors play as much a part as economic and technological factors' (Rubery et al. 1984, p. 8). Thirdly, greater attention is paid to 'supply-side' factors, which has led to a more developed theory of social reproduction. In the revised theory, labour markets are conceptualized as structured by the productive system, on the one hand, and by the system of social reproduction, on the other.

Clearly, the reformulated approach is far more sophisticated than earlier versions of the theory: emphasis has shifted from an analysis of supposedly typical forms of employers' behaviour to a much more comprehensive account of industrial organization; the analysis of secondary sector worker characteristics is grounded in a broader, more sociological view of social reproduction; conflict is now allowed for in the theory and trade unions have been introduced into the conceptual framework; and it is recognized that employment structures have developed in more divergent and complex ways than had previously been appreciated – divergencies which are revealed in the location of industries, the nature of product markets, technological developments and systems of labour organization. How adequate is this revised theory for analysing women's employment and, more specifically, for analysing part-time work?

A preliminary point to make is that it is not entirely clear what status the theory has in relation to women's employment and whether it is correct, therefore, to regard it as a potential tool for analysing part-time work. It can be argued, for instance, that the theory has been designed as a tool for analysing labour markets in general, and that it is not intended to deal with gender divisions. Against this it is worth noting that a number of writers have used dual and segmented labour market theories as a framework for analysing the 'demand' factors associated with women's employment. Furthermore, the emphasis on labour supply and the processes of social reproduction in its revised theory suggests that at least some members of the Cambridge Group believe that the framework can be used to analyse women's employment.

The critical contribution of the revised framework for analysing women's employment is its analysis of labour supply. The Cambridge Group makes the important point that for the most part labour has rarely been in scarce supply and that when scarcities have developed new supplies of labour have not been mobilized through the price system but through social and political changes such as changes in family organization or migration procedures. Labour is not intrinsically scarce. The supply of labour is constantly constructed by a variety of social and political factors. The Group also points out that the price of labour is not determined by the interaction between demand and supply but by the social costs of reproduction, which are themselves determined by customary standards of living. Thus, it is argued, certain people (married women, for instance) may be available to work at lower wages not because they are less efficient (as human capital theorists assume) but because they can rely for part of their reproduction on other workers or the state. It is through the system of social reproduction – the family system, the state welfare system and the education system – that the labour force becomes differentiated, according to the revised theory. By introducing an analysis of these institutions into the framework for analysing labour markets, divisions in the labour force, which writers like Barron and Norris (1976) treated as exogenous variables, are given a material basis.

The Cambridge Group's revised analysis of social reproduction is undoubtedly a very important contribution to the analysis of labour markets, especially since it underlines the fact that contemporary forms of labour organization can only be understood in the context of an analysis of wider social relations. In our view, however, the new theory is still problematic because it explains why women are secondary sector workers solely in terms of an analysis of social reproduction, ignoring therefore the gender construction of jobs within the production process itself. As Alison Scott (1985) has pointed out, men's and women's experience of work may differ substantially despite similar structural situations, and this can also affect their consciousness and political dispositions. Furthermore, gender can play a role in determining the forms of authority and supervision which are used in the workplace, it can affect the status, income and forms of contract of certain jobs, it can influence the skill categorization of particular tasks, and finally it can play a role in dividing the workforce, both structurally and politically.

Some of the problems of using labour market segmentation theories to analyse part-time work are illustrated in a paper by John Goldthorpe (1985) in which he argues that modern Western societies have used different strategies to cope with recession. Some (like Norway, Sweden and Austria) have displayed corporatist tendencies, while others (like France, Britain, Italy and West Germany) have pursued dualistic strategies. Goldthorpe (1985) argues that the presence of migrant labour has been a major source of dualism in many Western capitalist economies, helping to sustain economic growth until the late 1960s, and that recently this secondary labour force has been augmented by casual or marginal workers and married women part-time workers. While he accepts that not all women working part-time can be properly regarded as marginal workers (e.g. professional women in the public sector), Goldthorpe suggests that the growth of part-time work has led to a considerable expansion of the secondary labour force. He argues that 'non-standard' employment arrangements enable employers to reduce risk in the face of uncertain demand and provide workforces which are rendered flexible by the very terms on which they are engaged. He points out that opportunities for 'non-standard' employment serve to mobilize a previously latent supply of labour from among groups who would not otherwise regard themselves as being 'on offer'. He also suggests that the members of these groups have in common a strictly limited commitment to the work they take on, and that they have other sources of identity and satisfaction and perhaps also of economic support. Goldthorpe claims that such workers are functional for the economic system 'because they stand outside, and may not seek to become strenuously involved in, the "web of rules" which . . . represent the characteristically modern way of regulating employment relationships' (1985 p. 144), suggesting, therefore, that 'on account . . . of their location within the wider social structure, as well as the form of their employment, such workers are unlikely to constitute a labour force in which any very strong interest in developing greater organisational power and in curtailing managerial prerogatives either exists or can easily be developed' (p. 143).

It is true, by definition, that people performing 'non-standard' forms of work are generally located differently within both the wider society and the labour market from indigenous white male workers, who are the point of reference for 'standard' workers in Goldthorpe's analysis. It is also true that such workers often enjoy worse terms and conditions of employment than 'standard' workers. However, Goldthorpe's analysis of these 'non-standard' workers and forms of work suffers from being too general. It obscures the differences between the various categories of worker employed in 'non-standard' forms of work – for instance, between migrant workers who are essentially defined as non-indigenous and as transient in their 'host' countries, and women part-timers who live permanently in the countries in which they work, have citizenship there and sometimes limited employment rights. It also portrays casual, migrant and part-time workers as performing functionally equivalent kinds of work, yet it does not discuss what kinds of job each group is typically employed on or why they are employed to do these jobs, nor does it assess whether these jobs are central or marginal to the economy as a whole. In assuming that all 'non-standard' forms of work are marginal to the economy, Goldthorpe overlooks the extent to which whole sectors of the British economy have for many years been heavily dependent upon so-called 'non-standard' workers, part-time women workers in particular.

Goldthorpe also uncritically accepts stereotypical assumptions about 'non-standard' workers without reference to empirical evidence. He suggests that part-time women workers have a low attachment to the labour market (implying that they are somehow backward because they stand outside the 'characteristically *modern* way of regulating employment relationships' – our emphasis) without substantiating these claims. Evidence from small-scale studies is mixed, but the *Women and Employment* survey, the most comprehensive analysis of women's attitudes to work in recent years, suggests that part-time women workers have quite high levels of commitment to their paid work. That they sometimes have different priorities from full-time workers (emphasizing the importance of convenient hours, for instance) should not be taken as evidence that they are outside 'modern' employment relationships, but rather that they are differently located within them. Furthermore, it seems that women workers' attitudes to work may well change over the life cycle, becoming stronger in the later periods of their working lives, which is when they are more likely to work part-time (cf. Coyle, 1984).

Dual and segmented labour market theories have suffered from being too dependent on economics, from trying to compress a wide variety of forms of work into the 'primary-secondary worker' distinction or the 'standard-non-standard worker' distinction and from being too abstract. Interestingly, the Cambridge Group concludes a recent paper reflecting on its research with the comment that 'further progress [in the development of segmented labour market theory] can only be made by more detailed investigation of the determinants of the demand for, and supply of, labour' (Labour Studies Group, 1985, p. 123), a conclusion with which we wholly agree. It seems clear that such detailed investigations, which in our view also need to be historical, will require substantial modifications to analyses like Goldthorpe's. It also seems clear that further research into the labour market and the organization of work in public and private services will reveal that the theory, as developed so far, has been heavily biased towards manual work in manufacturing industries. Discussions of the service sector, especially within the welfare state, where part-time work is often central to the labour process, call into question the classification of part-time work as 'secondary' or 'non-standard' work which is marginal to the economy, and thus, in our view, challenge the whole notion of a secondary sector as currently conceived. They also pinpoint the central position of gender ideology in the construction of part-time jobs.

Part-time Work and Flexibility

The economic advantages of employing part-time workers are also touched on in recent discussions about flexibility and new forms of work organization, albeit in a slightly different way. In a paper which has received wide publicity, John Atkinson (1984) argues that firms are developing new forms of flexibility in order to reduce their labour costs, and that their workforces are increasingly being subdivided into core and peripheral workers. The core group consists of full-time workers who comprise the firm's primary labour market. This group contains managers, marketeers and technicians who are expected to be flexible and to switch from one job to another or one plant to another. In return for such functional flexibility, they are given job security and have good career prospects. Outside this core group are a number of peripheral groups which comprise the firm's secondary labour market. Unlike the core, which is relatively stable, the periphery expands and contracts with demand. Clerks, supervisors and assemblers fall within the first peripheral group. Here again jobs are full-time, but the people doing them do not have careers. High levels of turnover mean that numerical flexibility can be attained – that is, firms can reduce or increase their number of employees when necessary. It is in the second peripheral group that part-time jobs are found. This group consists of part-time workers, people on short-term contracts, public subsidy trainees etc. Job security is lower within this group and here again employers use labour turnover and contractual insecurity to attain numerical flexibility. Finally are the 'externals', people who work for outside agencies as temporary workers or are self-employed, and those who are subcontracted to do particular tasks. Job security is non-existent here, and employers gain flexibility by taking people on and disposing of them easily. Since they are employed by outside agencies or are self-employed, firms can reduce their overheads by employing them, and the employees never appear on the firms' books.

It is clear that many employers are interested in creating more flexible workforces, although as yet little research has been carried out to test the validity of Atkinson's arguments. There has been an increase in temporary work and in self-employment in recent years, and part-time work has increased its share of total employment in almost all modern capitalist countries while full-time work has been on the decline, as shown in chapter 1. Atkinson's analysis puts these changes in the foreground, linking them to an analysis of employers' strategies. His analysis of divisions within the workforce is more detailed than the analysis provided by most of the dual labour market theories and he gives more positive content to the category of peripheral jobs than many dual and segmented labour market theorists do.

Atkinson's analysis is of particular interest to us because we found that part-time workers were used as a flexible form of workforce in both manufacturing industry and the public sector, but our own analysis is rather different from Atkinson's because of the central place of gender within it. Indeed, our research suggests that the fact that it is overwhelmingly married women who are part-time workers is not a matter of contingency but that gender has been built into the structure of part-time work. We found that employers had devised different methods of attaining flexibility where men were employed from those used where women were employed. Likewise, Angela Coyle (1985) has suggested that the government's privatization measures in the health service have been easier to effect because the workers concerned are mainly women working part-time.

How far does gender enter into the construction of different kinds of core, peripheral and external jobs? And to what extent does its role change over time? These are important questions, but not ones that Atkinson (1984) is concerned with. It seems highly likely that core group workers and many workers in the first periphery category would be men – indeed, the core category is partly defined by reference to masculine attributes like the ability to move – and that women would mainly be found among second periphery workers and among some groups of external workers, but Atkinson does not discuss this possibility.

Clearly, economic considerations are very important in leading employers to introduce new forms of work organization, but there are certainly prima facie grounds for suggesting that flexibility may also have a gender-related dimension to it. Studies of flexibility need to be sensitive to the ways in which gender ideology and other non-economic considerations enter into the construction of different kinds of job, and they also need to analyse the role which other agencies – trade unions, and the state, for instance – play in the construction and demarcation of different kinds of job.

Gender and Work

The framework for analysing part-time work in Britain today needs to be considerably broader than the theories discussed so far in this chapter. It needs to theorize the ways in which gender enters into the organization of production, and it also needs to analyse the relationship between state policies and the family and to explain why in Britain women have participated in the labour market in a particular way. That is, it needs to provide a theoretical analysis of gender relations both within the sphere of production and the sphere of reproduction. We still do not have anything like an adequate theory of gender, but will conclude this chapter with some preliminary comments on what a theory of gender in the area of work might look like.

Most people writing about part-time work comment that in Britain this is mostly done by married women, but this observation has not been adequately incorporated within economic analyses which centre on production. The fact that part-time workers are women is usually thought to follow from other features of part-time work – for instance, because it is unskilled or because part-time jobs are concentrated in low-paying industries or in the secondary labour market or in peripheral jobs – or from a combination of these labour market factors and the sexual division of labour within the family. In our view this kind of analysis is problematic because it ignores the role of gender.

Our research revealed that it simply was not the case that employers used sex-blind criteria in their hiring practices, or in selecting people for training schemes, or in their definitions of what constitutes 'skill' or appropriate qualifications, but that they held very definite conceptions relating to gender. So did many trade unionists. Certain jobs (particularly manual ones) had been constructed as part-time jobs because they were seen to be women's jobs. Various things followed from this. Part-time jobs were invariably low graded, they were rarely defined as skilled even when they involved a range of competencies and responsibilities, women doing them lacked opportunities for promotion and training, and any training which the women had received (whether formally when they had been full-time workers or informally within the family) was neither recognized nor remunerated, even when the employer depended upon it. Whether their work was central or marginal to particular production processes, part-time workers were regarded as marginal, their work was not defined as skilled, and they were badly paid. The crucial fact to emerge from our research is that there is nothing *inherent* in the nature of particular jobs which makes them full-time or part-time. They have been constructed as such, and such constructions are closely related to gender.

The argument that gender enters into the construction of part-time jobs, and increasingly into the differentiation between full-time and part-time work, and the central role accorded to gender within the organization of production, is one of the features which distinguishes our analysis from the other theories discussed in this chapter. In emphasizing the ways in which gender enters into the organization of production we do not want to discount the importance of the sexual division of labour in the family as an important variable. On the contrary, the domestic division of labour is clearly an important part of the explanation of why women work part-time because it imposes real constraints upon women's participation in the labour market, especially when they are married and have dependent children or elderly or handicapped relatives to care for. We do, however, wish to counter the view that this is the only way in which gender enters into the organization of work relations, and also to suggest that the way in which the relationship between the sexual division of labour in the family and the organization of the labour market is analysed is often simplistic.

In order to analyse why married women with dependents to care for so often work part-time, it is necessary to analyse not only the domestic division of labour within the family, but also the ways in which this has been shaped through the operation of state policies. Crossnational evidence shows that it is only in certain countries, of which Britain is a prime example, that high women's activity rates are associated with high levels of part-time employment. France, for instance, has had almost the same level of participation by women in the labour market since the war, but this has mostly been on a full-time basis. In part, the differences between France and Britain can be explained in terms of their separate experiences of industrialization and by sectoral differences in the patterns of women's employment, but they are also very much a product of different state policies (Garnsey, 1984; Jenson, 1986). France has had family and labour market policies which have been much more favourable to women working than the equivalent policies in Britain throughout this century, and these have resulted in far better provision of preschool childcare facilities and maternity leave. The state plays a central role in determining what form the division of labour in the household takes and how this affects women's participation in the labour market. And in Britain it is the absence of adequate facilities for caring for children and for the elderly and handicapped that is one of the crucial determinants of the fact that most married women with dependents work part-time.

We believe that our research, like Cockburn's (1983, 1985) and Game and Pringle's (1984), demonstrates that gender enters into the sphere of production.[3] It is a big step, however, from demonstrating the empirical existence of a phenomenon to developing an adequate conceptual framework to explain it and as yet very little work has been done in this area. On the basis of theoretical and historical analyses which have already been undertaken, it seems clear that gender refers to a process in which social relationships which are based on perceived differences between the sexes are constituted. It is also a primary way of conceptualizing relations of power (Scott, 1985). Gender has a number of aspects which have been characterized in a variety of ways, but recent writings have indicated three important levels at which it operates: the level of gender symbolism, the process whereby gender is constructed through social institutions, and the construction of individual or collective subjective identities (Scott, 1985; Harding, 1986).[4] It has for many years been customary in feminist literature to give prominence to the family in analyses of women's oppression (for instance, in discussions of patriarchy), but theoretical analyses of gender (as well as recent research) suggests that gender is produced and reproduced on a number of different sites in modern capitalist societies (Scott, 1985; Beechey, 1986). The family and kinship system played an important part in the past in giving women a secondary and dependent status at the same time as it allocated them primary responsibility for day-to-day and generational reproduction, but this dependency has also been enshrined in a whole number of other institutions – in family law and other areas of state policy, for instance, and in the organization of production itself (cf. Kenrick, 1981; Scott, 1986).

From the time of the industrial revolution, if not before, women have been constructed as marginal workers. Many women have certainly worked, and often in jobs central to the economy and to particular labour processes. No matter what jobs they have done, however, their position has been defined as marginal because of a powerful form of gender ideology – the ideology of domesticity – which was deeply rooted in the emergence of bourgeois society and, indeed, became a defining characteristic of bourgeois class relations (Davidoff and Hall, 1987). This provided a moral justification for the forms of job segregation which emerged during the process of industrialization (Scott, 1986) and was taken up by middle-class reformers who were concerned to protect women and children from the effects of industrial capitalism by legally restricting their hours of work, and by a labour movement which defined a family wage as one of its central goals (Jenson, 1986). It was later incorporated in a whole range of state policies (cf. Lewis, 1980).

The fact that women's employment in the nineteenth century was affected by gender ideology, and by protective legislation and trade unions' attempts to secure a family wage, as well as by employers' desires for a cheap and malleable labour force, is well known to feminist historians. It is surprising, therefore, that few of the insights of these historical studies have been incorporated in contemporary theories of the labour market. Women today are no longer proscribed from participating in paid employment, as they were in the nineteenth century. And in the post-war world marriage is no longer a significant determinant of whether or not women participate in the labour market. None the less, the notion that there is a conflict between a woman's role as mother and worker is still pervasive. It is thought to be acceptable for women to be in the labour market so long as their paid work does not interfere with their main task, that of caring for their children, and part-time work has emerged as a major means of enabling women to combine these tasks. Because their main task is defined as a familial one, part-time women workers are defined as marginal workers. It certainly is not the case that all women workers, nor even all part-time workers, are marginal to the production processes in which they work. Nor is it the case that all women have interrupted work histories in order to care for their families, or that all women have spells of part-time working. It is the case, however, that all women are defined as if there were a conflict between their paid work and their domestic responsibilities and all women working part-time are defined as marginal workers, no matter what they actually do. Similarly, all men (with the possible exception of young men whose wages and conditions of employment have deteriorated significantly in recent years) are defined as if they have families to support, no matter what their actual situations may be.

In contemporary discussions of work, the association of married women with part-time working has attained a quasi-naturalistic status, and it is all too easy to ignore the processes whereby both men and women have been constructed as particular kinds of workers. It is difficult, therefore, to imagine how things could be different. It is worth noting in this context that the ideological assumptions about women working in France have been markedly different – a fact which partly explains the differences in the pattern of women's employment in the two countries. Quite different assumptions have existed about women's status as potential workers and mothers, both now and in the past. Neither the labour movement nor middle-class reformers tried to discourage women from engaging in paid employment in France, and the notion of the family wage, which has been so prevalent in Britain, is generally absent. In short, there appears to have been no real contradiction, within ideological discourse, between women's role as mothers and their role as workers (Jenson, 1986).

An analysis of gender can sensitize us to the ways in which men's and women's positions in the world of paid employment have been constructed within discourse and through the operation of institutions like the state and the labour market, and it can indicate some of the ways in which people's identities are formed within the labour market. The analysis of gender can also show how things can be different in different societies, thereby challenging naturalistic conceptions and economistic arguments, and pointing to possible alternative ways of organizing work relations, and indeed, social relations more generally.

6
Questions of Policy

Much of the concern about part-time workers in policy circles focuses on questions of pay and benefits. Part-time workers are concentrated in the lowest grades of the occupational hierarchy so far as pay and benefits are concerned, and large numbers of them are low paid. The New Earnings Survey shows that when the earnings of part-time women workers are calculated as a percentage of full-time earnings, women working part-time fare badly. According to recent data, the hourly earnings of women working part-time are 79 per cent of those of women working full-time and 58 per cent of those of full-time male workers.[1] The *Women and Employment* survey (Martin and Roberts, 1984) also found that average hourly earnings were lower among part-time women workers at both the manual and non-manual levels.

The earnings of part-time women workers are not only low relative to full-time earnings, especially those of men. They are also low in absolute terms. The Low Pay Unit has calculated that four-fifths of all women part-timers are low paid, and that the proportion has been increasing in recent years. In 1985, according to the Low Pay Unit, 8.6 million workers (comprising over 40 per cent of the adult workforce) were low paid, 68 per cent of these were women, and 45 per cent worked part-time (compared with 36 per cent in 1979) (*Low Pay Review* no. 24). Since the New Earnings Survey, from which these figures are calculated, excludes people whose earnings are less than the national insurance threshold, this figure undoubtedly involves considerable undercounting. The numbers of women working part-time whose earnings are too low to pay national insurance contributions has also risen markedly in recent years. Whereas in 1977 one-fifth of all part-time women workers earned below the threshold, by April 1984 the number had increased to over three-fifths, or 2.75 million workers (Land, 1986).

The reasons for the low pay of part-time workers are quite complex. In part, they have to do with direct discrimination by employers – in particular the exclusion of part-time workers from additional pay and benefits like sick pay and pensions. They also stem from job segregation – from the concentration of part-time workers in a narrow range of occupations and in low-paying industries, many of which are being severely affected by government measures to deregulate the economy and privatize services. Part-time workers are also deeply affected by state policies, not only policies towards the labour market, but also social policies. A comparison of Britain with other modern capitalist countries shows that the British government's policies in both of these areas have been more restrictive and less enabling than the policies of most other governments. Part-time workers in Britain formally have limited rights under the Employment Protection Act (1975) and the Sex Discrimination (1975) and Equal Pay (1970) Acts, but they are disadvantaged in numerous ways. Where they have won any improvements in their terms and conditions of employment this is because unions have fought hard to mitigate the effects of employers' labour market policies, because women have pushed employers and trade unions into pursuing equal opportunities policies, or because employers have pursued more egalitarian employment policies, as a handful of Labour-controlled local authorities have done recently.

Discrimination against Part-time Workers

There is little evidence of part-time workers receiving different hourly rates of pay from full-timers, although a few cases of different hourly rates do exist. The Agricultural Wages Board, for instance, has a separate rate for part-timers (now set at 95 per cent of the full-time rate). Generally, however, different hourly rates have been abolished as firms have introduced unisex grading systems for men and women to comply with the requirements of the 1970 Equal Pay Act (Robinson and Wallace, 1984).

This does not mean that pay inequalities have disappeared, however. Far from it. There is widespread discrimination in pay which is evident in the additional components of pay rather than in basic rates, as Hurstfield (1978) pointed out. Part-time workers rarely receive overtime payments for hours worked in excess of their normal weekly hours. We did not find a single instance of part-time workers receiving overtime pay, even though they were often expected to be flexible in their hours of work, and to do additional hours with little notice. A recent survey of employers conducted by the *Industrial Relations Review and Report* (IR-RR, May 1984) shows that this is a widespread practice, although the National Engineering Agreement is an exception to the rule. This specifies that where part-timers' hours of work are normally those of the full morning shift or the full afternoon one, they shall receive overtime pay when they work additional hours. The reasons which we were generally given for the exclusion of part-timers from paid overtime is that they would then be treated more favourably than workers who do a full working week. This point is also stressed by the Confederation of British Industry (CBI) in its evidence to the House of Lords Select Committee on part-time work (House of Lords, 1981–2).

Most of the part-time workers whom we studied did receive shift premiums and bonus payments, although these were generally lower than the premiums and bonuses paid to men. This, however, does not appear to be a widespread practice. Other studies (IR-RR, May 1984; Robinson and Wallace, 1984) show that part-time workers rarely receive payments for working unsocial hours, or get shift premiums, merit awards etc.[2] Robinson and Wallace (1984) suggest that the payment of premiums is an important mechanism which employers have often used to enhance men's pay since the Equal Pay Act formally required the abolition of discriminatory wage payment systems. The reasons given by the employers whom we interviewed, as well as by those interviewed for the IR-RR study, were that additional payments are not applicable to part-time workers because they *choose* their hours of work to fit in with their domestic commitments. It seems that employers often feel that they are doing the women a favour by offering them part-time work.

The Legal Manager of Sainsburys made a similar point in his evidence to the House of Lords Select Committee: 'What is unsocial hours for one person is social hours to another' (House of Lords, 1981–2, p. 38). One should not forget, however, how much part-time work takes place at hours which would be deemed 'unsocial' by well-organized male workers. Cleaners often start work at 5 or 6 o'clock in the morning, or else work in the evening, as do people working twilight shifts in factories, and nurses and residential workers work at all hours of the day and night, weekdays and weekends. Moreover, although they may choose (or be constrained) to work part-time for domestic reasons, many women's hours of work do not actually fit in easily with their domestic commitments, and it is becoming harder for women to work hours which are convenient to them as employers cut and reorganize hours to suit their own needs for flexibility. The point is that employment at different hours is often used to justify differences in bonus payments and shift premiums, and part-time women workers either do not receive these or receive lower ones than men. Moreover, the 8-hour working day, which was fought for by organized male labour and is much more commonly worked by men than women, still generally provides the basis for definitions as to what constitutes 'social' and 'unsocial' hours of work.

Many part-time workers are also excluded from other benefits. In the workplaces we studied some had paid holidays, but few were entitled to sick pay and none was included in her employers' occupational pension scheme. Britain is virtually the only country in Europe not to have any statutory paid holiday for workers, and entitlement to paid holidays is a matter for collective bargaining or employers' decision.[3] The situation in Britain contrasts sharply with countries like Denmark, France, Luxemburg and Sweden, all of which have a 5-week minimum entitlement for all workers. The IR-RR survey of part-time workers found that most part-timers in Britain had pro rata entitlement to paid holidays with full-time workers. However, when it examined which women actually benefited from holiday entitlements the *Women and Employment* survey found that three-quarters of part-time women workers had some holiday, although these were generally shorter than those of full-time workers, and that those part-timers who worked less than 16 hours a week were less likely to have any paid holidays (Martin and Roberts, 1984).

Fewer part-time women workers receive sick pay. The *Women and Employment* survey found that half of the part-time workers interviewed received sick pay, and here again those working less than 16 hours a week were less likely to be entitled to any (Martin and Roberts, 1984). Sixteen hours is a cut-off point for many firms which include some of their part-timers in their schemes. The IR-RR survey suggests that where companies have a sick pay scheme which covers the occupational groups in which part-timers work, the part-timers tend to be covered. However, many part-timers work in jobs which are segregated from full-time jobs (as our research clearly demonstrates) and it is these who are most often excluded from sick pay schemes.

It is in the area of occupational pensions that part-time workers suffer most. Only 9 per cent of the women interviewed for the *Women and Employment* survey belonged to an occupational pension scheme, a finding which our research strongly confirms and which seems to stem from a lack of entitlement to pension schemes rather than women's reluctance to participate in them. Only 12 per cent of the women interviewed in the *Women and Employment* survey said that they did not want to belong to a pension scheme. A study of occupational pension schemes conducted for the Equal Opportunities Commission in 1984 found that 62 per cent of its sample excluded all part-timers from membership, and a further 15 per cent admitted only those working a minimum number of hours (McGoldrick, 1984). An APEX study (1985) showed an even lower availability of pensions to part-time office workers.[4] Employers whom we interviewed claimed that it was far too expensive to include part-time workers in their pension schemes, although few seemed to have calculated the actual cost. Some employers singled out the cost of providing pensions pro rata to part-time workers as a major reason why they were opposed to the European Community's Draft Directive on part-time work (House of Lords, 1981–2).

The extent to which part-time workers have been selected for redundancy in preference to full-time workers is difficult to discern. We found one very clear case of this having occurred in the telecommunications firm we studied, and Robinson and Wallace (1984) found an equally clear case in a food factory. In both cases the procedures whereby part-timers were dismissed were negotiated with the relevant unions, and in both cases the redundancies occurred in situations in which the labour processes were being restructured. How typical these instances are is hard to say. We did not find any consistent practice of making part-time workers redundant first, and neither did Robinson and Wallace

(1984). What we did find, however, were many instances of part-timers' hours being cut and reorganized as labour processes were restructured, and there is every indication of this being a widespread practice. According to Robinson and Wallace (1984), this form of flexibility, which employers often impose on part-time workers, is a kind of disguised redundancy which may well be a more pervasive form of discrimination than dismissal, but in legal terms may actually be lawful.

The Law

The law has proved to be very limited as an instrument for ameliorating the kinds of discrimination discussed above. Britain has no legislation which deals specifically with part-time work, but part-time workers are protected in certain respects (including entitlements to redundancy pay, maternity pay and protection against unfair dismissal), under the 1975 Employment Protection Act, provided that they fulfil certain conditions (hours of work and length of service). As a general rule, part-time workers are protected if they work for 16 hours a week or more and have worked for the same employer for at least 2 years (or if they work for 8 hours a week and have worked for the same employer for 5 years or more). Although we did not find much evidence that employers had deliberately kept hours of work beneath the 16 hours threshold, this situation has undoubtedly changed since our fieldwork, at least in some industries. Official statistics show that the number of part-timers working for less than 16 hours a week has increased from 28 per cent in 1980 to 35 per cent in 1985.[5] Furthermore in some industries – privatized hospital cleaning, for instance – some employers appear to have attempted to reduce the hours of part-time workers in order to keep them below the level at which they are legally protected.

The position of part-time workers under the sex equality legislation is complex. The situation of part-time women workers under the old Equal Pay Act (1970) was unclear for a long time, but it gradually became clarified through a series of decisions by industrial tribunals, the Employment Appeals Tribunal and the European Court of Justice. Formally, part-time workers are entitled to equal pay, but case law shows this to be a qualified right. A part-time woman worker must be able to point to a comparable employee of the opposite sex before she can establish a claim. Furthermore, she must be able to show that the variation between her contractual conditions and those of the man with whom she is comparing herself is due to a material difference between her job and his, and not to some other factor which is independent of sex.[6]

In an important case which has clarified the legal framework so far as part-time workers are concerned, *Jenkins* v. *Kingsgate (Clothing Productions Ltd)*, the European Court ruled that the principle of equal pay for equal work should be extended to part-time workers, but also that different rates of pay for full-time and part-time workers could be justified if the differences between them were based on some factor other than sex. Thus, if an employer could prove that he paid different rates for reasons which were not to do with sex, for example, to discourage absenteeism or to keep the machinery running for longer (as Kingsgate Clothing Productions argued), then there would be a prima-facie case for concluding that the different rates of pay would be legal under the Act. The Equal Pay Act of 1970 has since been amended to comply with European Community Law, and a woman can now claim equal pay if she is doing 'like work' or 'broadly similar' work to a man, if she is doing different work which has been given an equal rating under a job-evaluation study, or if she considers her work to be of equal value to a man's. The new 'equal value' clause is a substantial improvement on the old Act, but no cases involving part-time workers have yet been brought under it. Given the ruling in the case of *Jenkins* v. *Kingsgate* that different rates could be justified if they could be shown to be necessary for economic reasons, and the ruling in another case (*Leventon* v. *Clywd CC*) that applicants and comparators must have common terms and conditions of employment, it is clear that there are many ways in which employers can circumvent the law. Furthermore, given the isolation of many part-time workers and the ignorance of many about their terms and conditions of employment, it may also prove difficult for them to find a male comparator and to go through the cumbersome process of bringing a legal case.

There have also been a number of cases where part-time workers have been made redundant before full-time workers and

have claimed that this is illegal under the 1975 Sex Discrimination
Act. In one case (*Clarke* v. *Eley (IMI) Kynock Ltd*) part-time
workers, all of whom were women, were made redundant by an
employer who used 'last in, first out' as a criterion for redundancy
and who required that an employee had to work full-time if she
was to benefit from the application of 'last in, first out' as a
principle of selection. In this case the resulting dismissals of
part-time workers were held to be unfair, and the Employment
Appeals Tribunal ruled that indirect discrimination had occurred.
A similar result was reached in the case of *Allan and ors* v.
Leyland Vehicles Ltd. However, in another case, (*Kidd* v. *DRG
(UK) Ltd*) the Employment Appeals Tribunal gave a different
judgement and refused to uphold Mrs Kidd's complaint that a
similar method of selection for redundancy in which part-timers
were selected for redundancy first, and 'last in, first out' was then
applied to full-timers, all of whom were also women, had a
disproportionately adverse effect on married women who could
not work full-time because they had to care for young children. In
this case Mrs Kidd failed to establish that indirect discrimination
on the grounds of marital status had occurred. The industrial
tribunal, upheld by the Employment Appeals Tribunal, thought
that any discrimination which occurred would have been justified,
since the employers could point to economic advantages which
occurred when full-timers rather than part-timers were employed
(*IDS Employment Law Handbook*, no. 31).

Because of the inadequacies of the existing legislation to deal
with discrimination against part-time workers, pressure has
mounted in recent years from a number of sources – from pressure
groups like the National Council for Civil Liberties (NCCL) and
the Low Pay Unit, from the European Commission and from a
number of trade unions and the Trades Union Congress (TUC) –
to extend employment rights to part-time workers. The main
thrust of these moves has been to attempt to make discrimination
against part-time workers illegal, thus bringing them directly
within the framework of employment law and industrial relations.
The European Commission's Draft Directive on Voluntary Part-
time Work has played an important role on the legislative front.
This outlines a legislative framework for the Community the aim
of which is to 'remove major abuses and discriminatory practices
. . . by requiring the extension to part-time workers of the rules

and provisions for full-time workers rather than by creating special rules for part-time work' (Commission of the European Communities, 1981, p. 2).

Given the evidence of widespread discrimination against part-time workers in bonus payments and benefits, and the evidence that part-timers are sometimes made redundant first, the introduction of legislation to include part-time workers within the framework of employment rights would be an important step forward. It would in principle extend the protection conferred under the 1975 Employment Protection Act to all part-time workers (and not just to those who fulfil certain conditions), and it would give part-time workers the right to equal pay and benefits and the right to equal treatment by bringing them within the general framework of employment law. This would be particularly important for women, so many of whom work part-time for at least a part of their working lives. The attainment of such rights in law will undoubtedly be an uphill struggle, however. There are powerful voices against such proposals, ranging from the government which has not only refused to ratify the Draft Directive, thus preventing part-timers in Britain from attaining many important employment rights, but has also vetoed the legislation for the whole European Community, to the employers' organizations which object to the proposed legislation, principally on grounds of cost.

The cost of extending employment rights to part-time workers is an important question, since it can affect whether part-time jobs would be lost if legislation were to be introduced, and opinions differ about how employers would balance costs versus benefits. In the House of Lords hearings representatives from the National Federation of Small Businesses said, when pressed, that they estimated that costs would rise by 15 to 20 per cent, whereas Sainsburys estimated a 3.3 per cent increase in their total wages bill (a figure deemed by Lord McGregor to be 'quite astonishingly low') and Barclays Bank estimated that the increase would only be 1 per cent (House of Lords, 1981–2). Our own research suggests that most employers had not actually calculated the costs, and it is not clear what the consequences of extending employment rights to part-timers would be. It may be that in industries which rely heavily on part-time workers and where they are central to the labour process, the employers' dependence on part-time labour and their need for flexibility will outweigh any increase in total costs, whereas in industries where part-time workers are more marginal to the labour process or where jobs can easily be abolished through introducing new technology part-time workers may be more vulnerable. On the other hand, it may be the case that where large numbers of part-timers are employed any increase in costs would be prohibitive. We just do not know.

At a time when the government is seeking to dismantle such employment rights as exist, and employers, like the government, are anxious to be rid of so-called 'rigidities in the labour market', the climate is not at all conducive to demands for further employment legislation, and it may be that trade union pressure to extend employment rights to part-time workers may be more successful than the law. Some unions have begun to campaign on the issue of part-timers' exclusion from additional components of pay. In many banks, for instance, part-timers are excluded from low-interest mortgages, staff loan schemes and territorial allowances, and the Banking, Insurance and Finance Union (BIFU) has recently won a 10 month negotiating battle to gain shift premiums for part-time workers to entitle them to full premiums for working outside the normal working day.[7]

Likewise, manual workers' unions in the public sector have been campaigning for some years for part-time workers to receive equal bonus payments to full-time workers, and have pointed out that the non-payment of these is one of the principal factors contributing to the low pay of part-time workers.[8]

The Women's TUC Conference has been arguing for a 'vigorous campaign' to include part-time workers in collective agreements and provide them with greater security, and a number of unions, among them NALGO, COHSE, NATFHE, BIFU, APEX, GMBATU and NUPE, now have policies which deal directly or indirectly with the problems of part-time workers. Furthermore, the TUC, which was originally sceptical about part-time workers and resistant to attempts to improve their conditions of work, now has a set of 'priorities for part-timers'. Some employers, too, (mainly Labour controlled local authorities) have devised policies to extend employment rights to their part-time workforces, and Sheffield City Council has included part-time workers in its proposal to create single status employment for its entire workforce.

These are clearly very important moves since in principle they would give part-time workers the same rights as other workers. It is important to point out, however, that both legislation and trade union policies of the kind described above are likely to be fairly limited in their capacities to change the situation of part-time workers unless they seriously tackle the question of job segregation. Just as the Equal Pay Act before its amendment proved to be a limited instrument for improving the situation of women workers in the long term because it could not tackle the existence of widespread segregation between men's and women's jobs, so attempts to improve the position of part-time workers through the law are also likely to be limited. Legislation could improve the earnings and benefits of some part-timers just as the Equal Pay Act, combined with pressure from women and from trade unions, improved some women's full-time earnings, but could not in itself do much to *change* the position of part-time workers because this is affected not only by directly discriminating practices but also by other, more structural features to do with organization of the labour market.

Trade union organization, too, tends to reflect more general features of the labour market. Part-time workers are far less likely to be members of trade unions than their full-time counterparts. The IR-RR survey (IR-RR, May 1984) found that only 7 per cent of part-timers in sales occupations, 9 per cent of part-time secretaries, 17 per cent of part-time clerical workers, 27 per cent of part-time health professionals, 31 per cent of part-time skilled operatives and 37 per cent of part-time other operatives belonged to trade unions. Furthermore, even when they are members of unions part-time workers do not necessarily have a strong voice in their local branches because branch organization often reflects the hierarchical organization of jobs within the workplace. It does not follow, therefore, that because a union has a strong policy on part-time work at a national level this will be reflected at the local level, as NALGO has pointed out (see also Fryer, et al., 1978). In many of the workplaces we studied the part-timers (who generally *were* members of unions) were not particularly involved in their unions. Occasional examples exist, however, of unions organizing part-time workers very successfully. In Coventry, for instance, the home helps were all in the TGWU, which waged an imaginative and highly successful campaign against the council and prevented it from cutting the home helps' weekly hours of work (and therefore their pay). Like home helps in Belfast who are members of NUPE, and who have successfully taken industrial action over their entitlement to paid holidays, this case illustrates an important point: part-time workers *can* be successfully organized, but this requires methods of organization which are sensitive to their situation and concerns.

We have suggested in this section that legislation and trade union policies to give part-time workers full-time rights, while important, are likely to be limited as vehicles for improving the situation of part-time workers because they do not deal with the more general determinants of their situation. Policies are therefore needed which tackle some of these determinants, like job segregation within workplaces and the concentration of part-time workers in low-paying industries like cleaning and catering. Policies are also needed to enable women to combine paid work with having children.

Equal Opportunities Policies

It has become clear over the past few years that one of the principal reasons why the sex equality legislation has been limited in its capacity to improve the situation of women in the labour force is because job segregation is deeply entrenched, and women's employment opportunities are thus severely restricted. Moves have thus been made in some workplaces, generally on the initiative of feminists, to introduce positive measures to improve women's situation at work. These have sometimes been instigated by employers and sometimes by unions, and have been more widespread in the public sector than in private industry. In recent years policies designed to promote sexual equality at work have often been linked with measures to promote equality for ethnic minorities, people with disabilities and lesbians and gay men.

Equal opportunities policies in Britain have mainly been concerned with countering discrimination in education and training schemes and employment discrimination within workplaces through which one class of people is denied access to higher-paying jobs solely or partly on the basis of social characteristics like gender.[9] They have mostly paid rather little attention to part-time workers, preferring instead to focus on promotion opportunities for women into managerial and higher-grade jobs, and, in some cases, encouraging women to enter into non-traditional jobs. However, there are several areas where equal opportunities policies have had an impact on the situation of part-time workers, either directly or indirectly. These are, broadly speaking, policies to lessen the effects which childbearing has on women's paid employment, to enable women to move out of low-level part-time jobs, and to increase the opportunities for part-time working at all levels of the occupational hierarchy.

Combining Paid Work with Having Children

Clearly the starting point for women to have any possibility of combining paid work with having children is adequate maternity leave. Britain, however, has the worst statutory maternity leave provisions of any country in the European Community. It has the strictest eligibility requirements (requiring national insurance coverage and at least two years' continuous employment with the same employer at the start of the eleventh week before the expected date of birth). Moreover, women have to notify their employer within a fixed time limit of their intention to take maternity leave, and a woman receives no pay at all for much of the period of entitlement. This contrasts sharply with other European countries. Ireland is the only other country in the European Community which requires a woman to give written notice, and Britain is alone among the countries of the European Community in not providing financial support for the entire duration of the leave. In Belgium, West Germany, Luxemburg, Portugal and The Netherlands, women are guaranteed 100 per cent of their earnings during their maternity leave, and in most other countries they receive 80–90 per cent (European Industrial Review and Report, 141, 1985). Furthermore, whereas in most European countries a woman is allowed to return to her former job, the British legislation permits an employer merely to offer suitable alternative employment, and if he employs five or fewer employees he is not legally obliged to take an employee back at all.

Britain has no provision for breaks for nursing mothers, and (like The Netherlands and Ireland) has no parental leave provision. Here again the situation contrasts sharply with that in a number of other European countries. In Sweden each family is entitled to 12 months' parental leave, the last 6 months of which may be taken as part-time leave at any time until a child is eight. Working parents are also entitled to 60 days paid leave per year for each child under 12, to care for sick children etc. West Germany has recently passed a new parental leave law, granting one year's paid parental leave to either parent, and Belgium now has a law granting all workers the right to a sabbatical year's leave, which can be used for parental leave or other purposes and can be taken at any point in a person's life.

Given such restrictive legislative provision, it is hardly surprising that many women in Britain leave paid employment rather than take maternity leave. Most women do not fulfil the stringent conditions of eligibility for leave. Only one in six women having babies qualified for maternity pay in 1984–5 (Land, 1986). Moreover, the number of part-time workers who are eligible for paid maternity leave is extremely low. A study by Incomes Data Services found that very few employers had extended eligibility for maternity leave to all their women employees irrespective of the hours they worked. The grounds given were that if the employee had not fulfilled the statutory service period, the employer could not claim a rebate from the Maternity Fund (Incomes Data Services Ltd, 1982).[10] Furthermore, even if women are eligible for paid maternity leave they have to return to work soon after giving birth, as the statutory period of leave is very short. Given the inadequacy of childcare provision this is impossible for most women and in any event women's wages are so low that it is practically impossible for most women to pay for childcare.

For women to have equality within the labour market it is very important that men are enabled and expected to take on their share of domestic responsibilities. However, very few employers in Britain make any provision for paternity or parental leave. Recently, the Confederation of British Industry examined a hundred agreements in the public and private sectors and found that only seven contained clauses giving paid paternity leave. The CBI, like the government, is strongly opposed to parental leave. It objected to the European Commission's recent Draft Directive on Parental Leave and Leave for Family Reasons (which was designed to give a minimum entitlement of 3 months' leave for each worker for each child and also to give leave for family reasons) on the grounds that such legislation would undermine industry's competitiveness, that it would be counterproductive to decreasing unemployment, and that it failed to recognize the importance of flexibility. The government also argued forcefully against the legislation on the grounds of cost and also argued that parental leave is not an appropriate area for legislation. Once again the government exercised its veto when the proposed legislation was considered by the Council of Social and Labour Ministers, thus killing the possibility of it being introduced for the whole European Community.

Improving maternity and parental leave has been a major area of equal opportunities work in recent years, and several unions have negotiated agreements which are better than the statutory minimum. Last year's TUC Council passed a motion calling for a draft model clause covering maternity pay and leave, adoptive leave and family responsibilities leave, and it pointed out that the inadequacy of maternity rights for women on short-term contracts and part-time employment was a particular cause for concern (Trades Union Congress, 1985). A few employers, in particular Labour-controlled local authorities, have introduced schemes which are considerably better than the statutory minimum (although seldom as good as those in other countries). Islington Council, for instance, gives its women employees 40 weeks' paid maternity leave (on a combination of full, nine-tenths and half pay), and all employees of the Council have the right to return to work to a similar job on the same grade as their previous one up to 5 years after having a baby, irrespective of their length of service and their hours of work (*Equal Opportunities Review*, no. 4, 1985). Given the widespread evidence of downward mobility among women who return to part-time work after having a baby, improved maternity and parental leave provisions are of critical importance.

If adequate maternity leave is the first condition which has to be met if women are to be able to combine paid employment with having children, adequate facilities to enable them to return to work are the second. There are very few workplace nurseries in Britain (although a few employers have introduced nurseries as part of their equal opportunities policies) and nursery provision is very limited. In 1984 there were only 168,327 day care places (in local authority day nurseries, registered day nurseries and with registered childminders) in England, catering for just 5.3 per cent of the population aged four or less (Land, 1986). This is among the lowest provision in the European Community. France, for instance, has far higher provision. In Canada 95 per cent of nursery places are state-assisted. Public provision of nursery places in the United States is lower, but parents can claim tax relief on childcare expenses. In Britain there is no allowance for childcare expenses to be deducted from taxable income except for single men with dependents who have resident housekeepers. It is hardly surprising, therefore, that most childcare in Britain is done by relatives without pay, and most mothers of young children are obliged to work part-time, fitting their paid work around their childcare responsibilities. Childcare in Britain is seen as an essentially 'private' matter, of concern to the state only where children are thought to be 'at risk'. Employers generally see children as a woman's own responsibility, although we found that the employers of women working part-time wanted to know what arrangements the women had made.

Most employers do little or nothing to help women returning to work, even when they rely heavily on a female workforce. We found that whereas in the period of labour shortage after the war some employers took women's own needs for flexibility into account (e.g. in the timing and organization of shifts), in recent years they have tended not to pursue enabling policies. There are, however, occasional exceptions, and a few employers have made moves to encourage women to stay in, or return to, the labour market after having children. One or two Labour-controlled local authorities, for instance, have issued statements expressing a wish to accommodate women returning to work as part of their equal opportunities policies.[11] Such statements of intent have generally been accompanied by specific policies. The Greater London Council (GLC), for example, gave women who left to have a baby but who subsequently decided that they wished to return to work the right to return to a job at the same grade and salary point within 2 years of their resignation (subject to the availability of jobs), and also stated that it would treat sympathetically any woman who wished to return to work between 2 and 5 years after resigning. It also organized refresher courses for women on extended maternity leave and established a women returners' scheme. This consisted of lunchtime and full-day sessions at which women were encouraged to return to work after having a baby, and were given information about finding childcare and encouraged to form support groups.

Women returning to the labour-market after a break for childrearing are generally downwardly mobile. Women leaving the full-time labour market have few opportunities to return to it, and those who do manage to move into part-time employment in the same organization generally move into lower-grade jobs and lose employment protection because the part-time job is generally considered to be a new job. It is extremely important, therefore, that the possibility is created for women to move between full-time and part-time employment over their working lives, and also that part-time working is extended to higher-level jobs.[12]

Extending Part-time Working

Our research showed quite clearly that part-time jobs were seldom linked into career ladders, and that many part-time jobs were dead-end jobs without opportunities for training or promotion. We found no evidence of part-time women workers eligible for training schemes or for promotion, and the National Training Survey suggests that this is widespread. Fewer than one part-timer in 20 had received on-the-job training on a part-time basis (Elias and Main, 1982). It appears, however, that women working part-time are interested in both training and promotion.

Many of the women whom we interviewed expressed a desire for further training. Moreover, just over one-third of the women working part-time who were interviewed for the *Women and Employment* survey said they would like further training, and a roughly equivalent proportion expressed an interest in promotion (Martin and Roberts, 1984). As yet very few equal opportunities programmes have tackled the question of increasing training and promotion opportunities for part-time workers, and here again the Greater London Council broke new ground. In addition to encouraging women to move into higher-level management and professional jobs and into non-traditional manual jobs and creating paths of accelerated development for people stuck in clerical and junior executive posts, it devised schemes to teach manual workers basic skills (literacy and numeracy). It also devised an innovative scheme to enable women to move out of catering and cleaning work and into clerical work. Unlike most equal opportunities programmes, which tend to be biased towards enlarging opportunities for women in white collar and professional and managerial jobs, the GLC scheme gave new opportunities to part-time women manual workers.

The most common means of extending part-time working to higher-level jobs which has been introduced in Britain in recent years is job-sharing. In a pamphlet on job-sharing the Equal Opportunities Commission (EOC) suggests that job-sharing provides an 'imaginative variant' on the 40-hour normal working week, and that it enables women to move into higher-level part-time jobs which are adequately paid and properly protected (Equal Opportunities Commission, 1981). Job-sharing has undoubtedly enabled some women wanting to work part-time to work in jobs which are commensurate with their skills, experience and qualifications. It has also contributed to a situation in which some more 'responsible' jobs have been opened up to part-time working. Job-sharing is also one of the few practices that can encourage men to share domestic responsibilities. A number of unions now have job-sharing policies, and job-sharing is available in quite a few workplaces, especially in the public sector. Almost all posts in the GLC were in principle open to job-sharers, as are some teaching posts in the Inner London Education Authority (ILEA). Sheffield City Council has an agreement with NALGO, the white collar union, which allows job-sharing in all white-collar grades, and the CPSA (one of the Civil Service unions) has negotiated a pilot job-sharing scheme in the Department of Health and Social Security. In the private sector some banks allow alternate week working, which is a kind of job-sharing, but this is not supported by the BIFU, the banking union. Job-sharing has generally been introduced with the needs of women in mind, but Leeds City Council has recently been considering introducing a job-sharing scheme for disabled people. Unions which have job-sharing policies generally try to protect the position of their full-time members. The National Association of Teachers in Further and Higher Education (NATFHE), for instance, explicitly states in its job-sharing policy that any introduction of job-sharing should not diminish the amount of full-time employment and it should not adversely affect the conditions of service of other people. Like most union policies it states that the employment protection, continuity of service and pension rights of somebody who starts job-sharing should not be adversely affected, and (unusually) it stipulates that any agreement reached should specify clearly the conditions in which a person can return to full-time work. Unions sympathetic to job-sharing have generally drawn a sharp distinction between job-sharing and the government's job-splitting scheme (which was introduced in 1983 but seems to have been quietly dropped on the grounds that job-sharing involves subdividing a job in order to meet the needs of employees whereas under the job-splitting scheme it is the employer who takes the initiative in splitting up a job. The unions argue that the latter often involves deskilling and dilution, and that the jobs are seldom adequately paid and properly protected.

Given the high profile which job-sharing has had in discussions of new forms of work, and the assumption which is sometimes made that it constitutes a solution to the problem of part-time work, it seems important to point out that job-sharing is not appropriate to all kinds of work. It is far more common among professionals and in the public sector than in lower-level white-collar and manual jobs. Indeed, since many of these have been constructed as part-time jobs, it is difficult to see how they could be further subdivided. Job-sharing is limited too because it does not challenge the notion of the 'normal' working day or week. It merely assumes that a 'normal' full-time job can be done by two people instead of one. A more radical approach to the restructuring of work would need to challenge the notion of the 'normal' working day and working week, for men as well as women, and to devise a wider array of different options to full-time working.

Workplace equal opportunities policies in Britain have generally been concerned with employment discrimination, and with trying to extend the opportunities for women within the existing hierarchy of occupations. Some policies have affected the structure of occupations in a limited way (for example, by extending career ladders between secretarial and administrative jobs, and by opening up new opportunities for part-time working) but they have not been generally concerned with wage discrimination, with the ways in which the structure of occupations is organized and graded.[13] The fact is, however, that even if a few women manage to move out of secretarial jobs and into administrative ones, or out of cleaning and into clerical work, there will be large numbers who do not. Many part-time jobs will continue to exist, particularly at the lower level of the occupational hierarchy. These are generally dead-end jobs without promotion prospects, and they are often badly paid and inadequately protected.[14] Two different kinds of policy have been used to tackle these jobs: policies to ameliorate low pay, and policies to revalue women's jobs.

Tackling Low Pay

Low pay among manual workers has been a major concern of several public-sector unions (e.g. NUPE) in recent years. These have been involved in negotiating measures to alleviate low pay at the workplace level, and have also been strongly behind moves to put pressure on Trades Union Congress and the Labour Party to support the demand for a national minimum wage. As a result of union pressure and industrial action by manual workers, several local authorities have recently developed policies which are specifically designed to deal with low pay in the areas within which they have discretion, e.g. in the payment of bonuses (see IR-RR, February 1984). Thus, for example, Haringey Council has introduced a Low Pay Supplement, and Camden and Sheffield Councils have introduced Minimum Earnings Guarantees to supplement low rates of pay. Sheffield City Council (like Camden) found that the vast majority of its part-time staff earned less (pro rata) than the weekly threshold figure, and that school meals staff, cleaning staff, office cleaners, home helps and care assistants were heavily concentrated among the low paid. The supplements in each of these schemes are paid pro rata to part-time workers (and the Haringey scheme also specifies that term-time employees in educational establishments should not be treated as part-time in respect of periods for which they receive half pay or are not paid). A major problem, however, in introducing the schemes has been fears about their possible knock-on effects for more highly paid workers (who are usually men and tend to be better organized), and the employers found that they had to tread carefully in order not to wipe out existing differentials. In most cases, therefore, the supplements have been graduated, with higher levels being paid to the lower-paid workers and lower levels to the higher-paid.

Much of the recent growth in part-time work has been in private service industries like laundries, the retail trades, hotels and catering and cleaning, and these are all low-paying industries in which statutory forms of protection have been severely weakened in recent years. In these industries there are often no better paid men with whom a part-time woman worker might compare herself, and the whole workforce is often badly paid.

The hotel and catering industry is in many ways typical of women's employment in the private sector, as a recent *Low Pay Review* points out (MacLennan, 1984). Three-quarters of the workforce are women, and half the workforce works part-time. The majority of firms are small and the level of union organization is low. It has been estimated that only 6 per cent of hotel and catering workers are members of unions. (Counter Information Services, 1980). In many firms there is a high proportion of seasonal and casual workers, and turnover is high. This makes union organization difficult, and it also means that most of the workforce falls outside the scope of the 1975 Employment Protection Act.

The fast food industry has been one of the most sensational areas of growth in recent years, and exemplifies an important form of employment in the hotel and catering industry (see Gabriel, 1985). Over 1,000 hamburger, over 1,350 pizza and over 650 chicken outlets have opened in Britain in the past 15 to 20 years. McDonalds alone has 165 outlets, an annual turnover in excess of 100 million, and a workforce of 12,400 people, of whom 75 per cent are under 21 years of age and the majority work part-time. Staff turnover is extremely high, and most people working in the outlets see their employment as temporary. Employers like McDonalds are very hostile to moves to unionize the workforce, and are said to employ special consultancy agencies to keep unions out (Gabriel, 1985). In some areas of the United States, McDonalds has had such difficulty in recruiting labour because the wages it pays are so low that even its 'traditional' sources of part-time labour (college students) have dried up, and employers have been forced to experiment with other ways of attracting workers: bussing people out from the cities to the suburbs and paying married women an allowance for childcare expenses in order that they can be induced to work during the day. In such firms low pay and part-time work are inextricably interwoven.

A second example of an industry in which many women work part-time for extremely low wages is the cleaning industry. Unlike the fast food industry, most of the women working as cleaners are older. A study of cleaners in the Civil Service found that the vast majority were between the ages of 35 and 59 and were married with family responsibilities (Beardwell et al., 1981). Cleaning is mainly done by women with domestic responsibilities returning to the labour market, although cleaning hours are often not convenient for wives and mothers, tending to disrupt rather than accommodate family relations and activities (Coyle, 1985).

Over the past two decades the contract cleaning industry has expanded rapidly. Cleaning is a highly profitable business and the industry is extremely competitive. Employers thus keep wages as low as possible. As we found in Coventry, many large companies have sub-contracted cleaning and catering services to private firms in recent years, and the government too has subcontracted its office cleaning. The 1980s have seen a massive onslaught on in-house cleaning and catering as the government has required all district health authorities to put hospital cleaning, catering and laundry services out to tender. Private contract cleaners have often provided cleaning services much more cheaply than the National Health Service, and they have accomplished this in a number of ways: by reducing women's hours of work, increasing the intensity of their work, lowering rates of pay, and removing their entitlements to sickness and holiday pay. Furthermore, the introduction of sub-contracting has altered the nature of the employer/employee contract. Labour can be hired and fired at will without entitlement to redundancy and severance pay, and agreed rates of pay, hours of work and place of work can be changed at the employer's will. The poor standard of service and the bad conditions of employment in hospitals where cleaning has been sub-contracted have achieved widespread publicity in recent years. The women cleaners at Addenbrookes Hospital in Cambridge, for instance, went on strike in October 1984 when the cleaning services were contracted out because their hours were almost halved, they lost their sick pay entitlements, pension rights and bonus payments, and suffered a reduction in their holiday entitlement. As in the hotel and catering industry, it is difficult for unions to organize in the contract cleaning industry. Privatization is proceeding at a local level, and unions are often unable to protect their own member's pay and conditions if in-house tenders are accepted, or to organize among the contract cleaners, if the work is sub-contracted out. This is especially true if there is no strong local branch organization (Coyle, 1985).

In situations like this the only protection the part-time workers have has been provided by legislation. While not all employers wish to keep wages as low as possible and to evade paying benefits to their workforce, many do, and the general climate of competition in private service industries (and the specific directive from the government in the case of cleaning in the National Health Service that employers must take the lowest tender) means that there is heavy pressure on employers to keep down costs.

Government policies to deregulate the economy, however, are likely to lead to further deterioration in part-time workers' conditions of employment in private sector service industries. The government has removed schedule 11 of the 1975 Employment Protection Act which provided for the 'going rate for the job' in private sector industries, and it has also abolished the Fair Wages Resolution which stipulated that private contractors had to pay at least the same level of wages and conditions as employers in the public sector. Although both of these were hard to enforce, and wages in the public sector were already low, such legislation did give some indication to workers in the private sector as to what they *should* be earning. After a long period of uncertainty,[15] the government has also decided to whittle down the powers of the Wages Councils which determine the pay of about 2.75 million workers, removing young workers from their protection and simplifying the regulations relating to adults.[16] Thus, most of the people working in firms like McDonalds will be removed from the protection of the Wages Councils, and there will be no legal floor to the practice of paying low wages.

Britain already has far less protection for workers against the payment of low wages than most other European countries even before the government's measures to deregulate the economy were introduced. Five countries in the European Community – France, Luxemburg, The Netherlands, Portugal and Spain – have a statutory minimum wage, Belgium and Greece have a general minimum wage laid down by national level collective agreements, and Denmark, West Germany and Italy have set minimum rates of pay established by industry through collective agreements. Only Ireland and Britain have minimal protection for low-paid workers with Wages Councils setting minimum rates for certain industries which pay especially low wages.

It is because statutory protection against low pay is now virtually non-existent in Britain that some local authòrities have recently begun to counter government policies and to try themselves to influence the wages and terms and conditions of workers in the private sector. The GLC, for instance, passed a Fair Wages Resolution which stipulated that people employed by outside contractors from whom the Council purchased goods and services had to be paid the same rate as local authority rates of pay. And a number of local authorities have introduced contract compliance regulations based on the US model. These stipulate that suppliers of goods and services to the authority must adhere to the race relations and sex equality legislation. These measures have proved difficult to enforce but they are potentially quite powerful. Where part-time workers are concerned, the local authorities have generally expected that their pay and conditions should be pro rata those of full-time workers. Some trade unions and feminists have also begun to argue that a statutory minimum wage should be a major plank of an alternative economic policy, and that this is necessary if the interests of the most vulnerable sections of the workforce are to be protected.

Re-valuing Women's Jobs

Moves to ameliorate low pay have clearly improved the earnings of part-time workers in those local authorities which have introduced schemes to supplement basic wages, and a statutory minimum wage would undoubtedly improve the earnings of many more part-time workers in all sectors of the economy. Policies which focus solely on low pay, however, do not tackle the grading of occupations and their hierarchical organization, and they do not touch the content of jobs. Since the introduction of the equal value amendment to the Equal Pay Act in 1984, however, some unions have begun to press employers to tackle the underlying grading structures more fundamentally by building equal value claims into their annual pay claims.

Both NUPE and GMBATU have argued that employers should ensure that women's jobs are not undervalued simply because they are done by women, and have suggested that lower-paid women workers should compare themselves with higher-paid men: nurses with ambulance staff, technicians or administrative staff employed by the National Health Service, canteen assistants with labourers, and cook/chefs with craft workers. Recent pay settlements in the public sector have begun to implement these principles. In a recent settlement for hospital ancillary staff, the lowest grades have been merged so that women working part-time who were mainly on the lowest two grades were brought on to the same grade as male manual workers like porters, and the 1985 pay claim for local authority manual workers involved forming a new general grade which merged the bottom three grades and examining the entire grading structure using job-evaluation techniques.

Isolated attempts to re-grade women's occupations are not new. The struggle by Ford sewing machinists to have their work graded as equivalent to semi-skilled male production workers was first set in motion in 1968 (taking 17 years to win). What is new, however, is a wider concern with re-evaluating grading systems, and the move, in a few cases, to take up equal value cases which span the blue-collar/white collar divide.

It is likely to be difficult for part-time workers to bring successful cases under the equal value amendment to the Equal Pay Act and the moves being made by some trade unions look more promising as a means of getting part-time jobs re-graded. However, there are a number of problems which arise in this area which research like ours makes it possible to highlight. There is a danger, first, that part-time workers will be left out of union-sponsored equal value legal cases and re-gradings unless the unions have already taken measures to organize part-time workers and to represent their interests, not only nationally but also locally. A second problem is that job-evaluation schemes may well be used to rationalize the status quo rather than to change it, as happened in many workplaces when the Equal Pay Act became law (Snell et al., 1981). A third danger is that attempts to re-grade occupations will not transcend the manual – non-manual divide because non-manual and manual workers are very often subject to different negotiating conditions and are organized in separate unions. For equal value moves to make any real in-roads into sexual in-equalities at work they have to include part-time workers and also to transcend the division between manual and non-manual workers.

In North America, in particular, challenges to the overall grading structure of occupations have been far more advanced than in Britain, and in the United States the idea of comparable worth has been taken up by a number of unions as a mechanism for drawing comparisons between women's and men's jobs. Comparable worth offers a new concept of the value of women and of women's work (Feldberg, 1984). It asserts that 'the relative worth of jobs reflects value judgements as to what features of jobs ought to be compensated . . . Paying jobs according to their worth requires only that whatever characteristics of jobs are regarded as worthy of compensation by an employer should be equally so regarded irrespective of sex, race or ethnicity of job incumbents' (Treiman and Hartmann, quoted in Feldberg, 1984, p. 139). A good example of the use of the concept of comparable worth in re-valuing women's jobs occurred in a case brought by the state employees union against the state of Washington. This requested that a study be undertaken, using job-evaluation techniques, to compare the jobs held mainly by men (for example, traffic guide and electrician) with those held mainly by women (for example, secretary, clerk typist and nurse). The study found that for jobs which were rated equally by the job-evaluation system those held mainly by men were paid 20 per cent more on average than those held mainly by women, and that the difference occurred largely because the state's pay scales had been developed by using area wage surveys. The federal judge hearing the case ruled that the state was guilty of 'overt and institutionalized discrimination' and ordered it to remedy its actions. The case has now been settled out of court (Treiman and Hartmann, 1981; Feldberg, 1984).

The theory of comparable worth rests on the argument that remuneration should be independent of the social characteristics of the workers. It poses a challenge to economic explanations of women's position in the labour market which ignore the ways in which the structure of the labour market incorporates prejudices, customs and ideologies 'that connect the worth of different kinds of work with ideas about the inherent worth of workers who vary by sex, race, age, ethnicity and other social characteristics' (Feldberg, 1984, p. 319), and it provides a mechanism for tackling job segregation. Comparable worth reveals that there is often little relationship between the skills involved in women's work and the wages paid, that economic laws that are supposed to describe the relationship between workers, work and wages do not operate in the same ways for women's work as they do for men's, that particular skills required in many women's occupations are not recognized as skills, and that women are not seen as fully entitled to fair wages because the assumption is made that they are economically dependent on men. It has potentially far-reaching effects on how women's work is regarded and remunerated.

Wider Considerations

Although the past few years have seen a greater commitment to formal equality between the sexes, a marked increase in the number of women in the labour force, and (perhaps surprisingly, in view of many people's predictions to the contrary) women largely holding on to their jobs in the recession better than men, the dominant climate is extremely inhospitable to egalitarian policies. The present Conservative government has steadfastly pursued policies which are in sharp conflict with egalitarian social goals – deregulation of the economy, cutbacks in the public sector and the privatization of services. Like previous administrations, both Labour and Tory, it has pursued social policies which are predicated on the notion of a male breadwinner/dependent wife and which reinforce women's position in the family and their dependence upon men. Moreover, it has cut back on social services for the elderly, the handicapped and the sick and on childcare provision, and has systematically blocked a number of attempts by the European Commission to pass legislation which would contribute to the improvement of the situation of women within the European Community as a whole.

In this context, it can be difficult to think positively about alternative ways of organizing work, and many people would say that all one can do is to try to hang on to the gains introduced by previous governments, or bury one's head in the sand and wait for a different government. We dissent from these views, partly because we think that the current situation does present new opportunities for change because work is being fundamentally restructured, and partly because there are few guarantees that future governments will engage in the kind of radical thinking about the nature and structure of work which we think is needed.

It is beyond the scope of this book to discuss policies about the future of work in any depth, but we will conclude by raising a number of broader issues about work which in our view need wider discussion.

The first issue is flexibility. Two things are clear from our reseach into part-time employment. The first is that part-time women workers are used by employers for reasons of flexibility. Employers need a flexible workforce and they often take advantage of women's willingness to be flexible in their hours of work, frequently without remuneration. The second is that women, too, often need flexibility in their hours of work, especially when they are trying to combine paid work with caring for children or for sick, elderly or handicapped dependents. At present there is considerable interest in the question of flexibility by the government and by some employers. 'Flexibility' has become a buzzword in management circles. It is seen as a good thing, as something which other countries (the United States, for instance) have and which Britain lacks, and which generally connotes 'modern' forms of labour process, an absence of restrictive practices and a rolling back of the state's intervention in the labour market.

What is interesting about the current debate about flexibility is how entirely 'masculine' it is. There has been little interest in the question of the extent to which flexibility is related to gender, and little recognition of the fact that women already are (and probably always have been) an exceedingly flexible form of labour force. In chapter 5 we discussed some of the theoretical implications of the association of flexibility with masculinity in recent discussions about the future of work, but here it is important to point out that this question also has policy implications. For unless the terms of the debate are changed and women's interests are made central to the discussion, it seems unlikely that women will benefit from the higher pay and other rewards which are frequently promised to other groups of workers – technicians, for instance, and skilled workers – who change their work practices when new technology is introduced and work is reorganized. It is those men who give up the 5-day week or the 'normal' working day who are likely to benefit financially from moves to introduce flexibility (the so-called 'core' workers) and not the part-time women workers who have grown accustomed to having their work restructured, their hours changed and even their places of work altered with little or no consultation, let alone remuneration.

The flexibility debate is only just beginning in Britain. As yet, trade unions have mainly been hostile to attempts to increase flexibility since this is seen as involving a deterioration in their members' terms and conditions of employment. It seems likely, however, that flexibility is here to stay, and there is an urgent need, therefore, to develop more positive policies towards it. These need to take women's interests into account as well as men's.

The flexibility debate does allow issues which are of concern to women to be placed on the policy-making agenda, both ideologically and in practice. The Greater London Council's London Industrial Strategy recognized this, to a certain extent, and it developed a rather different kind of analysis of flexibility from most of the analyses which are currently popular. It placed domestic work at the centre of its alternative economic strategy, and advocated a form of restructuring based on alternative production for need rather than on market criteria. Thus, it argued, industries like retailing do not have to follow a path in which modern supermarkets, hypermarkets and out-of-town shopping centres have pioneered the new principles of flexible specialization, employing mostly casual, part-time labour and serving poor-quality food, while local shops are being put out of business. And it is suggested that it is perfectly possible for computer systems to be applied in the interests of need rather than profit, and for new technology to be used to bring the advantages of the supermarket to the local corner shop (Murray, 1985).

Some employers have recently shown an interest in ideas which call into question the notion of the 'normal' working day and week: among them the abolition of paid overtime in favour of time off in lieu, the notion of annual working time (in which people are paid at a regular rate each week but in fact do variable hours of work) and the notion of a 7-day week (in which people work a certain number of days, but in which Saturday and Sunday are no longer considered sacrosanct). As yet there have been few, if any, moves to introduce such measures, and trade unions have generally been rather hostile to them. It is perhaps not surprising that policies such as these are not particularly popular with men who, after all, were in the forefront of the struggles to establish the 8-hour working day in the nineteenth century and who continue to gain from this today – through additional payments for overtime and for work done in unsocial hours and the notion of a clearly defined weekend which can be used for leisure. However, such moves to challenge the notion of the 'normal' working day have considerable potential for women. They call into question the prevailing notion of full-time work. They create the conditions in which women can demand that work which is undertaken at a range of different times of the day and week is properly remunerated. And in the longer term they may well lead to a situation in which a wider array of forms of work organization will exist and be considered as 'normal'.

The second issue we wish briefly to discuss overlaps with the question of flexibility, but as a general policy it is rather more remote from the political agenda at the moment. This is the shortening of working time. The organization of working time has been a matter of major political and industrial debate in a number of European countries (France, Belgium and The Netherlands, for example) in recent years, but in Britain, despite the fact that the Trades Union Congress has a policy on reducing working time and the Labour Party's Jobs and Industry Campaign has a target of a 35-hour working week, it has generally been absent from discussions of unemployment. These have centred on trying to save jobs and on job creation in the future rather than on reorganizing and restructuring working time.

Reducing working time can also be a profoundly egalitarian policy. As we showed in chapter 1, we presently live in a world in which the working population is increasingly subdivided among a group of people (mainly men) who work long, full-time hours (many of them doing overtime), a second group (almost exclusively women) who work part-time, an ever-increasing group which is condemned to long periods on the dole at immense cost both to themselves and to the state, and a final group (which is not usually included within the category of the 'working population'), consisting mainly of housewives, people on training schemes and retired people. Shortening working time would provide a means of distributing the available work more equitably between these different groups in the population. It would also provide a means of meeting women's desires for paid work which can be combined with domestic commitments, and a mechanism (in the longer term) for breaking down the distinction between full-time and part-time work which is so overlaid with gender and the domestic division of labour.

It is clear that shortening working time will not be easy. In fact, working time has increased rather than decreased in the recent past. Although there was a general move in the early 1980s to introduce a 39-hour week for manual workers, this began to slow down in 1983, and the Confederation of British Industry reports that agreements to reduce the length of the basic working week were at a record low in 1984. Furthermore, the total weekly hours of overtime worked in manufacturing industry rose from 9.79 million in April 1982 to 11.47 million hours a week in June 1984, a period in which unemployment continued to rise (Beechey, 1985). A study (White, 1981) which looked at the different means which firms have used to reduce working time (decreasing the working week by 2 hours, increasing annual holiday entitlement by 10 days and decreasing the pensionable retirement age by 2 years) found that most of the workplaces studied had actually increased their hours of work rather than decreased them. Managers were said to be particularly resistant to shortening the working week, and the majority thought that lowering the pensionable age of retirement was the most acceptable means of reducing working time.

It seems that men and women have different preferences as to the best means of reducing working time. A study by the Trade Union Research Unit (1981) found that men overwhelmingly favoured reductions which would give them useful blocks of time off – typically a whole day or series of days – whereas women tended to favour earlier finishing times. It appears, therefore, that it is not simply shortening working time per se which would benefit women, but shortening the working day – say to 6 hours – which would enable them to combine different kinds of work which they currently do (paid, unpaid and voluntary). It would also make it easier for men to participate in domestic work and childcare.

As yet, little has been done to reduce working time, and indeed in many workplaces policies have been pursued which point in the opposite direction – towards increasing working time for those in full-time work and disposing of other workers (especially older workers) from the labour force. The prognosis for reducing hours of work or developing a more flexible approach to working time is not good. The government and the CBI are implacably opposed to reducing working time, and the government has recently vetoed a Recommendation on the Reduction and Reorganization of Working Time which was proposed by the European Commission. Clearly, money is a crucial reason why it is so difficult to reduce working time. Employers have been reluctant to reduce working time without loss of pay, and workers have been reluctant to lose any of their earnings. It may be, therefore, that it will only be possible to reduce working time, or to make it more flexible, if the state takes on some of the responsibility for this – by providing sabbaticals so that people can have periods out of the labour market in which they are paid, or by introducing some form of minimum income which will sever the link between work and earnings and will be paid to people regardless of whether they are in paid employment of how many hours they work. It is extremely unlikely that the present Conservative government, with its appalling record on a whole range of social policies and its explicit commitment to deregulation of the economy, would make any moves in such a direction, but these are issues which future governments should be pressured to take up. Several European governments have recently introduced progressive policies in this area. The Mitterand government in France introduced a shorter working week, while periods out of the labour market, with pay, are provided for in West Germany under the new parental leave law (which was in fact introduced by Chancellor Kohl's right-wing government) and in The Netherlands by a new law which provides for all workers to have a year's sabbatical leave. Such provision for people to spend periods out of the labour market are very important. They break with the notion that full-time work must inevitably be continuous throughout a person's working life. They also break the link between work and earnings which the present British government has tried so hard to protect.

   In the course of researching into, and thinking about, part-time work our emphasis has shifted. Whereas at first we saw part-time work as a distinctive (and highly exploitative) form of women's work which deserved investigation in its own right, we have become very aware in the course of our research of its interconnections with full-time work. We have also become acutely aware of the relationship between women's work and men's work. It has become very common in feminist writings to emphasize the ways in which women's situation is socially constructed and throughout this book social constructionist arguments have been advanced. Part-time work, we have argued, should be seen as a social construct. But it is important to point out that similar arguments can be applied to full-time work. Instead of being taken for granted as the norm, as it generally is in studies of the labour market, full-time work needs to be treated as problematic, and analysed as a social construct. Moreover, the question of whether gender enters into the construction of full-time work requires investigation.

Our argument that gender is important in the construction and organization of work is both a theoretical argument and a political one. It is extremely important therefore that analyses of restructuring should consider the ways in which gender enters into the organization of work and that strategies to transform work and work relations are developed which will eliminate the negative consequences of gender. We need new concepts which can account for the complexities of work in the world today and a vision of the future and set of policies for moving towards this which will enable both men's and women's relationships to work to be transformed.

Notes

Introduction

1　When we use the term 'marginal' here, and elsewhere in the book, we do not wish to imply any judgement about the relative value or importance of such jobs. We are rather referring to how such jobs are located within the overall organization of work in particular establishments and sectors.

2　The research was funded by the EOC/SSRC Joint Panel for Equal Opportunities Research, and was carried out by both of us.

3　We decided not to place any of the conventional restrictions on our definition of what counted as part-time work, and took part-timers to be all those who did not work full-time hours in any particular workplace. Our part-timers ranged from one who came in for 2 hours a week in a baking firm to some who worked 35 hours (compared to a norm of 40), although most of our part-timers in fact fell below the 30-hour mark. While clearly the situation and conditions of a 35-hour-a-week part-timer are very different from a 2-hour-a-week part-timer, we felt that in order to understand how part-time workers were used the crucial distinction was that between the 'normal full-time day' and all other less-than-full-time hours.

4　These arguments are developed at greater length in Beechey (1978, 1985). Similar arguments have been advanced by Brown (1976) and Siltanen and Stanworth (1984).

5　The distinction between job and gender models is made in Feldberg and Glenn (1979).

6　It is very rare for studies of male workers to be concerned about their family obligations, although studies of unemployed men do sometimes consider their relationships with their families and the wider community, normally from a concern with financial support.

7　See, for example, Pollert (1981), Cavendish (1982), Cockburn (1983, 1985), Wajcman (1983), Coyle (1984), Westwood (1984) and the essays in West (1982).

8　In many respects our approach has similarities with the new approaches to the labour market outlined in Roberts et al. (1985). These tend to be interdisciplinary and to be concerned with 'the new challenges which people and institutions face in the changing economic patterns of the contemporary world' (Roberts et al., 1985, p. 13).

Chapter 1: Part-time Work in a Changing Labour Market

1   See Beechey (1985) for a further discussion of these changes.
2   Although official statistics have improved somewhat in their coverage of women's employment as increasing numbers of women have entered the labour force, it is still difficult to be precise about the changing patterns of women's employment because the available statistics are less reliable for women's employment (and far less reliable as a measure of part-time employment) than for men's. Joshi and Owen (1984) suggested that the 1951, 1961 and 1981 censuses (on which Beacham's calculations are based) have considerably underestimated the extent of women's employment in post-war Britain, and they have endeavoured to generate what they call a 'less inconsistent series' of female activity rates as follows:

Age group	The less inconsistent series				Unadjusted census data			
	1951 revised	1961 revised	1971[a] census	1981 labour force survey	1951	1961	1971	1981
20–24	64.50	61.55	60.22	69.21[b]	65.39	62.34	60.22	69.21
25–29	44.15	43.97	43.11	56.27	40.45	39.51	43.11	55.45
30–34	38.46	40.96	44.98	55.99	33.47	36.57	45.98	53.39
35–44	39.41	46.51	56.15	68.00	35.15	42.42	57.15	65.49
45–54	40.21	49.87	59.40	68.10	34.42	43.38	60.40	66.03
55–59	30.36	40.44	49.46	53.40	27.56	36.89	50.96	52.26
20–59	42.11	47.44	53.68	62.80	38.31	43.26	54.47	61.47

[a] Activity rates for age groups over 30 revised by the following factors: 35––1.00, 55–59: –1.50, 20–59: –079.
[b] Census 1981

Source: Joshi and Owen (1984).

The most noticeable effects of this revision are to decrease the amount of the rise in the activity rates between 1961 and 1971 and to increase it slightly between 1971 and 1981. There is no dispute, however, that the activity rates of women did rise, and rise substantially. Although there is some disagreement between the two versions as to the amount of the overall rise for particular age groups, two noticeable changes emerge from both versions. First, over the period as a whole it is the activity rates of the over-35s which have increased most. Secondly, since 1971 the rise in the activity rates of older women, especially the over-55s, has slowed down while the activity rates of younger women have increased much more rapidly.

3   Joshi and Owen's revised calculations (1984) suggest that the rate of increase in the women's activity rate would be higher between 1971 and 1981 if the 1981 census figures were adjusted to take account of the under-representation of women's employment and were brought into line with the Labour Force Survey. Also, the General Household Survey comments that if the numbers of women over state retirement age are excluded from the calculations (as they are in Joshi and Owen's analysis), the decline in the married women's activity rate between 1980 and 1982 is not statistically significant. As is so often the case in this area, what conclusion one draws depends in part upon which statistical series one uses.

4   Earlier studies suggested that single parents are caught in a poverty trap in which they are forced to work very few hours and remain dependent on supplementary benefit, or to work full-time in order to qualify for Family Income Supplement (see Finer, 1974, vol. 1; Hurstfield, 1978, p. 14).

5   It is worth noting the importance of women's employment in Coventry's manufacturing industry during the war. Female employment in Coventry rocketed: it increased much more during the war than it did nationally, and although its decline after the war was also greater, the increase in women's employment over the whole period, 1939–48, was 18,106 (or 63.6 per cent).

6   Analysis of table 1.5 and of the sources from which it is derived (British Labour Statistics Historical Abstract Tables 142 and 137) showed that for most of the 1950s there was a gradual increase not only in the proportion of part-timers but also in the numbers of part-timers employed in most manufacturing industries. There was a sharp decline between 1951 and 1953 which was accounted for by substantial reductions of part-timers in just four industries (textiles and clothing in 1951–2, and metals and engineering in 1952–3). Only two industries, textiles and clothing, ended up with fewer part-time women workers in 1961 than they had in 1950. Both of these industries also suffered a decline in full-time female employment. In

the textile industry, this decline affected full-time women workers more than part-timers, whereas in the clothing industry it affected part-timers more so that in 1961 the clothing industry also had a smaller proportion of part-timers than it had in 1950. Although in most industries both the numbers and the proportion of part-timers increased between 1950 and 1961, in two (vehicles, and paper, printing and publishing), the proportion of part-time workers to full-time women workers declined slightly (though the numbers of part-timers actually increased). (see also *Ministry of Labour Gazette*, Dec. 1962.)

7   As Denise Riley (1984) has pointed out, the task of discerning what women might have done if different conditions had prevailed is fraught with problems. All one can do, therefore, is suggest that different public provision for children might have affected women's patterns of work without any absolute certainty that this would in fact have happened.

8   Audrey Hunt's figures for the proportions of women working full-time and part-time in different occupations in 1965 are as follows:

	All Workers %	Full-Time %	Part-Time %
Miscellaneous services	19.5	12.6	31.2
Distribution	18.2	18.3	18.4
Professional and scientific services	16.7	15.8	19.2
Engineering etc.	10.3	11.9	7.1

Source: Hunt (1968) vol 1, p. 33.

9   In discussing part-time employment in manufacturing industry it is important to underline the fact that many part-time women workers in manufacturing do similar work to that done by part-time women in the service sector of the economy. Many of the women in manufacturing industries who were interviewed for the *Women and Employment* survey worked in service occupations, particularly as clerical workers. Indeed, the survey found that only in the textiles, clothing and footwear, and food, drink and tobacco industries were over half the women employed clearly engaged in production jobs (Martin and Roberts, 1984). One simply cannot tell from industry-level statistics whether the women part-timers in an industry work as clerks or

cleaners, receptionists or operatives.

10   An analysis of full-time equivalents can give a much better idea of the
      extent to which the expansion of part-time working is in fact part of a
      real expansion.

11   Here again different patterns of employment occurred in different
      industries. Betwen 1978 and 1981, as the recession deepened, the
      clothing industry and the food, drink and tobacco industries experi-
      enced greater declines in men's and women's part-time employment
      than in full-time employment, while women's full-time employment
      declined more sharply than part-time employment in the textiles
      industry.

12   It would be interesting to know whether there is evidence of
      part-time women workers being substituted for young male workers
      or whether it is young women's jobs which are being lost to married
      women part-timers. In Britain, unlike some other countries (e.g. the
      USA) there are very few young workers of either sex working
      part-time.

13   Figures calculated from *Employment Gazette*, Historical Supplement
      no. 1, August 1984, and *Employment Gazette*, May 1986, table 1.4.

14   It also shows that there are significant differences in the patterns of
      women's activity by age. Britain has a higher proportion of women
      returning to the labour force than most other countries, although the
      Japanese pattern is fairly similar to the British one, as the following
      figure shows.

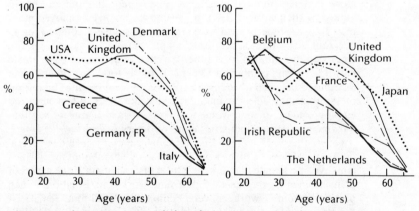

International comparison of female activity rates, by age, 1983.
Source: Central Statistical Office (1986), p. 63.

Chapter 2: Manufacturing Industry

1   Both our findings and our analysis in this chapter owe a great deal to
    Colleen Chesterman, who analysed women's part-time employment
    in Coventry for her unpublished MA thesis. In particular, the section
    on part-time employment in Coventry's textiles industry relies
    heavily on evidence which Colleen Chesterman collected in 1977–8.
2   In fact, 'metal goods n.e.s.' (not elsewhere specified) had more
    women part-timers working in it than food, drink and tobacco, but
    we excluded this from our sample because it is very much a
    miscellaneous category, containing a variety of different kinds of firm
    which do not fall within the other engineering categories.
3   In order to map out where women worked part-time in Coventry's
    manufacturing sector we used the Census of Employment for
    Coventry for 1971–6. These statistics were made available to us at the
    level of both Standard Industrial Classification (SIC) and the more
    detailed Minimum List Headings (MLH). In table 2.1 we show how
    many women worked part-time in each industrial group (SIC) along
    with the number of women working full-time and the total number of
    men. As table 2.1 shows, only seven of the 17 SICs employed more
    than 100 women part-timers. These seven SICs accounted for over
    three-quarters (1,729) of the 2,018 part-time women workers
    employed in Coventry's manufacturing industries. When we analysed
    the statistics at the level of MLH this concentration became both
    more and less marked. First, we discovered that out of the 76
    industries (defined by MLH) in Coventry, only five employed more
    than 100 part-time women workers, and these five accounted for 49
    per cent of women's part-time manufacturing employment. Ten
    employed no women part-time. So the remaining 1,035 female
    part-timers, who comprised 51 per cent of the total part-timers, were
    distributed between 61 industries. While it would be true, therefore,
    to say that in 1976 most manufacturing industries in Coventry did
    employ some part-time women workers, it is also true to say that
    most manufacturing industries employed very few.
        Given that a Minimum List Heading generally includes several
    different employers, there were clearly a large number of firms which
    employed no female part-timers. The statistics illustrate one aspect of
    many women's experience of part-time work – its isolation. When
    part-time women workers were compared to full-time female or
    full-time male workers, it was evident that the part-timers were more
    likely to work in industries which employed very few other part-
    timers. While 15 per cent of women part-timers worked in industries
    employing between 0 and 20 part-timers, only 0.1 per cent of
    full-time male and 1.3 per cent of full-time female workers were

engaged in industries employing 0–20 full-time men or women workers respectively. By contrast, in Coventry, 99.2 per cent of full-time male and 87.2 per cent of full-time female workers were engaged in industries which employed more than 100 full-time men or women workers, compared to only 48.7 per cent of the part-time women workers. These differences are a salutory reminder that (contrary to conventional wisdom) it is in some respects harder to describe the 'typical' part-timer than it is to describe the 'typical' full-timer.

4   Calculated from Census of Employment for Coventry, 1971 and 1976.

5   Calculated from Census of Employment.

6   Calculated from statistics kindly supplied by the management.

7   Calculated from Index of Insured Employees, 1958–70, and Census of Employment, 1971–6 (both by MLH).

8   Note that the detailed pattern since 1970 is not absolutely clear, since the different sets of statistics show differing fluctuations. According to the Census of Employment statistics, employment fell from 1970 to 1972, rose slightly from 1972 to 1973 and fell sharply from 1974 to 1976. According to the statistics of the firm's management, however, employment fell steadily from 1974 to 1978. Since 1978 the trend has levelled out, and it may have begun to be reversed. The broad trend, however, is clear from both employment and unemployment statistics: employment rose steeply from 1968 to 1970, then fell sharply from 1974 to 1978. In the following discussion we use employment statistics supplied by the management, since these enable a far more detailed breakdown of employment trends than the Census of Employment statistics.

9   Published in *Coventry Evening Telegraph*, 13 February 1968, and quoted in Chesterman (1978), p. 153.

10   While the numbers of employees classified as 'staff' may have been affected by groups of workers successfully negotiating staff status for themselves rather than being entirely the result of changes in the occupational structure, our fieldwork suggests that these changes have been significant over this period, and that the statistics therefore largely reflect real changes in the occupational structure.

11   Calculated from Census of Employment, 1971 and 1976.

12   Since the 1950s the baking industry has undergone a process of extensive concentration and has been dominated by two giants whose plant bakeries produce over two-thirds of all the country's bread and 85 per cent of the standard white loaves. Master bakeries are usually old family businesses. Both types of bakery produce bread and confectionery (cakes, tarts, pies etc.), although the master bakeries produce considerably less bread than they used to and most of this is speciality lines (such as rolls, small loaves etc.). Production in master

bakeries has shifted substantially over the past 30 years to confectionery. Although there are differences between the two types of bakeries (in terms of size and product quantity, for instance), these are not as great as might be expected since many master bakeries have adopted methods of production previously associated with plant bakeries (e.g. mechanical mixing devices and accelerated fermentation procedures) and many plant bakeries have grown by taking over master bakeries.

13   The fourth firm (another master bakery) employed only women, seemingly because it was a small family firm which produced very little bread. The proprietor himself did all the preparation and mixing of the dough before the women came to work.

14   In 1980 basic rates of pay ranged between £54.00 (group F) and £65.00 (group A). Most men were in groups A–C; most women were in groups E–F. These figures relate to plant bakeries, wages in master bakeries being somewhat lower (£48.60–£62.00). Figures quoted are from National Agreements between the Bakers Union and the two employers federations, The Federation of Bakers and the National Association of Master Bakers.

15   In the plant bakery there were about ten male part-timers (three paying-in clerks who came in on Saturdays, three security men, and four van cleaners). In the master bakery there were eight male part-timers, two of whom were retired men who did odd maintenance jobs, two van drivers (also retired men), and four Saturday boys who washed bread trays.

16   Bonuses were said to be given for responsibility, long service or for early starting. Most of the women's bonuses were between £2.60 and £3.60, while the men's were £8.40–£10.40. There appeared to be little system to the award or non-award of bonuses.

17   The National Federation's arguments are at variance with those made to the Select Committee by the CBI and large employers like Sainsburys who argued that part-time workers were too expensive (House of Lords, 1981–2).

18   Men were also employed as machinists, but they generally worked on different machines making different products.

Chapter 3: Welfare Services

1   Our research in the public sector was greatly assisted by discussions with Mick Carpenter on the health service, and Bob Fryer supplied considerable information on manual workers, especially in education. Our analysis of education, however, was somewhat limited because the local education department would not give us any information about teaching.

2 Statistics derived from the Census of Employment.
3 Statistics supplied by Coventry Area Health Authority. In contrast to the Education Department, the Area Health Authority was extremely cooperative in providing access to statistics and helping us to understand them. Unless we specify to the contrary, all analyses of occupational data in the health service are calculated from payroll data supplied by Coventry Area Health Authority.
4 Within paramedical occupations there was considerable occupational segregation. The eight occupational groups in fact contained 53 subdivisions (representing pay and status points). There were only 11 groups in which women worked part-time. In eight of these no men were employed, and in seven there were no women working full-time. The category of radiographer comprised six full-time female, three full-time male and three part-time female workers. With this exception, female part-time employment in paramedical occupations at the hospital occurred only in those occupational subgroups in which there were only women employed full-time, or (in two cases) where there were no full-time employees at all. It was rare to find a female part-timer in the same occupational category as male full-timers.
5 Summary of all staff of Coventry Social Services Department in post, September 1979. Unfortunately, these statistics do not distinguish between male and female, full-time and part-time in the same series but it is quite clear that the vast majority of the part-timers were women. Unless otherwise stated, statistics in this section are derived from this Summary which the Social Services Department kindly let us see.
6 Manpower in local authorities' statistics', *Department of Employment Gazette*, September 1981.
7 We are indebted to Bob Fryer for help with this section and for providing us with information about the school meals service.
8 Derived from statistics on manual workers supplied by Coventry City Council Treasurer's Department. Unless otherwise specified, all statistics from this section come from this source.
9 The numbers employed in the school meals service varied according to the demand for meals and depending upon the kind of meal or other service provided. Until the 1980 Education Act, local authorities were obliged to provide a main midday meal for all pupils. The 1980 Act relieved the local authorities of this statutory burden and obliged them only to provide meals to those pupils whose parents or guardians were in receipt of Social Security or Family Income Supplement Benefits, and to provide facilities for pupils to consume their own food. The 1980 Act also gave discretion to authorities in respect of prices to be charged and the form and content of the meals.

In addition to changes in statutory provision, staffing in the service is subject to variation from changes in demand associated with the seasons, the introduction of convenience foods, the spread of cafeteria systems, increases in charges, the growth of sandwich consumption and the use of 'cook-freeze' systems of central preparation of meals.

Chapter 4: Attitudes of Employers

1   This, and subsequent definitions, are taken from the National Agreements of the Baking Industry in England and Wales.

Chapter 5: Theoretical Perspectives

1   These arguments are developed by Tessa Perkins (1983), who argues that the reserve army of labour thesis cannot be adequately tested simply by numerical shifts in the numbers of employees and that in any event such shifts are particularly difficult to interpret where part-timers are concerned. That the concept of the industrial reserve army has been tested mainly in terms of a statistical analysis of job losses and gains reflects the ways in which a masculine concept of work continues to prevail today despite the enormous changes in the organization of work which have taken place since the nineteenth century.

2   Other criticisms which have been levelled against dual labour market theories are that they relegate the sexual division of labour to the status of an exogenous variable and place too much weight on an inadequately theorized notion of feminine characteristics in explaining labour market differentiation; that they abstract employer's behaviour from a broader analysis of production and provide an over-simplified account of employers' strategies which ignores the positive advantages to employers of hiring women in certain kinds of jobs; that they cannot explain why women do certain jobs while men do others (that is, they cannot explain occupational segregation) because they ignore the role of gender ideology; and finally that they take no account of the role of trade unions and male workers in creating and maintaining segmented labour markets.

3   Since this chapter was written, *Gender and Stratification*, edited by Rosemary Crompton and Michael Mann, has been published. This includes some excellent articles (including Alison Scott's) which demonstrate the centrality of gender to production relations.

4   Joan Scott (1985) identifies four inter-related aspects: culturally available symbols that evoke multiple representations, normative conceptions that set forth interpretations of the meaning of the

symbols, social institutions and organizations and individual/collective (subjective) identities.

Chapter 6: Questions of Policy

1 Calculated from the New Earnings Survey, 1985, part E, table 125, and part F, table 179. The figures refer to average gross hourly earnings. Note that these figures exclude those whose earnings are beneath the national insurance threshold, so the real situation is likely to be worse.

2 The IR-RR study (which tends to be biased towards employers with good practices) found that in almost half the organizations studied no bonuses existed in the jobs done by part-time workers and that part-timers rarely received shift premiums.

3 Until recently, low-paid workers in industries covered by Wages Councils have in principle been granted paid holidays, but this statutory protection is to disappear when the powers of the Wages Councils are reduced.

4 In only 18 per cent of the cases surveyed was membership of a pension scheme open to part-time workers.

5 New Earnings Survey 1980, part F, table 183, and 1985 part F, table 183.

6 The Employment Appeals Tribunal has ruled that lower productivity and an earlier entitlement to overtime pay amounted to a material difference in the case of *Handley V. H. Mono Ltd.* And in the case of *Kearns* v. *Trust House Forte Catering Ltd* the Employment Appeals Tribunal ruled that the difference between part-time and full-time workers was *in itself* a material difference other than a difference of sex. This ruling should, however, be regarded with suspicion in the light of the ruling by the European Court of Justice in the case of *Jenkins* v. *Kingsgate (Clothing Productions Ltd)*.

7 The employers were extremely resistant to the union's demand, and insisted on introducing new conditions for future shift-working part-timers as the price for bringing part-timers' overtime pay into line with that of full-timers.

8 It has been estimated that less than 10 per cent of local authority manual workers who are women have access to bonus schemes, compared with 80 per cent of men.

9 Equal opportunities policies generally involve reviewing criteria of recruitment, promotion etc., and changing these when they are found to be actually or potentially discriminatory, auditing the composition of the workforce in order to identify areas of action (promotion barriers, high turnover rates etc.), developing positive discrimination

proposals in order to rectify imbalances, evaluating the progress of policies by monitoring the composition of the workforce and job applicants, and providing training and guidance for decision-makers.

10   Under the present law this is correct, but it should be pointed out that the Maternity Fund is constantly in surplus, and some loosening of the conditions of eligibility could easily be afforded. In 1981 the surplus was so high – at £51 million – that the government diverted some of its income to the Redundancy Fund (Land, 1986).

11   The Greater London Council, for instance, stated in its Equal Opportunities Code of Practice that it 'gives employees the entitlement to maternity leave and the opportunity for child-responsibility leave, job-sharing, part-time work and flexible working arrangements to provide greater opportunities for people who need or wish to combine employment with domestic or other responsibilities' (GLC, undated). Camden Council's maternity leave agreement states that 'wherever practicable, special efforts will be made to accommodate women who wish to return to work after maternity leave but wish only to work part-time' (quoted in Incomes Data Services Ltd, 1982).

12   There have been few, if any, moves to implement one of the most radical clauses in the European Commission's Draft Directive on part-time working. This states that part-time workers should have priority over outside candidates with similar skills when full-time jobs become available, and that full-time workers should have greater opportunities to transfer to part-time employment. Our research suggests that the right to transfer to part-time employment never exists as a general right, although occasionally an individual woman had managed to arrange to go part-time after having a child. Moreover, the right for part-timers to have priority over outside candidates in transferring to full-time employment is unheard of. Even in organizations like the GLC, which pursued many enabling policies towards women, this did not exist because it was thought that any restriction of hiring to an internal labour market would go against policies to extend employment opportunities to ethnic minorities. In this case a policy which would undoubtedly help to improve the situation of women who were already on the Council's payroll was in direct conflict with policies designed to broaden the basis of recruitment and to improve the position of ethnic minorities.

13   The distinction between employment discrimination and wage discrimination is made by Treiman and Hartmann (1981, pp. 8–9): 'Employment discrimination exists when one class of people is denied access to higher-paying jobs solely or partly on the basis of social characteristics . . . Wage discrimination exists when individuals of one social category are paid less than individuals of another social category for reasons that have little or nothing to do with the work

they do'. The Committee on Occupational Classification and Analysis of the National Research Council, whose study is reported in Treiman and Hartmann (1981), found two major kinds of wage discrimination:

(i)   when one class of people is paid less than another class for doing exactly and substantially the same job;
(ii) when the job structure within a firm is substantially segregated by sex, race, or ethnicity, and workers of one category are paid less than workers of another category when the two groups are performing work that is not the same but is, in some sense, of comparable worth to their employer.

14   A study of low pay among Camden Council manual workers conducted in 1983 found that low pay was especially prevalent among those (like cooks and home helps) who did not do overtime, and that it was pervasive among part-time workers (Metcalf, 1983).

15   The fate of the Wages Councils has been unclear for some time, with the government threatening to abolish them altogether. However, strong lobbying, by pressure groups and the TUC, and even by the CBI (which recently voted three to one in favour of keeping the Wages Councils) forced the government to change its mind, and now the Wages Councils are to be kept, but with limited powers.

16   Wages Councils have provided some protection against low pay and exploitative conditions in some of the industries in the private sector in which women's part-time employment is particularly concentrated: the retail trades, hotels and catering, hairdressing, and the clothing and textiles industries. There are presently 26 Wages Councils which determine the pay of about 2.75 million workers. The three largest are in the retail, hotels and catering and clothing trades, and these together comprise 90 per cent of the total labour force protected by the Wages Councils (EIRR, January 1986). Part-time workers are in principle protected when an industry is covered by a Wages Council, although there is widespread concern that the Wages Councils are not very effective in enforcing minimum wage levels. The Wages Inspectorate, whose duty is to enforce the minimum rates, has been cut by one-third since 1979, and in 1984 two-fifths of the employers visited by the inspector (and one-third of those in hairdressing) were found to be paying their staff illegally low wages.

References

Armstrong, Pat and Armstrong, Hugh (1986) 'More for the money: redefining and intensifying work in Canada'. Paper given at Conference on Work and Politics; the Feminisation of the Labour Force, Harvard University Center for European Studies.

APEX (1985) *Pensions Survey 1985*. London, APEX.

Atkinson, John (1984) *Manning for Uncertainty – Some Emerging UK Work Patterns*. Institute of Manpower Studies, University of Sussex.

Ballard, Barbara (1984) 'Women part-time workers: evidence from the 1980 Women and Employment Survey', *Employment Gazette*, September, pp. 409-416.

Barrett, Michèle and McIntosh, Mary (1980) 'The family wage', in E. Whitelegg et al. (eds) *The Changing Experience of Women*. Oxford, Martin Robertson.

Barron, R. D. and Norris, E. M. (1976) 'Sexual divisions and the dual labour market', in Diana Barker and Sheila Allen (eds) *Dependence and Exploitation in Work and Marriage*. London, Longman.

Beacham, Roland (1984) 'Economic activity: Britain's workforce 1971–81', *Population Trends*, Autumn, pp. 6–13.

Beardwell, I., Mills, D. and Worman, C (1981) *The Twilight Army*. Low Pay Pamphlet no. 19. London, The Low Pay Unit.

Beechey, Veronica (1978) 'Women and production: a critical analysis of some sociological theories of women's work', in Annette Kuhn and Ann Marie Wolpe (eds) *Feminism and Materialism*. London, Routledge and Kegan Paul.

Beechey, Veronica (1980) 'The sexual division of labour and the labour process: a critical assessment of Braverman', in Stephen Wood (ed.) *The Degradation of Work*. London, Hutchinson.

Beechey, Veronica (1985) 'The shape of the workforce to come', *Marxism Today*, 29, no. 8, pp. 11–16.

Beechey, Veronica (1986) 'Rethinking the definition of work'. Paper given at Conference on Work and Politics: the Feminisation of the Labour Force, Harvard University Center for European Studies.

Beechey, Veronica and Perkins, Teresa (1985) 'Conceptualising part-time work', in Bryan Roberts, Ruth Finnegan and Duncan Gallie (eds) *New Approaches to Economic Life*. Manchester, Manchester University Press.

Benenson, Harold (1984) 'Victorian sexual ideology and Marx's theory of the working class', *International Labor and Working Class History*, 25, Spring.

Birmingham Feminist History Group (1979) 'Feminism or femininity in the nineteen-fifties?', *Feminist Review*, no. 3, pp. 48–65.

Braverman, Harry (1974) *Labor and Monopoly Capital*, New York, Monthly Review Press.

Brown, Colin (1984) *Black and White Britain* (the Third PSI Survey). London, Heinemann.

Brown, Richard (1976) 'Women and employers: some comments on research in industrial sociology', in Diana Barker and Sheila Allen (eds) *Dependence and Exploitation in Work and Marriage*. London, Longman.

Bruegel, Irene (1979) 'Women as a reserve army of labour: a note on recent British experience', *Feminist Review*, no. 3, pp. 12–23.

Bruegel, Irene (1983) 'Women's employment, legislation and the labour market', in Jane Lewis (ed.) *Women's Welfare, Women's Rights*. London, Croom Helm.

Cavendish, Ruth (1982) *On the Line*. London, Routledge and Kegan Paul.

Central Statistical Office (1976) *Social Trends*. London, HMSO.

Central Statistical Office (1984) *Social Trends*. London, HMSO.

Central Statistical Office (1986) *Social Trends*. London, HMSO.

Chesterman, Colleen (1978) 'Women's part-time employment in Coventry'. Unpublished MA thesis, University of Warwick.

Clark, George (1982) 'Working patterns, part-time work, job sharing and self-employment'. Manpower Services Commission unpublished report.

Cockburn, Cynthia (1983) *Brothers*. London, Pluto Press.

Cockburn, Cynthia (1985) *Machinery of Dominance*. London, Pluto Press.

Commission of the European Communities (1981) *Proposal for a Council Directive on Voluntary Part-time Work*. COM 81 775 final, Brussels, 22 December 1981.

Connelly, Patricia (1978) *Last hired first fired*, Ontario, The Women's Press.

Counter Information Services (1980) *Hardship Hotel*. CIS Anti-Report no. 27.

Coyle, Angela (1984) *Redundant Women*. London, The Women's Press.

Coyle, Angela (1985) 'Going private: the implications of privatisation for women's work', *Feminist Review*, no. 21, pp. 5–23.

198   References

Crompton, Rosemary and Mann, Michael (1986) *Gender and Stratification*. Cambridge, Polity Press.

Davidoff, Leonore and Hall, Catherine (1987) *Family Fortunes: Men and Women of the English Middle Class, 1780–1850*. London, Hutchinson.

Davidson, Marilyn J. and Cooper, Gary L. (1984) *Working Women: an International Survey*. Chichester, Wiley.

Department of Employment and Productivity (1971) *British Labour Statistics, Historical Abstract 1886–1968*. London, HMSO.

Dex, Shirley and Perry, Stephen M. (1984) 'Women's employment: changes in the 1970s', *Employment Gazette*, April.

Dex, Shirley and Philipson, Chris (1986) 'Older women in the labour market: a review of current trends', *Critical Social Policy*, no. 15, Spring.

Doeringer, Peter B. and Piore, Michael, J. (1971) *Internal Labour Market and Manpower Analysis*, Lexington, D. C. Heath.

Doyal, L, Hunt, G, and Mellor, J. (1984) 'Your Life in their hands: immigrant women in the National Health Service', *Critical Social Policy*, vol. 1 no. 2.

Elias, Peter and Main, Brian (1982) Women's working lives: evidence from the National Training Survey. University of Warwick Institute for Employment Research Report.

Elias, Peter and Wilson, R. A. (1985) 'Employment prospects in the UK, 1985–90: an exploration of industrial, occupational and regional trends'. Unpublished paper produced for the University of Warwick Institute for Employment Research.

Employment statistics, *Employment Gazette* Historical Supplement no. 1. August 1984.

Equal Opportunities Commission (1981) *Job Sharing. Improving the Quality and Availability of Part-time Work*. Manchester, EOC.

European Industrial Review and Report (October 1985), no. 141. 'Time off for family responsibilities'.

Feldberg, Roslyn (1984) 'Comparable worth: towards theory and practice in the United States', *Signs* 10, no. 2, Winter pp. 311–328.

Feldberg, Roslyn and Glenn, Evelyn Nakano (1979) 'Male and female: job versus gender module in the sociology of work', *Social Problems* 26, no. 5, June pp. 524–538.

Finer, Sir Morris (1974) *Report of the Committee on One-parental Families*, 2 vols. London, HMSO.

Fogarty, Michael P., Rapoport, Rhona and Rapoport, Robert N. (1971) *Sex, Career and Family*. London, Allen and Unwin.

Fryer, B., Manson, T. and Fairclough, A. (1978) 'Notes: employment and trade unionism in the public services', *Capital and Class*, no. 4, Spring pp. 70–77.

Gabriel, Yiannis (1985) 'Feeding the first food chain', *New Statesman*, 12 April.

Game, Ann and Pringle, Rosemary (1984) *Gender at work*. London, Pluto Press.

Gardiner, Jean (1976) 'Women and unemployment', *Red Rag*, no. 10.

Garnsey, Elizabeth (1984) *The Provision and Quality of Part-time Work, the Case of Great Britain and France*. A preliminary study carried out for the Directorate – General Employment, Social Affairs and Education of the Commission of European Communities.

Greater London Council (1983–4) *On the Road to Equality*. First Annual Equal Opportunities Monitoring Report. London, GLC.

Greater London Council (1985) *The London Industrial Strategy*. London, GLC.

Greater London Council (undated) *Equal Opportunities Code of Practice*. London, GLC.

Goldthorpe, John (1985) 'The end of convergence: corporatist and dualistic tendencies in modern western societies', in Bryan Roberts, Ruth Finnegan, Duncan Gallie (eds) *New Approaches to Economic Life*. Manchester, Manchester University Press.

Grim, James W. and Stern, Robert N. (1974) 'Sex roles and internal labour market structures: the "female semi-professions"', *Social Problems*, 21.

Hakim, Catherine (1979) *Occupational Segregation*. Department of Employment Research Paper no. 9, November.

Hallaire, Jean (1968) *Part-time Employment, its Extent and Problems*. Paris, OECD.

Harding, Sandra (1986) *The Science Question in Feminism*. Milton Keynes, Open University Press.

Hartmann, Heidi (1976) 'Capitalism, patriarchy and job segregation by sex', in Martha Blaxall and Barbara Reagan (eds) *Women and the Workplace*. Chicago, Chicago University Press.

House of Lords (1981–2) *Voluntary Part-time Work*. Report of the Select Committee on the European Communities, Session 1981–2, 19th Report. London, HMSO.

Humphries, Jane (1983) 'the "emancipation" of women in the 1970s and 1980s: from the latent to the floating', *Capital and Class*, no. 20.

Humphries, Jane and Rubery, Jill (1986) 'Recession, disablement and exploitation: British women in a changing workplace, 1979–85. Paper given at a Conference on Work and Politics: the Feminisation of the Labour Force. at Harvard University Center for European Studies.

Hunt, Audrey (1968) *A Survey of Women's Employment*, 2 vols. London, HMSO.

Hunt, Audrey (1975) *Management Attitudes and Practices towards Women at Work*. London, HMSO.

200 References

Hurstfield, Jennifer (1978) *The Part-time Trap*. Low Pay pamphlet no. 9, London, The Low Pay Unit.

Incomes Data Services Ltd (1982) *Part-time Workers.* IDS Study no. 267, June. London, IDS.

Incomes Data Services Ltd (1985) *Part-timers, Temps and Job-Sharers*, Employment Law Handbook no. 31, London, IDS.

Industrial Relations Review and Report (February 1984) 'Low pay Initiatives by local authorities', 21 February.

Industrial Relations Review and Report (May 1984) 'Part-time work, a survey', 20 May.

Jenson, Jane (1986) 'Gender and reproduction: or, babies and the state', in *Studies in Political Economy: a Socialist Review*, Summer.

Joshi, H. and Owen, S. (1984) *How Long is a Piece of Elastic? The Measurement of Female Activity Rates in British Censuses 1951–1981*. London, Centre for Economic Policy Research, Discussion Paper no. 31.

Kenrick, Jane (1981) 'Politics and the construction of women as second class workers', in Frank Wilkinson (ed.) *The Dynamics of Labour Market Segmentation*. New York, Academic Press.

Klein, Viola (1965) *Britain's Married Women Workers*. London, Routledge and Kegan Paul.

Labour Studies Group (1985) 'Economic, social and political factors in the operation of the labour market', in Bryan Roberts, Ruth Finnegan and Duncan Gallie (eds) *New Approaches to Economic Life*. Manchester, Manchester University Press.

Land, Hilary (1986) 'The unwelcome impact of social policies on women in the labour market'. Paper given at Conference on Work and Politics: the Feminisation of the Labour Force, Harvard University Center for European Studies.

Lewis, Jane (1980) *The Politics of Motherhood: Child and Maternal Welfare in England 1900–39*. London, Croom Helm.

McGoldrick, Ann (1984) *Equal Treatment in Occupational Pension Schemes: a Research Report*. Manchester, EOC.

McIntosh, A. (1980) 'Women at work: a survey of employers', *Employment Gazette*, November.

MacLennan, Emma (1984) 'Why are women low paid?', *Low Pay Review* 21, Spring.

Martin, Jean and Roberts, Ceridwen (1984) *Women and Employment, a Lifetime Perspective*. London, HMSO.

Murray, Robin (1985) 'Benetton Britain: the New Economic Order', *Marxism Today*, November, pp. 28–32.

Myrdal, Alva and Klein, Viola (1956) *Women's Two Roles*. London, Routledge and Kegan Paul.

OECD (1980) *Women and Employment*. Paris, OECD.

OECD (1985) *The Integration of Women into the Economy*. Paris, OECD.

Office of Population Censuses and Surveys (1981) *Census*. London, HMSO.

Office of Population Censuses and Surveys (1983) *The General Household Survey*. London HMSO.

Paukert, Liba (1984) *The Employment and Unemployment of Women in OECD Countries*. Paris, OECD.

Perkins, Teresa (1983) 'A new form of employment: a case study of women's part-time employment in Coventry', in Mary Evans and Claire Ungerson (eds) *Sexual Divisions, Patterns and Processes*. London, Tavistock.

Phillips, Anne and Taylor, Barbara (1980) 'Sex and skill: notes towards a feminist economics', *Feminist Review*, no. 6, pp. 79–88.

Pollert, Anna (1981) *Girls, Wives, Factory Lives*. London, Macmillan.

Popay, J., Rimmer, L. and Rossiter, L. (1983) *One Parent families: Parents, Children and Public Policy*. Study Commission on the Family, Occasional paper no. 12.

Reskin, Barbara F. and Hartmann, Heidi I. (eds) (1986) *Women's Work, Men's Work: Sex Segregation on the Job*. Washington DC, National Academy Press.

Riley, Denise (1984) *War in the Nursery*. London, Virago.

Roberts, Bryan, Finnegan, Ruth and Gallie, Duncan (eds) (1985) *New Approaches to Economic Life*. Manchester, Manchester University Press.

Robinson, Olive and Wallace, John (1984) *Part-time Employment and Sex Discrimination Legislation in Great Britain*. Department of Employment Research Paper no. 43.

Rubery, Jill (1980) 'Structured labour markets, worker organisation and low pay', in Alice Amsden (ed.) *The Economics of Women and Work*. Harmondsworth, Penguin.

Rubery, Jill, Tarling, Roger and Wilkinson, Frank (1984) 'Labour market segmentation theory: an alternative framework for the analysis of the employment systems'. Paper delivered at the BSA Conference on Work, Employment and Unemployment.

Rubery, Jill and Tarling, Roger (forthcoming) 'Women and employment in Britain', in Jill Rubery (ed.) *Women and Recession*. London, Routledge and Kegan Paul.

Scott, Alison MacEwen (1986) 'Industrialisation, gender segregation and stratification theory', in Rosemary Crompton and Michael Mann (eds) *Gender and Stratification*. Cambridge, Polity Press.

Scott, Joan W. (1985) 'Is gender a useful category of historical analysis?'. Paper given at the meeting of the American Historical Association.

Siltanen, Janet and Stanworth, Michelle (eds) (1984) *Women and the*

Public Sphere. London, Hutchinson.

Snell, M. W., Glucklich, P. and Povall, M. (1981) *Equal Pay and Opportunities*. Department of Employment Research Paper no. 21.

Summerfield, Penny (1984) *Women Workers in the Second World War*. Beckenham, Croom Helm.

Thomas, Geoffrey (1944) *Women at Work*. Wartime Social Survey. London, Office of the Ministry of Reconstruction.

Thomas, Geoffrey (1948) *Women and Industry*. An inquiry into the problem of recruiting women to industry, carried out for the Ministry of Labour and National Service. London, The Social Survey.

Trade Union Research Unit (1981) *Working Time in Britain*. Anglo-German Foundation.

Trades Union Congress (1985) *Report of the Annual Trades Union Congress*. London, TUC.

Treiman, Donald J. and Hartmann, Heidi (1981) *Women, Work and Wages: Equal Pay for Jobs of Equal Value*. Washington DC, National Academy Press.

Trown, Ann and Needham, Gill (1980) *Reduction in Part-time teaching: Implications for Schools and Women Teachers*. Manchester, EOC.

Wajcman, Judy (1983) *Women in Control*. Milton Keynes, The Open University Press.

Walker, Alan (1984–5) 'Conscription on the cheap: old workers and the state', *Critical Social Policy* no. 11, Winter.

West, Jackie (ed.) (1982) *Work, Women and the Labour Market*. London, Routledge and Kegan Paul.

Westwood, Sallie (1984) *All Day Every Day*. London, Pluto Press.

White, Michael (1981) *Case Studies of Shorter Working Time*. London, PSI.

Wood, Stephen (ed.) (1980) *The Degradation of Work?* London, Hutchinson.

Index

absenteeism, 21, 22, 62, 64, 102
Addenbrookes Hospital, 171
age factor, 12, 13–15, 184–5, 187
Agricultural Wages Board, 151
agriculture (France), 41
Allan and Ors v. *Leyland Vehicles*, 157
ancillary staff
  baking industry, 65–6
  health service, 10, 80, 84, 86–90, 144,
    155, 171–2, 174
apprenticeships, 63, 64, 69, 107, 110
Armstrong, Pat and Hugh, 130, 132
Asians, 20, 58–60
Association of Professional, Executive,
  Clerical and Computer Staff, 154,
  159
Atkinson, John, 142–4

Baker's Union, 64
Baking Hours of Work Act, 63
baking industry, 60–7, 75, 104–5, 108,
  113, 114, 116–17, 189–90
Ballard, Barbara, 32
Banking, Insurance and Finance Union
  (BIFU), 159, 167
Barclays Bank, 158
Barrett, Michèle, 127
Barron, R. D., 134–5, 139
Beacham, Roland, 11, 13, 14, 184
Beardwell, I., 171
Beechey, Veronica, 122, 125, 127, 132,
  147, 180, 183, 184
benefit payments, 19–20, 44, 185
  maternity, 3, 155, 164
  retirement, *see* pension (retirement)
  sickness, 3, 67, 95, 151, 153–4, 171
Benenson, Harold, 125

Bevan, Aneurin, 23
Birmingham Feminist History Group,
  122
Black and White Britain, 20–1
bonuses, 3, 64, 87–8, 152–3, 158–9, 169,
  171, 190, 193
Braverman, Harry, 123, 124–5, 126–8
bread manufacture, 61–4, 104, 189–90
British Labour Statistics, 27, 185
Brown, Richard, 20–1, 183
Bruegel, Irene, 5, 35, 45, 129–31, 132,
  135–6
'buffer hypothesis', 131
Burnham system, 93

Cambridge Labour Studies Group,
  138–9, 142
Camden Council, 169, 194, 195
capital
  accumulation, 131, 133
  human (model), 134, 135, 139
  –labour relations, 124–8
  structure, 48–9, 51, 56, 60, 123–5
capitalism, 123–5, 128, 140, 147–8
car industry, 4, 67–8, 70–2, 73, 76
care assistants, 91, 92, 98
care role (female), 15, 78–9, 81–2,
  90–1, 100–1, 111–12, 125–6
Carpenter, Mike, 190
casual work, 41, 78, 94, 140–1, 143, 170
  baking industry, 62, 64, 67
catering work, 73, 74, 75
  welfare services, 78–9, 86–7, 91–2,
    95–7, 99
Cavendish, Ruth, 183
Census (1981), 16, 185
Census of Employment (1976), 47, 56,
  188, 189, 191